Will: The Autobiography of Will Greenwood

To my two boys Freddie and Archie and my wife Caro

Will: The Autobiography of Will Greenwood

Will Greenwood

arrow books

Published by Arrow in 2005

1 3 5 7 9 10 8 6 4 2

Copyright © Will Greenwood 2004

Will Greenwood has asserted his right under the Copyright, Designs and
Patents Act, 1988 to be identified as the author of this work

First published in the United Kingdom in 2004 by Century
The Random House Group Limited
20 Vauxhall Bridge Road, London SW1V 2SA

Random House Australia (Pty) Limited
20 Alfred Street, Milsons Point, Sydney,
New South Wales 2061, Australia

Random House New Zealand Limited
18 Poland Road, Glenfield
Auckland 10, New Zealand

Random House South Africa (Pty) Limited
Endulini, 5a Jubilee Road, Parktown 2193, South Africa

The Random House Group Limited Reg. No. 954009

www.randomhouse.co.uk

A CIP catalogue record for this book is available from the British Library

Papers used by Random House are
natural, recyclable products made from wood grown in
sustainable forests. The manufacturing processes conform to
the environmental regulations of the country of origin

ISBN 0 09 9476487

Typeset by SX Composing DTP, Rayleigh, Essex
Printed and bound in Great Britain by
Bookmarque Ltd, Croydon, Surrey

Acknowledgements

There are a few very important thank-yous that I must make: To the fantastic team at Century books for their enthusiasm for the story, and to my literary agents Luxton Harris. To my manager Nick Keller for his advice and support, despite me taking the micky out of him consistently for eight years, he has been a true friend and a constant companion. To all the team at Benchmark Sport, especially Matt Jones. Thank-you to Action Images and Getty Images for their help in researching photographs for this book.

To Niall Edworthy whose expertise, craft skills, and hard work have ensured that this book is of the quality I strived for when this project began: patience, humour, and sensitivity in abundance. Niall has helped me try and write something more than just a rugby book.

To my dad, Dick, whose storytelling skills and sharp memory demonstrate the contribution he has made not only to this book but also to my life and career. And of course to my mum, Susan, my greatest fan. To Mrs T (mother-in-laws rarely get a mention but this is well deserved) and my sister and brother Emma and Tom.

Finally to my family, Freddie, Archie and Caro, who make rugby seem so wonderfully irrelevant.

Scene-setter

I WAS IN THE team room at our hotel in Perth playing pool with some of the boys when my mobile phone rang. It was my wife Caro and, not for the first time since we had arrived in Australia two weeks earlier, I felt a slight tightening in my stomach. It was about five in the evening on the Monday before the South Africa game, one of the most hyped internationals in recent years. Our bodies were still a bit sore from the physical battering we had taken from the Georgians the day before, but our minds had quickly turned to the great challenge that now lay just five days ahead.

When the World Cup draw had been made eighteen months earlier, there had been a sharp intake of breath throughout the rugby world when the names of England and South Africa were called alongside each other. Our 53-3 victory over them eleven months earlier was without question the most brutal senior international in which I have ever been involved and it cranked up the fierce rivalry between our teams to unprecedented levels. Once they had had a player sent off for taking out Jonny Wilkinson, Twickenham became a virtually lawless territory, and the violence was too much for one referee alone to try to contain. As one of the girls in the backs I had done my best, as always, to try to avoid getting involved in the Wild West stuff, but there was nowhere to hide in this very public brawl with swinging knees and elbows, cheap shots, sly punches and late hits all over the pitch that afternoon. It was one of those matches when you shuddered to think what was going on in the depths and shadows of the rucks and mauls.

'We'll see you in Perth,' their captain Corne Krige had said, spitting defiance after his country's most humiliating day on a rugby field. And now we were here and the tension in and around the England camp was starting to mount. Saturday was going to be not so much a rugby match as a collision.

I put down my pool cue and walked away from the table to take the call from Caro, who rang every day at about the same time, when it was early morning back in England, not just for a chat but also to give me an update on how the pregnancy was going. After what had happened to Freddie, we had both felt, in equal measure, powerful waves of anxiety and excitement over the past three months or so, and it was with a mixture of those feelings that I pressed the answer button.

'Are you alone?' asked Caro.

'No.'

'Well, it's probably best if you were. I've got some news and it's not great. It's happening again.'

I felt a blast of nausea as I quickly strode over to the door and punched in the security code to get out of the room, with the phone pressed to my face like an icepack. I got out into the corridor and there seemed to be about half as much air in my lungs as there had been thirty seconds earlier.

'It's happening all over again,' said Caro, her voice bouncing off the satellite somewhere deep in space. 'The contractions have started again. They are admitting me straight away.'

She was trying not to freak me out. I could tell that. She had always been brilliant at hiding her own anxiety and panic, but it wasn't difficult to read between the lines. She was about twenty weeks pregnant, just as she had been when her contractions had started with Freddie. We were still mourning him when Caro had got pregnant for a second time. Freddie has never been out of our thoughts since he passed away, but right then the full intensity of that grief came flooding through me and I found myself sprinting up to my room, seized with panic. I slammed the door behind me and broke down as I fell on to my bed, my hands over my face. 'Not again, please not again,' I found myself saying over and over. 'You've taken one from us, you bastard. Is that not enough? How many do you effing want?'

I had to get home. You can keep the World Cup, I thought. I tried to compose myself by taking deep breaths and splashing my face with cold water, but I still had bloodshot eyes as I walked out of the room to try and find Clive Woodward. He was in a meeting with the forwards in the 'war room' when I knocked and walked in. 'Can I have a word, Clive?' You don't interrupt these meetings unless it's very important and Clive only had to take a sideways glance at me to know that something was terribly wrong.

About two hours later I was lying on my hotel bed staring at the ceiling and trying to go to sleep, completely unaware of the drama that was rapidly unfolding 12,000 miles away back home in south-west London. It was only the following morning that I discovered that Caro was unconscious in intensive care after being rushed to theatre for an emergency operation shortly after our telephone conversation. I spoke to the doctor, Mark Johnson, a saint of a man who we had got to know very well over the past eighteen months or so. I wanted hard facts and data from him, some concrete figures to work with so that I knew where we stood. I didn't want vague reassurances or half-truths. There was about a 30 per cent chance of our second child surviving, I was told.

Chapter One

IT SEEMS STRANGE now, looking back on a childhood spent mainly in my native Lancashire and the bleak landscape of Cumbria, that my first memories and words were Italian. It feels even weirder when I go back with England to the Stadio Flaminio on the outskirts of Rome to play Italy and I look around at the steep terraces of that largely unchanged arena where I had spent so many of my weekends as a young child. It never occurred to me back then to question why my father liked to entertain himself there by rolling around in the mud with thirty or so other angry looking, grown men in shorts in pursuit of a ball that didn't even bounce properly when you dropped it. Eating ice cream and annoying Mum and my older sister Emma seemed a far more obvious and enjoyable way of killing time.

I was born in Blackburn but we moved to Rome when I was about ten months and did not return until 1978, when I was almost six. I spoke Italian then but not much remains of my first language today; should I ever wish to, however, I can still invite people out for a game of Cowboys and Indians – *'Andiamo gioca Cowboy e Indiani'* – which is hardly going to get me a job at the United Nations when I finish my playing career, especially when you hear it in broad Lanc. Emma went on to study Italian at Cambridge and my younger brother Tom, another Cambridge graduate like our father and mother before him, wasn't born until we returned to England, but taught himself to speak the language. My Italian, sadly, remains confined to the kindergarten although I can just about understand what someone is saying to me so long as he is talking fairly slowly and doesn't have a mouthful of pizza.

It is difficult now to distinguish in my mind between the genuine memories of my Roman childhood and the images planted there by the dozens of stories I have heard my parents and Emma recount down the years, but, either way, Italy stirs up good feelings for me. We lived in a block of flats in Villa Bonelli out by the airport and my best friend, fellow street urchin and fierce football rival was a boy called Ugo who taught me lots of swear words, which a child of that age really shouldn't have known. Dad's England career having been brought to a premature end by a rocketing squash ball to the eye, he had headed abroad for the adventure and to play pseudo-pro, or 'shamateur', rugby while earning a few quid in the wine trade. Mum taught at a local school, just as she continues to do today, in between looking after me and Emma.

I thought Dad played for a team called Algida until I discovered, when I was much older, that Algida was the name of the ice-cream maker that sponsored the club. In fact he was involved first with Roma, and then Lazio, two glamorous names in the world of football, but unheard of then in rugby circles beyond the Italian frontier. Dad also got involved in coaching out there, as did a number of other foreigners, including Brian Ashton (whose wife used to babysit me), the Frenchman Pierre Villepreux and Welshman Carwyn James, coach of the victorious 1971 Lions tour to New Zealand. All four of them would later be hailed as among the most visionary and intelligent coaches of their generation and it's weird that they all happened to be in Italy, an infant rugby nation then, at the same time.

I am not sure whether I actually remember Dad being jailed or if I just heard the story a few years later, but either way it is a fact that he spent a few nights as a guest of the Italian authorities, to Mum's crimson-faced embarrassment. The story of a former England rugby captain being imprisoned after a brawl in a Roman bar was one that our newspapers needed little encourage-ment to pick up. A team of his old Cambridge buddies had come out for a brief tour and, boys being boys, and beer being beer, a brawl broke out in a bar after one of their matches. Being the only Italian speaker among them, Dad tried to break it up and then spoke to the owner and the policemen who had arrived on the scene

7

of the demolished bar. For his trouble he was promptly carted off to the clink.

He gets a much warmer reception when he goes back to Italy these days and so, to my great embarrassment, do I. I have played against Italy in Rome twice, in 2002 and 2004, and on each occasion there were lots of my father's old pals and their wives in the crowd. I go there as an international athlete, a 6-foot 5-inch, 16-stone England back with, I like to kid myself, something of a steely glint in my eye and a granite jaw. Any illusions of machismo I might like to give out, however, are destroyed in an instant when, one after another, my parents' friends grab the fat of my cheeks between thumb and forefinger, or ruffle my hair, and coo, 'How is my little bambino, Willino?'

I like the Italians a lot and if there is one international team I haven't enjoyed stuffing down the years, it's them. You don't feel sympathy in Test rugby at the best of times because the people you are playing against are generally trying to ruck your head off and bury you into the earth in the tackle. In my experience the Italians are as physical a side as any in world rugby but on the couple of occasions when England have racked about forty or fifty points against them, or other less developed teams for that matter, I tend not to go hunting for openings in a way that I would, say, against New Zealand or South Africa. I hope that doesn't sound patronising, but thrashing another team (especially Italy, for me) simply isn't as much fun as you might think. When we beat Romania 134–0 not long ago I felt positively depressed afterwards. It was as if I had spent the afternoon clubbing seals.

Back in Lancashire, the centre of my life for the next twelve years or so would be the village of Hurst Green in the Ribble valley north of Blackburn. Even when I got sent off to boarding school, home was only a couple of miles down the road. My parents have a house there to this day and whenever I am asked where I come from I reply, 'Hurst Green, Lancashire'. Beers I have drunk elsewhere have never tasted quite as good as those I have enjoyed in the Bayley Arms. Work has brought me down south for the past decade or so but I will always be a Lancastrian and a northerner to the tips of my size twelve boots.

After a year at the local primary school, I went to St Mary's Hall prep school where my mother taught mathematics and from where most pupils went on to the Jesuit-run Stonyhurst College next door. I was a dayboy for two years, but at ten I became a boarder. Dad became the rugby coach at Stonyhurst and, like all school rugby coaches, taught a bit of geography, too. (If you have ever wondered about the link between rugby and geography, it is because in the 1950s and 1960s many of the leading universities, including several colleges at Cambridge and Oxford, used to take on a handful of promising rugby players to study 'land economy'. The practice died out for a number of years thanks entirely, legend has it, to the one-time England back-rower Chris Sheasby, whose staggering lack of commitment to his studies led to a revision of the Oxbridge selection process. That, anyway, is my excuse for being the only member of the Greenwood family not to get into Cambridge, and I'm sticking to it.)

St Mary's, like Stonyhurst, attached a lot of importance to outdoor pursuits and I soon found myself playing a variety of sports and loving them all. At that age I wasn't particularly tall or obviously athletic, but by the time I left on a sports bursary to go to Sedbergh, I had become a reasonably good cricketer, rugby player and triple jumper. To this day my mother says that her proudest moment in my sporting career was watching me in my green and white hooped shirt score a hat-trick in the final of the Malsis Under-11 Sevens competition at the age of nine. I remember receiving the trophy after our victory and thinking at the time that it was roughly the same size as the old, jug-eared European Cup in football, but I saw a picture of it not long ago and it's no bigger than a coffee mug.

In those days I was probably as tidy a cricketer as I was a rugby player, and it wasn't until my late teens that rugby began to exert a greater hold over me. As a middle-order batsman and first-change bowler, I managed to win a call to the Under-13 North Lancashire team to play our South Lancashire rivals at

Old Trafford in the summer of 1984. My captain that day was a run machine called John Crawley and in the opposition line-up was a swaggering, bushy-haired all-rounder called Ronnie Irani, both of whom went on to play for Lancashire and England. I still have a copy of the scorecard today. We lost by 21 runs, Ronnie hit an unbeaten 75 and took 3 for 22. He actually had me plumb LBW first ball, but the very nice umpire, reluctant to give a kid out for a golden duck, shook his head and pointed down the leg side. Later that summer I played alongside the two future Test players for Lancashire Under-13s. I promise that I don't go round boasting about my prep school sporting achievements today, but, for the sake of historical truth, I have to record here that I also won the triple jump competition in the National Prep School Athletics championship in Haringey.

In sport, I had found something that I was fairly good at and, although it increased my confidence, I remained a painfully shy child throughout my time at St Mary's and for a long time into my teens. The fact that my mother taught there made me that little bit more self-conscious; it was only through my dad putting me in so many positions where I simply couldn't be shy that finally I stopped going red and squeaky whenever some-one spoke to me. Roughly twenty years after leaving St Mary's, it seems that I have come a very long way on the shyness front in the intervening years, at least according to an anonymous letter I received in April 2003. It read as follows:

> *Greenwood,*
> *You are a fucking arrogant arse and too self-centredly blind to see the harm which your attitude is doing to the game of rugby. Grow up.*

And if you think that's bad you should see some of the hate mail I get. I certainly couldn't fault my correspondent for frankness, but even if he had had the courage to leave a name and address what are you meant to say in reply to abuse like that? Playing for England in recent years gets you used to being hit with the 'arrogant' line of insult from time to time. I suppose it's meant to wind us up and provoke a response but we tend to yawn or mutter the words 'change the record' at the mention of it. International sport is a very unforgiving, black and white world: if you fail to win everything, you're a 'loser'; if you win, you're arrogant. Being called arrogant is a sign that your team is doing well. Losers never get called arrogant.

The older I get the fonder my memories become of my time at boarding school, but I hated it at first and as soon as term was over I was straight home and out with my mates on our street, Smithy Row, playing football in the winter and cricket in the summer. Recently, during a rare gap in my schedule, I went back for my mum's birthday and as I walked back into the Bayley Arms there were all the mates I used to play with as a scabby-kneed, snot-smeared youngster – the Hayhursts, the Youngs, the Boltons and Neil Brown . . . I love going 'home' and catching up with all the local news. On this occasion I was as interested to know how they got on in the recent local football derby against Longridge as they were to know what had gone wrong in England's Six Nations defeat against Ireland.

Back then I had a very strong Lancastrian accent; it has been diluted by living down south for so many years but it comes straight back whenever I return. Lancashire meant everything to us as young sportsmen. You were Lancastrian first and English second. It wasn't exactly Basque separatism, but the county certainly forged our identity and this was fuelled by the fierce rivalry with neighbours Yorkshire. One of the most stirring pre-match talks I have ever experienced was delivered by a man called John Burgess, one-time President of the RFU and a man so Lancastrian he could almost pop. He gave me my first cap for Lancashire at the age of eighteen, and it was in the changing room before we played a Cumbrian side in a charity game, all of us pulling on our red and white hooped shirts, when he gathered us around and delivered the words which still resound in my ears today. 'I have three things to say to you, gentlemen: Lancashire, The North, England – in that order!' he bellowed.

Perhaps I risk upsetting my southern paymasters and I may well be making a horrible, biased generalisation but I've always thought the best English rugby players over the years have come from the north. The nature of rugby is changing rapidly in the professional era, but the superiority of the north as a rugby breeding ground certainly seemed to hold true when I was making my way up through the junior and representative ranks. Will Carling's excellent England teams of the late 1980s and early 1990s all had a hard core of northerners to them. Perhaps that's all changing now as the England team that won the World Cup was dominated by southerners and Midlanders. Tindall, Balshaw, Jason Robinson and myself were the only players of the twenty-two that day to be born and brought up in the north.

The older I got the more I enjoyed St Mary's and when I went off to Sedbergh on that sports bursary, an hour and a half to the north in the middle of the Cumbrian wilderness, my little prep school seemed like Disneyland compared to the outwardly chilling institution where I was to spend the next six years. For some reason I had always been in the year ahead at St Mary's and so I was just twelve years old when my parents dropped me off at my new school, where the motto *Dura Virum Nutrix* (Hardy Nurse of Men) didn't exactly put a spring into the step of fresh-faced, homesick newcomers. I absolutely hated it at first.

Say what you like about public schools – and I personally don't feel that strongly about them one way or the other – but I know for a fact that Sedbergh hardened me up, emotionally if nothing else. Unlike many professional sportsmen on tour, I've never suffered from homesickness when abroad. Going to boarding school also meant that I spent the better part of a decade running around outside playing sports – a dream for a lot of young kids as well as a privilege and an opportunity that is no longer available in most state schools. I was never bullied or abused, I got into one of the country's best universities with four good A levels to my name and I made some very good friends while I was there. As school experiences go, at Sedbergh mine was a pretty good one, though it took me a couple of years to find my feet and feel truly comfortable there.

I was lucky to have a great housemaster called Angus McPhail in my last two years, and by the time I left his charge in 1991 I was a happier, more confident, better rounded and higher achieving individual than I had been on the day of his arrival. Angus – can I call him by his christian name now that I am almost thirty-two? – is a double blue (at cricket and rugby) and a man who doesn't have to work hard for his respect – you just give it to him instinctively. He was also my economics teacher and he had a tremendous influence over me in all areas of my life. He has since gone on to become the headmaster at Radley, or The Warden to give him his official title. His predecessor was a strict man called Mr Thomas and I always seemed to be in some kind of trouble with him, mainly for drinking at weekends.

On one occasion I said I was going to spend Saturday with my aunt in the nearby town of Kirkby Lonsdale but she, in fact, was abroad on holiday and we headed straight to the pub and drank ourselves into a stupor, as had been our intention all along. It was the day my dad's Stonyhurst team played Ampleforth in one of the biggest fixtures of the school rugby calendar. Stonyhurst won. In his enthusiasm – bless him and curse him all at once – Dad called Mr Thomas later that evening and asked him to go and tell me the result. I wasn't, as Mr Thomas soon discovered, especially interested in hearing the great news as I was busy hanging out of my window enjoying a bout of alcohol-induced sickness. He was distinctly unimpressed and promptly grounded me for two weeks.

Sedbergh has produced a number of talented pupils who have gone on to enjoy successful careers in different spheres, but it is as a producer of great rugby players that it has perhaps been best known in recent years. Its most famous rugby son is probably Will Carling, but twenty-nine others who have worn the school's brown jersey have also gone on to pull on the white shirt of England. You only have to look at the fixture list to appreciate that the rugby education there was about as good as it gets at schoolboy level:

Newcastle Grammar School, Bradford Grammar School, Lancaster Grammar School, Ampleforth, Stonyhurst, Durham, Uppingham, Rossall, Loretto and Wellington. Traditionally the school had always attracted a lot of beefy sons of equally beefy northern farmers, and we always seemed to have big, fierce packs of forwards who spent their holidays tackling bulls and shoulder-charging other cattle.

I played in the 1st XV for three years, most of the time at fly-half or full-back, and one of the highlights of the season was the weekend clash with Ampleforth when both schools put out fourteen teams against each other, some at home, some the three-hour coach journey away. One year we were 16–0 down at home to Ampleforth but fought back to 16–12 when I was tackled and broke my collarbone and I was taken off in a fair amount of pain. I remember my old man gave me his Barbarians scarf to use as a makeshift sling, but, after a minute or two, with the match still hanging in the balance, he said: 'Right, son, I think you can go back on. Just kick it if you get it.' The referee that day, though, wouldn't allow it. Thank heavens. Four weeks later Lancashire Schoolboys were scheduled to take on our Yorkshire rivals and, desperate for me not to miss the match, Dad had me out tackling him in the back garden even though my collarbone had not fully mended. It certainly wasn't any better after that session and, luckily, the match was frozen off. Thank God he never became a doctor.

Dad has been called a lot of things down the years but 'soft' or 'unmotivated' do not feature among them. One summer I went backpacking with my sister and her boyfriend and, after a month or so sleeping on beaches and drinking beer, I arrived back at Llandudno in North Wales where my parents were on holiday, at about one o'clock in the morning, feeling a little the worse for wear. At seven o'clock I felt a tap on my shoulder and heard a familiar voice: 'Welcome back, son, I'll see you on the promenade for training in fifteen minutes.' He's a great organiser and a motivator, Dad, and has always had his family's best interests at heart in everything he has done for us. At Sedbergh, the coaches for some reason never put us forward for schoolboy representative rugby and it took my old man to make them release us, telling them in no uncertain terms that they were guilty of holding back myself and one or two others from developing as players.

Before I left Sedbergh I represented Lancashire Schoolboys at both rugby and cricket. I still have my Lancashire cricket jersey and caps, but to be honest I never did that much, mainly because John Crawley scored all the runs and Ronnie Irani took all the wickets. Some say I should have chosen cricket instead of rugby, but I'm not convinced I ever stood out quite enough to have ever made it to the top of the sport. I did go on to captain Cumbria Under-19s, but I suppose that's about as impressive as saying 'I am the Tiger

Woods of the Faroe Islands' or the 'Michael Schumacher of Ascension Island'.

At school I had the great experience of being coached by West Indian fast bowler Kenny Benjamin, who was over playing for Kendal in the Lancashire League one season. He's an absolutely top man, Kenny, but you messed about in his net sessions at your peril. If you were foolish enough to horse about, he'd bowl at you, coming in off just one yard and fire down the fastest ball you've ever faced. He would then walk down the wicket and, in a lazy West Indian drawl, say, 'Don't mess about in my net sessions.'

I still play a bit of cricket today, on the rare occasions I get a chance, and it remains a niggling regret that I have yet to score a century. Eighty-odd is my highest score. I once took nine wickets against Ampleforth at Under-15 level but my favourite cricketing memory came playing against the MCC at Sedbergh when I smashed an abusive former county player for one of the biggest sixes ever hit on the ground. The ball landed in the garden of my house, Evans House, and they tell me that the shot is still spoken about today. (Or am I imagining that?) I had played and missed a couple early on when I took a swipe and found only air against this particular bowler, a leg spinner; he walked down the wicket and said: 'Next time, why don't you bring a fucking bat with you?' Next ball, I put him into the garden and muttered under my breath, 'Fetch that, you big ex-county hero', or words to that effect. It's weird how memories of schoolboy incidents like that can be as vivid and compelling as any of my experiences in my club and international rugby career. I suppose it's all about what it meant at the time and that little encounter definitely had me pumped up.

I captained the Sedbergh cricket XI for two years but was stripped of my responsibility towards the end of the second season after an unfortunate incident during my A level revision programme. I had a history paper to sit on the Monday and was given permission to miss Saturday's 1st XI match against a school called Giggleswick in order to knuckle down to some last-minute revision. At about three o'clock that afternoon I was found 'revising' in the Snooty Fox in Kirkby Lonsdale, on the wrong end of about five creamy bitters, and was promptly stripped of the captaincy and banned from going on the end-of-season tour. That, I suppose, was the end of my fledgling cricket career. Every game of cricket I have played since has been purely recreational.

While I was still at school Dad decided my rugby education demanded a few lessons on the northern club circuit and so it was that, at the age of seventeen, still as thin as a beanpole, I found myself in the changing room with the men of the Preston Grasshoppers 4th XV for a match against Vale of Lune. It was certainly a different world from the changing rooms at Sedbergh and other

schools – for one, we never had a schooner of sherry
before kickoff. As far as I could work out, the general
idea of 4th XV club rugby was that you turned up, had
a fight, drank thirty pints and went home singing 'She'll
Be Coming Round The Mountain'. Most of the players
were veterans, good or even great players in their days
but now well over the hill – men like my dad, a former
England captain and coach to boot, all of them strapped
and bandaged from head to foot and reeking of Deep
Heat and beer.

Dad, who was a flanker, played alongside me that day
and he rushed to my defence when I got walloped early
on by a late tackle from my opposite man at fly-half. I'll
never forget the sight that followed. Dad came haring
out of the scrum, steam pouring out of him, and chased
this man across the field before picking him up by his
nostrils and shouting, 'Stand up and take your punishment!' He then whacked him about four times as I
looked on, feeling proud, shocked and mildly amused
all at once by this exhibition of summary justice.
Needless to say, the guy never touched me again and I
ended up having a half-decent game. The day obviously
made a big impression on me because the images of it
are still very clear in my mind, not least of sitting in the
big bath afterwards, singing our heads off as Dad handed
me a pint of lager.

I played with my old man just three times in all and he
always seemed to be in the thick of the action and the

controversy. Once, playing for a team called the Anti-Assassins in a charity game, Dad, who must have been getting on for fifty at this time, stiff-armed the scrum-half who'd come running up his channel on the blind side. The referee that day was the former Scotland inter-national referee David Leslie, who immediately warned my father about his future conduct. At the next line, Dad shouted from the back: 'The next lineout call is "the referee's a prat".' Everyone laughed, including Leslie, but his seventeen-year-old son was standing at fly-half going red, thinking, 'Oh God, is that really my dad?'

It was around this time that I started going to representative trials, first at county level, then at regional and national and, helped by my brief foray into club rugby, I was starting to play against and alongside some seriously talented footballers. In the autumn of 1990 I played for Lancashire Under-18s at fly-half against Warwickshire and, although I had a reasonably solid game, I was dropped for the next match and replaced by a guy called Neil Ryan from Mount St Mary's College, a Jesuit school near Sheffield. This, I can assure you, was no cause for shame as Neil was one of the most talented rugby footballers I have ever seen. In a way he was perhaps more suited to rugby league because he could pass with both hands, had a great nose for a gap and was a very clever grubber kicker, too. If he had a weakness it was in the contact area and I don't think I will be sued for libel if I say that Neil hated tackling even more than

I did in those days. But what a player. There are a handful of players I remember from my youth who everyone was convinced would go right to the top of the game if the will took them. Neil was one of them and another was a bloke called Diccon Edwards who went on to play once or twice for Leicester before fading from the game. I played alongside him a few times in trials and representative games and he was absolutely outstanding. I have no idea why neither Ryan nor Edwards went further than they did because at the time they were the ones to watch.

I captained Lancashire Schools on a couple of occasions, once against a Yorkshire side who we would have thrashed had it not been for a lanky lad called Tim Stimpson on their wing. I couldn't have known at the time as I watched this incredible athlete score a try, a penalty, a conversion and a drop goal to give his side a 22–18 win over us, that, years down the line, we would become good pals. Stimpson was absolutely devastating as a schoolboy and genuinely shone brighter than the rest of us, like a beacon. He looked every inch a world-class player, and although he went on to win nineteen caps for England and to forge a highly successful club career, he has never quite reached the standards he was setting the rest of us back then. I remember saying to someone at the time that if I had the chance to steal someone else's natural gifts and body shape, I would have taken Stimmo's.

When I was about seventeen I began to get invited to various RFU get-togethers for my age group and, quite frankly, they were a bit of a nightmare. It was like being sent to a new, even stricter boarding school where everyone was a stranger and each boy was desperate to make an impression on the coaches. To them, we were just numbers on a sheet or players in a position to be run through a series of exercises and disciplines and then graded accordingly. Some of the more confident, mature boys thrived in the competitive atmosphere but many others, including me, retreated a little into themselves and never really did themselves justice.

Below is my assessment written up by an RFU coach at the end of an under-18 North of England meeting. I seem to have done OK that week, although I remember my judge's comments right at the end about my handling skills sticking in the gullet. That was meant to be one of my strengths!

Handling: A/B. Showed some nice touches, good
    weight and length of pass.

Running: A/B: Straightened back division up well

Kicking: A/B. Very safe touch kicking/good place
kick

Contact: A/B. Strong tackle

Game skills: A/B. Good reading of the game

Fitness: A/B

Attitude: A/B

Keen to learn: A

Competitive: A
Size/speed: A/B
Potential for national week: Yes
Comments: A sound report but must continue to develop his handling and kicking skills through constant practice.

A few weeks later I was invited to take part in the national get-together at Trent College in Nottingham for a two-week meeting. I hated it from beginning to end. Nowadays I am often the annoying, vocal, bossy one in training, but back then I used to stand at the back and let others grab the limelight. Perhaps I hadn't quite shed my childhood shyness by then, or perhaps I was surprised to discover that there were actually lots of other fairly talented players from parts of England other than Lancashire. But, there again, it might just have something to do with being what someone in the England set-up called me a few years later: namely, a less than committed trainer. As you will see from my results below, somebody that fortnight wasn't overly impressed by the potential of W. Greenwood. The comments at the end are particularly galling and it's interesting to note that for my entire professional career the handling, passing and angles of running he mentions have been the strongest part of my game.

Body fat: 12.5 per cent

Speed and acceleration over 15m: 2.39 seconds
Speed and acceleration over 30m: 4.19 seconds
Handling: B
Running: B/C
Kicking: B
Contact: C/B
Reading the game: B
Attitude: Keen to learn B, competitive C/B
Comments: Needs to improve speed of ball through hands and then take-up angles of support. Should be encouraged to feel that he has other skills apart from kicking. Not competitive enough to warrant selection at divisional level. [!?!]

Ouch. I can't quite remember my reaction to this assessment at the time, but I wonder how many other players of roughly my ability and confidence took one look at their mediocre results and thought they lacked what it took to perform at the highest level and then drifted away from the game. Today there are probably dozens of middle-aged men sitting at their office desks who, with the right encouragement and guidance in their teenage years, might have gone on to be successful sportsmen. I was lucky to have my father to drive me on.

The following year I reached the final trial for England Under-18s ahead of a match against Australia at

Twickenham and was selected to play for the Possibles against the Probables. Alongside me in the backs that day were my fellow northerners Neil Ryan and Diccon Edwards and, helped by a powerful pack, we set about making a mockery of the selection process. Barely five minutes into the contest it had become clear that the Possibles were considerably stronger than our supposedly superior opponents and when the final whistle went we had beaten them by fifty points, much to the embarrassment of the coaches. Even though I had scored a hat-trick and directed operations pretty well from fly-half, I was the only player in the team not to be promoted to the first-choice XV and I had to settle instead for a place on the bench. The fly-half who kept his place in the final XV was my long-time Quins team mate Paul Burke, and I have never tired of reminding him of the injustice of it all.

We played Australia at Twickenham in January 1991 and there were some interesting names on the squad sheets that day. In the Australian side was a certain Matt Burke at centre, who would go on to win the World Cup in 1999, and Craig Polla-Mounter, who later switched to rugby league and starred for Canterbury Bulldogs. In our squad we had a towering lock, Barrie-John Mather, a fellow Lancashire lad, who later picked up a full England cap and also played rugby league for Wigan and Great Britain. Tony Diprose started at blindside flanker while the scrum-half was a cocky, dark-haired boy called Matt Dawson. (For the record, I feel it my duty to point out that in the match programme it said of young Matt: 'His interests outside rugby include driving cars and other forms of transport.') But the most interesting name of all is Colin Charvis, a future Wales captain, who I never realised sat alongside me on the bench that day until I came across the programme while researching this book. I have spoken to Colin a great deal down the years, and I like the man a lot, but he has never mentioned that he used to sup with the English devil. I look forward to asking him a few searching questions about his true ancestry when we next meet up.

I was involved in the Under-18 Five Nations Championship that year and went on my first rugby tour to Limerick for the Ireland game and to Colwyn Bay for the Wales game. It was a great honour to be involved in the national set-up, but it remains a source of minor irritation that I never came off the bench to win a cap. Towards the end of the tournament I asked one of our two coaches why I wasn't getting a short run-out in any of the games. His answer will stay with me forever. 'Greenwood,' he said solemnly, 'you'll never be anything more than a carthorse.' And cheers to you, too, you great motivational guru, genius diplomat and man-management supremo.

Throughout my career that comment resurfaces from the depths of my mind from time to time, generally when I have done something reasonably well, such as score a try or play a part in an important victory. It certainly popped into my mind when I was running around Sydney's Olympic Stadium holding the World Cup trophy aloft in November 2003 singing 'We Are The Champions'. The words of my former chemistry teacher and school Under-15 coach, Mr Bennett, also returned to me that day. We had been humped about 70-0 by Bradford Grammar School one afternoon and, because I was full-back, the last line of defence, and had missed a couple of tackles, I was handed all the blame. Afterwards Mr Bennett promptly dropped me to the 'B' team with the words, 'Greenwood, you're pathetic. You'll never play for my team again. Be gone.'

I don't remember that much about that Five Nations Championship, perhaps because my bitter disappointment at the time of not winning a cap led me to blank the experience from my mind. If you're not playing, there's not much to remember except sitting on the bench, wandering around like a spare part in the dressing room and getting on and off buses. My most vivid memory from that period was the post-championship party after we had lost to Wales in Colwyn Bay. We all ended up drinking far more than our young heads could manage and I dimly remember ending up going back to a local woman's house for what I thought was going to be a continuation of the festivities. As it turned out it was just the two of us and, when she sidled across the room and said, 'Don't worry, my husband's on nightshift at the factory and won't be back until six o'clock', in one motion I dropped my glass, opened the door and took off into the night and didn't stop running until I was back in bed with the sheets pulled over my head.

As my six largely happy years at Sedbergh in the wilds of Cumbria drew to an end I had no real idea about what to do next. I was vaguely aware that one day I would have to get a proper job but, after getting my A level results and achieving a creditable AABC in Maths, Economics, History and French, I gained a place at Durham University having failed to get into Magdalene College, Cambridge. (The fact that I gave the worst interview in history is entirely irrelevant, of course.) The interviewers, I'm sure, took one look at the word 'rugby' in my CV, thought 'idle bonehead' and wished me a good day with watery half-smiles. In hindsight, it was the best thing to happen to me up to that point. It wasn't actually my decision to go to Durham – it was Dad's – and to this day I remain deeply grateful to him for making up my mind for me. My three years at Durham, which began in the autumn of 1991, were quite simply the best of my life. Fact.

It wasn't just the freedom to do pretty well what you liked, or the sheer enjoyment of endless days in the pubs and evenings at parties, or the legions of beautiful girls, or lying in bed until midday, or the beauty of the historic surroundings, or the camaraderie of the rugby club . . . but a combination of all those things. The vast majority of my closest friends today are those I made at Durham. I have made plenty of great pals through rugby and other areas of my life, but what's special about university is that you live, eat, drink, play, breathe (and occasionally study) together day in, day out for three, sometimes four years, at a time when you're feeling set free for the first time after fifteen years of confinement at school. Your adult life is just beginning and university is a kind of prolonged coming-of-age party. As far as I'm concerned the man who invented British university education should be given a knighthood. They should make it compulsory for everyone, not simply to raise the standard of learning in the population or to give everyone a roughly equal start in their careers (though that would be great, too), but just so that, for three years or so, people can enjoy their lives among friends of their own age, without a real care in the world.

I was invited to go on a Durham University pre-season rugby tour over the summer so that when I turned up as a fresher a few weeks later I already knew the 1st XV lads and didn't feel like a complete loner or stranger on arrival. In my first year I lived with a guy called Warwick Ryan who was going out with Lucy Heald (now married to Tim Henman) and after a few weeks I was going out with the captain of lacrosse, Poppy Adams, who remains a great friend to this day. I had never really met any girls until then. They were like an alien species to me at eighteen. At Sedbergh we were surrounded by lots of sheep and other lads, neither of which was really my cup of tea romantically speaking, and I had to keep rubbing my eyes and pinching myself when I arrived at Durham and found myself surrounded by walking, talking, living girls. You wanted to prod them in the ribs just to make sure they were real. In no particular order my great passions at Durham were beer, girls, rugby, sleeping, eating poorly, destroying the horrible little houses we lived in and borrowing other people's essays and lecture notes to get me through my exams. Incredible as it might seem today, I somehow managed to leave there with a 2:1 in Economics and I am in line to receive an honorary doctorate.

During my first year at Durham I made my debut for Preston Grasshoppers firsts in a Division Four match against Wrexham, and played at full-back in a 35-9 victory. I combed the local match report the following day and was mildly put out to discover I was a 'former Stonyhurst player' but delighted to read that I 'never put a foot wrong' in a 'splendid' debut. But the most enjoyable rugby I played that year was with Durham as we somehow managed to reach the 1992 UAU final, now known as BUSA, beating a number of supposedly superior sides along the way. On paper our team was distinctly average: we had a prop who weighed about 8 stone and a fly-half with the build and running skills of a prop. Getting to the final was without question one of the most remarkable and odds-defying achievements of my career. We won a tough quarter-final away against Cardiff after my old buddy (now my manager) Nick Keller, aka 'the Ferocious Ferret', scored the winning try and promptly cried his eyes out at the final whistle. Victory over Imperial College London in the semis sparked a ten-day bender which, in hindsight, was probably not the best preparation for the final against Loughborough University. To be fair, they would probably have beaten us anyway even if we had retreated to a fitness camp for the build-up. Besides, our training sessions in the pub had served more than adequately to get us to the final in the first place. Why change a winning formula?

Loughborough had some seriously useful players in their line-up for that final at Twickenham, including future internationals Niall Malone and Derwyn Jones. During the warm-up my old man took one look at them and came over to deliver the private message to me: 'Damage limitation, lad.' We had brought about five thousand down from Durham and the whole of the West Stand was swathed in purple and, although we got absolutely stuffed, it was a great day out. We reached the semi-finals in the following two years with Tim Stimpson and Scotland's Duncan Hodge now on board, going out to Bristol in 1993 after Kyran Bracken scored a try and their fly-half slotted five drop goals. Our new captain, Ben Fennell, later best man at my wedding, still can't talk to Tim Stimpson on account of a crucial oversight in the dying minutes. Stimmo thought we were four points down when we were actually just two in arrears, and he decided to kick and run rather than slot a relatively easy penalty. 'You've got the World Cup winners' medal,' Ben says today. 'That was my World Cup.'

There have been a number of critical turning points in my rugby career and one of them happened in my second year at Durham when my captain, Ben, suggested I try playing at centre, in order to accommodate Duncan Hodge in my usual position at fly-half. I have been playing in that position ever since. God knows why it took my agoraphobic prop friend to point out that centre might be a more suitable position for me to play. After all, how many 6-foot 5-inch fly-halves do you know? I suppose in a way I owe everything I have achieved in the game to Ben.

By the end of my first year at Durham I was playing for the university on Wednesdays and for Waterloo on Saturdays but occasionally I was forced to decide between the two. One occasion has made me regret that decision ever since. Waterloo, who were then in Division Two, had drawn Bath in the cup. Bath were the most dominant club side in England at the time but I opted instead to play for Durham against Oxford because they had never beaten them. It proved to be a dreadful decision on two counts. Firstly, I dislocated my shoulder and in doing so triggered an injury problem that has dogged me ever since. Secondly, Waterloo, with a young Austin Healey and Paul Grayson in their line-ups, pulled off one of the great cup upsets of all time by beating a Bath team dripping with internationals.

My shoulder popped out another four or five times in this period and was threatening to wreck any future I might have had in the game. It was a major problem and nobody seemed to have a clue what to do about it. I even remember one doctor making me lie on the ground and then looking up at him, incredulous, as he put his foot on my chest and tried yanking my arm back into its socket. Isn't that what they did to rugby players in the Middle Ages?

In the end it was thanks to the brass of my mum, a no-nonsense Lancastrian, that the problem came to be addressed properly. One morning she read in the papers that the England back Ian Hunter had solved his shoulder problems after going to see a certain Dr Stuart Copeland and undergoing an operation. By lunch she had tracked down Ian's telephone number, called him up out of the blue and, before I knew it, I was in the car on the way down to Reading to see Dr Copeland. The operation that followed was a great success and, although I lost a little bit of mobility, the work he performed has stood up to a thousand tackles and heavy falls ever since. When my shoulder popped out again in December 1997 it was out of the back socket, not the front, which Dr Copeland had tightened up for me five years earlier.

Having missed out on an Under-18 cap, I was chuffed to pieces to get called up for England Students and even more delighted to score two tries in my first match against Scotland at Basingstoke. I was now the proud owner of the famous purple tracksuit, or 'the purple nasty' as it was known, which used to be handed out to England players of all levels. At this stage I never seriously entertained the idea of playing for England, but, like many young men of that age, I certainly dreamed about it – just as I dreamed about scoring a hat-trick for Manchester City in the FA Cup final against Man United or hitting a century against the Australians before lunch at Lord's. I knew I was good at rugby, but I was just enjoying what came along in those days. I was twenty-one and playing rugby and drinking beer with my mates. As far as I was concerned, life had nothing more to offer.

Throughout the early nineties I used to watch Will Carling and Jerry Guscott on television playing in that highly successful England team and I would have laughed in your face if you told me that it was going to be me, muggins with his umpteenth pint in his hand, who would be pulling on their shirts in just a few years' time. Rugby then was as much a social activity as it was an athletic one – we liked playing and winning, but we liked socialising in the clubhouse even more. Even when I joined Quins after Durham, there were some fabulously talented players there like Jason Leonard, Pete Mensah and Darren O'Leary, but none of us could be described as models of virtuous living in those days. We trained, we played matches, we partied heavily – and we loved every minute of it. There's no use pretending otherwise. Some of us trained on Tuesday evening, some didn't. Most of us trained on Thursday, then we played on Saturday and in the evening we went down to the Pharaoh and Firkin on Putney Bridge.

It all changed pretty damned quickly with the advent of professionalism in the mid-nineties but the senior rugby world I entered was an entirely different place from the one I now inhabit. For pints of aftershave, read pints of isotonic energy drinks. The drinking culture has not disappeared, but the sessions are far fewer and further between and they certainly don't happen if there is a big game in the offing. You have to time your run to the pub to perfection these days. With England, the drinking is nearly non-existent, partly because so many Test matches now are back to back and your body simply wouldn't recover in time if you filled it full of lager after eighty minutes of gruelling contest. At the end of a tour or the autumn series of internationals or the Six Nations then, yes, we all go out and live it up a bit. But that's it. It used to be the case when I first got involved with England that after a match at Twickenham, you'd hit the West End after the post-match dinner; nowadays we get on the coach and head back to Pennyhill Park Hotel in Bagshot and by the time you get there you're half-asleep. Drinking is a good way for a team to bond, but the old social bonding has now been replaced by bonding on the training pitch.

The party spirit was still very much alive in the summer of 1993 when I was selected for the England Under-21 squad's seven-match tour of Australia. For many of us that tour will always hold very special memories because it saw a whole generation of us come together for the first time. Often when you look at old junior international squads and team sheets you are struck by how many of the names have disappeared into the shadows, but many of the 1993 boys were there for England at the World Cup ten years later. It was a highly talented young squad and included Austin Healey, Mike Catt, Tim Stimpson, Lawrence Dallaglio, Tony Diprose, Simon Shaw, Mark Regan, Richard Hill and Kyran Bracken.

I found an old photograph from that trip long ago and was highly amused to see Mike Catt, who had just arrived from South Africa, sporting a very fetching pair of dungarees and white socks, while Dallaglio was wearing as much denim as it's possible to wear without actually being a cowboy. He also had his belt about three inches above his belly button and I had great pleasure in bringing the picture along to his testimonial dinner shortly after we got back from the World Cup.

In 1993 I remember scoring twice as we thrashed Western Australia 80-8 in the opening game but we went on to lose as many matches as we won. It was our first proper tour and none of us were really thinking about making the step-up to the senior side at that stage for the simple reason that there wasn't much point. Nowadays youngsters are given a taste of senior international rugby at a much earlier age, but back then you were made to serve out an unofficial apprenticeship with your clubs and at junior England levels before you were deemed to have earned yourself a cap. As a twenty-year-old student, that tour felt like a free holiday to Australia with a bunch of like-minded lads with the odd bit of rugby thrown in between the fun.

We did, however, step up to the plate when it really mattered and in the one-off Test against our Australian equivalents we emerged 22-12 winners, a victory sealed, incredibly, by a late drop goal by me, albeit from about two yards out. I was allowed to keep the match ball that day and donated it to my local, the Bayley Arms in Hurst Green, where it remains to this day. I remember the match vividly because I had a terrible dead leg, should never have played and spent most of the afternoon hopping rather than running.

Bizarrely, when I got my World Cup photographs developed there was one shot that was virtually identical to the one I had taken almost exactly ten years earlier: Catt, Bracken, Dallaglio and Greenwood in the same pose, on the same beach, outside the same hotel, the Manley Pacific. If, back on that boozy tour in 1993, someone had told us that we would one day be mobbed outside that very hotel after winning the World Cup we would probably have bought him a pint, slapped him on the back and told him he was a very, very funny man.

Chapter Two

WILL CARLING WAS probably only dimly aware of my existence at the start of the 1994/5 season, but if he had chanced upon a copy of my CV at this time, he could have been forgiven for thinking that I was some kind of weird career stalker. Having followed him from Sedbergh to Durham University, I continued the trail by joining his club side, Harlequins – and, as if that wasn't quite enough, I had also converted myself into a centre by then. Perhaps I should have changed my surname to Carling as well and moved into the house next door so as to really freak him out. Had he known that, three years later, I was effectively going to take his position in the England team he had served so magnificently for a decade, he might not have been quite so friendly and welcoming as he was on my arrival at The Stoop that first summer.

There are a handful of former England internationals I'd sprint across the street to avoid, but Will Carling is not one of them. Our careers overlapped only briefly and so I'd be lying if I said we became great friends, but

I always got along very well with him when our paths crossed and today I listen to and read his opinions on the game with interest and respect. That is certainly not something I could say about the punditry skills of other former players who feel obliged to earn their media shillings by saying something 'controversial', regardless of whether or not it has any basis in truth or fairness. There can be an element of bitterness and envy in some commentators from Carling's generation because they missed out on the money that came with pro-fessionalism. You could never accuse Carling of that, or my other former Quins team-mate Brian Moore for that matter, because, apart from anything else, they both have highly successful careers outside rugby as a businessman and lawyer respectively.

In signing for Quins I succeeded in embarrassing my father who, at the time, was involved in a campaign to stop the best northern rugby players migrating south, but the game was still amateur then and I had to put my business career before my rugby. More by accident than design I had somehow managed to get a job as a trader in the City with Midland Global Markets (later HSBC). Like many students, I hadn't given a great deal of thought to what I was going to do with my life after graduation, busy as I was drinking beer, chasing girls and lying in bed until midday. In fact, I didn't have a clue what I wanted to do but it wasn't so much down to a lack of focus as the lack of a calling. There had been no shimmering visitations from my guardian angel in the middle of the night instructing me to become a pioneering heart surgeon, human rights lawyer or Middle East peace negotiator. Nor, sadly, did it seem likely that I would ever be able to make the step-up from mediocre/crap weekend footballer to professional with Manchester City and England which, if I had had any say in these matters, would have been my career of choice.

And so it was, like tens of thousands of other undergraduates up and down the country, I got out of bed and began to apply for jobs offering good prospects and reasonable amounts of money, but about which I knew precisely nothing. Although I was an Economics graduate, I had barely the faintest notion about how the City and all its different markets operated, but everyone else seemed to be heading that way and so I just jumped aboard. Since leaving school, life had been dealing me some pretty impressive hands. I had had a brilliant time at university; I'd made some friends for life; I'd represented my country at Student and Under-21 level; been signed up by one of England's leading clubs, and then virtually walked into a job with a starting salary of £18,500, which, as a student with only enough cash to buy Pot Noodles and toilet paper, seemed like an impossibly huge fortune. Sportsmen are fond of saying that they can only play what's in front of them and that's the way I saw the true beginning of my adult life. When

I boarded the train for Euston to begin my new life in London, I could see no further than the months immediately ahead of me. I was to work in the City with a bit of rugby at the weekend – and, if that sounds boring, you'll have to take my word for it that it most certainly was anything but.

I worked on 'the floor' of the LIFFE building near Cannon Street station where hundreds of millions of pounds, liras and Deutschmarks in futures were traded every working day in an atmosphere which could only be described as an orderly riot. This is not the place to give you a precise and detailed breakdown of how the market worked but suffice it to say I spent the majority of my working day in front of flashing screens, screaming down telephones in a booth surrounded by hundreds of other people doing exactly the same thing in scenes reminiscent of the final moments of the film *Trading Places*. I didn't understand what I was doing half the time but it was like one long adrenalin rush, exciting and terrifying in equal measure as you could lose or gain thousands of pounds in a matter of minutes.

The year before I remember screwing up a big sterling/yen trade when I was back in the HSBC building as a graduate trainee and when I realised that I had lost £50,000 in an instant I wanted the floor to open up and swallow me. I was selling when I should have been buying – and it doesn't get much more wrong than that. I fronted up immediately and admitted my error to my boss, Bobby Barnett, who was quite an intimidating character; but, luckily for me, the bank had just made well over a million pounds from the day's dealings and my losses were comfortably cancelled out by the massive gains my colleagues had made.

It may sound strange but there is a good deal of similarity between an international rugby match and a trading session in the City in the days before it became fully computerised: the pressure in both instances is enormous, you have to make quick and critical decisions on the hoof, you have to keep a cool head and you need to be bullish and brave. The only major difference between the two worlds as they were back then was that, after a day in the City, you tended not to end up in a big bath together singing lewd songs and throwing soap at each other.

One of the things I liked about the City was the mix of people you found there. I had imagined it to be full of public schoolboys, but in my field at least there were loads of Essex boys, East Enders and foreigners. I was actually one of the odd ones out, a northern monkey among streetwise Cockneys. The work was exhilarating but, combined with my rugby commitments, it was also absolutely shattering. Had I carried on living as I did for those two years, I would almost certainly have had some kind of breakdown by the age of thirty and no doubt ended up living under Southwark Bridge, drinking from puddles and introducing myself to passers-by as Napoleon Bonaparte himself.

My working day began when my alarm went off at five-thirty; for someone who loves his kip as much as I do, that daily bleeping sound was a truly cruel punishment. I would finish work at about six in the evening, already fairly exhausted after a nerve-shredding day on the floor, and on Mondays and Wednesdays I headed straight to the gym where I would work out for a couple of hours, then grab some food on the way home before going straight to bed. On Tuesdays and Thursdays I jumped on the tube to Waterloo from where I caught a train to Twickenham for Quins training and wouldn't get back home to Clapham until around midnight. If Saturday's match was up north or down in the West Country, we used to travel there the night before and then, straight after the game, win or lose, we would go out and drink ourselves daft because that, for most of us, was the only downtime we had all week. On Sundays I always had a dog of a hangover and felt even more exhausted than normal. When I finally dragged myself out of bed I'd spend an hour or two ironing my shirts for the week ahead – very, very slowly. Throughout that two-year period I had virtually no social life to speak of (barring the Saturday night sessions with my team mates) and almost never saw my family.

I was also representing the North of England at this time, and occasionally the bank would give me a couple of hours off to make the long journey to West Yorkshire for a training session. In hindsight, that trip seems like sheer madness. I used to catch the train from King's Cross to Wakefield where I'd collect a hire car, drive to the rugby club, do the training session, shower and change, drive back to London, get to bed at three in the morning, get up at five, drive the car to Kensington in west London to drop it off, get on the tube and be at my desk by seven o'clock.

The only time in my life that I've smoked was during my two-year stint in the City. As soon as I walked out of my front door in the morning on the way to the tube station at Clapham Common I would light up a cigarette, not because I enjoyed the experience but just to kill the terrible hunger pangs I always felt. (In the City, it wasn't so much that breakfast was for wimps, but you generally ate it on the go.) If you had seen this pale, miserable, hollow-eyed character puffing away on his cigarette as he sleepwalked his way to the station, you certainly wouldn't have been thinking: 'Now, there goes a World Cup winner in the making as sure as I'm an Englishman standing here today!' I must have cut a wretched figure.

In my first year at Quins I played at full-back most of the time as Will Carling teamed up with Pete Mensah in the centres, but I slotted into my preferred position whenever one of them was missing. I also played full-back for Emerging England and then centre for England

'A' on the end-of-season, six-match tour to Australia. That squad was probably not the most successful representative party ever to return to England's shores but it might well have been the most hung-over. In these days of professionalism we would, in all likelihood, be sent home and have our contracts and sponsorship deals terminated if we behaved as we did on tours back then. If our attitude sounds unprofessional, well, quite frankly, it was. Having fun was as important to us as winning and if that meant taking the field in a provincial game nursing a mild hangover, then so be it. We played as hard as you like once the opening whistle sounded, as hard as we would do in any kind of representative match today, but our preparation was, er . . . how shall we put this? . . . not exactly a blueprint for all young sportsmen trying to make their way in the world.

After we had lost a string of provincial games and gone out most evenings, the tour manager, Peter Rossborough, a former England full-back, made the connection between the two and called us all in for a dressing down: 'Do you want this tour to be remembered as the biggest boozing and shagging tour of all time or do you want it to be remembered for your achievements on the field?' he asked us. It was a no-brainer and, although no one dared say it, we were all thinking: 'We'll take the boozing and shagging trophies, please, Peter.' We all shuffled our feet, looked at the ground and muttered something about trying harder not to go out so often and then promptly walked out of the meeting and went straight down to the pub for a few beers to reflect on Peter's advice. You had to feel a little sympathy for the management on that tour but occasionally you also had to say they brought the trouble upon themselves. On one occasion, they organised a boat trip around Sydney's many harbours and put the Leicester prop Darren Garforth in charge to make sure we didn't have anything to drink. Let me repeat that – they put the Leicester prop Darren Garforth in charge to make sure we didn't have any-thing to drink. Why not make Herod chief babysitter while you're about it? Darren Garforth, Beer Monitor? I don't think so, somehow.

In the one match that really mattered on that tour, the one-off Test against Australia 'A' at Ballymore, Brisbane, we prepared reasonably sensibly and our discipline was rewarded with an impressive victory. I was a substitute that day, coming off the bench like a yo-yo warming up but never managed to get on. That was the one match in which we really didn't want to let ourselves down, the one result that anyone would ever remember or pay any attention to back home. For the rest of the time on that tour we were effectively playing in a vacuum, as all eyes in the rugby world were focused on South Africa.

The day after our triumph and the post-match

celebrations we had a long, painful journey to Fiji, where the thirty of us transferred on arrival to five six-seater planes to take us to Suva on the other side of the island. It rained in buckets for almost our entire stay there until the afternoon of the match itself when the cloud evaporated, the temperature hit 100 degrees centigrade and effectively boiled all the rain and turned the Pacific island into a giant sauna. Doing anything remotely active in a sauna is a major challenge under normal circumstances, but playing rugby against men the size and speed of trains after a night of no sleep and plentiful beer followed by a long plane journey is not an experience I can honestly recommend. We lost 59-25 to the full Fiji team and were lucky not to concede even more. We were dead on our feet.

The 1995 World Cup finals were taking place in South Africa at the same time as our boisterous tour to Australia and we watched as many games as we could on the television. The senior England set-up and that tournament seemed worlds apart to me at the time and it's extraordinary that I hadn't quite clicked that we, on that 'A' tour, were effectively the next generation. Carling, Guscott, De Glanville were the England centres for that tournament and for some reason it hadn't properly dawned on me that they were all much closer to the ends of their careers than the beginning. The idea that I should be competing with them, those icons of English rugby who I had watched as a schoolboy, for a place in the full national team must have been so ridiculous to me that I never entertained it as a serious thought.

At the start of the following season, with the game on the cusp of turning professional, Dad wrote to me setting out certain goals for me to consider. Thank God somebody was taking my career seriously. Among a number of points, he suggested that I consider alternative clubs if I didn't feel that Quins were quite up to the mark; that I develop my upper body strength; understand the limits of my troublesome left shoulder; work on my speed/power/plyometrics; improve my diet and, finally, make sacrifices in my social life. All this, he said, was a long-term plan with a view to getting into the 1999 World Cup squad. What social life? I asked myself, but I took Dad's point to be that traditional rugby culture was going to be swept away by the advent of professionalism. Rugby was about to get very serious. Dad once said it was the inalienable right of the amateur to 'play like a pillock'. I suppose you could say it was the inalienable duty of the professional not to.

I played some of the best rugby of my career in that 1995/6 season and by the end of it I had attracted a few supporters in the game and in the press who felt that I should be chosen ahead of the veteran England triumvirate of Carling, Guscott and De Glanville – or 'the old gits' as it once slipped out while I was on live television. The England coach of the day, Jack Rowell, however, was not entirely convinced that it was time for the tall, skinny lad at Quins to push aside his favourite old campaigners. Loyalty died hard in rugby back then and once you were well established in the England club you had to try pretty hard or grow fairly old and infirm before being politely shown the door. Today they virtually pluck kids off climbing frames in playgrounds to blood them at senior international level. The prevailing philosophy is 'if you are good enough, you are old enough', whereas the attitude then was more 'if you're not a total embarrassment and I like you, then you're in'.

In December 1995 I scored a hat-trick for England 'A' in a 55-0 win over the Samoans at Gateshead. It was a bitterly cold night and the tourists weren't in the least bit interested so our victory was not quite as impressive as it might appear on paper. In the New Year I captained the side in a brutal match at the Stade Jean Bouin near the old Parc des Princes in Paris. We won 25-15 but not before playing our part in one of the biggest legalised mass brawls I have ever witnessed. It was as if there were no touch judges in attendance that day and fights were erupting all over the pitch. The French, often poor travellers in my experience, are always a formidable proposition on their own turf and they have a great expression along the lines of 'No defeat within the sound of our church bells'. The only bells around that January day, however, were the seven that each side was trying to knock out of the other. I remember one incident – amusing in a dark kind of way – when Tim Stimpson was jumped on by a pack of Frenchmen who promptly started taking lumps out of him. Garath Archer, our giant lock, piled into the mêlée to help him and, as he explained later, followed what he thought was a French arm up to the owner's face which he then proceeded to give a good squeeze. There followed a terrible screaming noise and, once the ruck broke up, Stimmo came running over and said: 'Will! Will! You've got to do something as captain. They're trying to gouge my bloody eyes out.' As he trotted off, Garath, who had heard Stimmo's complaint, whispered in my ear: 'Easy, Will, I think there may have been a case of mistaken identity there, if you get my drift.'

That season I played a lot of games for Quins as well as two for the Northern Division and four for England 'A', and by the end of it I had received some flattering appraisals of my form which boosted my confidence enormously. I was never going to be a powerhouse player in the Carling mould or a jet-heeled one in the style of Guscott, but it was acknowledged I could read the game reasonably well, my distribution was sound, I could stand up and offload in the tackle and I could run a good line. Those have always been my strengths as a rugby player. Raw power and pace were never options.

It was at this time that the long drawn-out saga of shedding the game's amateur status came to an end and a brief transitional period followed in which some players, but by no means all, began to give up their day jobs and turn fully professional. They were strange days because you didn't quite know how the game would develop from then on. The big question facing us was: did you really want to give up your fairly well-paid job and steady career prospects to sign up for an uncertain future at clubs whose finances were limited by the absence of a major television deal and by weekly crowds of just a few thousand? Furthermore, it would take only a split second to wreck your cruciate ligament and your new career with it.

I decided to see what was on offer at Quins before making any hasty decisions, but it became clear very early in my negotiations with coach Dick Best that, if I was to have a place in the professional game, it wasn't going to be at the London club. His offer, quite frankly, was insulting – it was roughly half the modest salary I was earning in the City. I loved my rugby but not enough to play it for free. Best was an extremely good coach, especially with the forwards, who he would work into the ground, and, to be fair to him, there was no reason why he should have become a financial expert and professional contract negotiator overnight. I didn't fall out with him over the contract and no angry words were exchanged, but if another big club came in for me and could offer me more than a peppercorn salary, I was definitely off.

I must have been very naïve in those days because I only found out years later that, towards the end of the season and during the summer months, I was being discreetly sounded out by Leicester about a possible transfer. It was all change in rugby then as the merry-go-round of player transfers gathered momentum, while agents, go-betweens and club officials were sniffing about trying to recruit the best players. That May I played for the Barbarians against Ireland in Dublin in a Peace International organised by the former international Hugo McNeill. The match was my first genuine taste of the international scene and I loved every moment of it. There was a full house of 55,000 inside Lansdowne Road and there were some great players on display that day, including Philippe Sella, a personal hero of mine, and Eric Rush. I came on in the eighth minute after an injury to Phil de Glanville and I had a half-decent game in a 70-38 win for the Baa-Baas.

The day before we had gone to the Guinness factory – only the Barbarians can prepare for a match in a brewery – and I don't know how any of us were able to take the field the following day. I've never seen such commitment. There were about four or five Leicester lads in the Barbarians squad but not for a minute did I question why they seemed to enjoy my company so much that day. Later that summer I was invited to join Harvey Thorneycroft's tour party to West Africa to raise money for Max Brito, the Ivory Coast player paralysed during the World Cup finals. The playing party was made up almost entirely of Leicester and Northampton players and I still didn't click when I ended up rooming with the Leicester captain Dean Richards, who dropped a number of subtle hints about Leicester and made polite enquiries about my future as a professional and so on. It wasn't until shortly after I returned to England and Peter Wheeler, the Leicester chief executive, called me up, that I became aware that the Tigers were interested in signing me.

That little trip to Africa proved to be an eye-opener in other ways, however. Our first match was in Ghana against a South African XV and my opposite man that day was the great Danie Gerber, the daddy of all centres, who had scored a hat-trick in the first half against my old man's England team at Ellis Park in Johannesburg back in 1984. This might have been a charity match but someone obviously forgot to tell Danie, who beat me up pretty tidily early on. Before the referee had even blown the opening whistle, we were all in need of medical attention as it was, having had to stand in the blistering sun for almost an hour while the Ghanaian president – no doubt a keen disciple of Fidel Castro, the great rambler himself – warbled on about anything that happened to be passing through his mind at the time. It was so hot they had to stop the game every ten minutes to allow us to rehydrate and catch our breath, but we managed to sneak a victory thanks to a highly dubious decision by an extremely pleasant English referee we had brought out with us. But any satisfaction we might have felt at playing a part in a good cause was ruined when we found out later that, when they came to add up the gate receipts, there was only 7,500 tickets' worth in the coffers even though there had been a massive 80,000 in the stadium.

The following day we endured a terrifying flight to the Ivory Coast. We were all set to take off when the pilot announced he was not prepared to fly because the plane's radar had broken. It looked as if we would have to cancel the match because kickoff was at 7.30 that evening, just a few hours away, when another pilot, grinning from ear to ear, appeared on the scene and announced everything was fine because he knew the route from memory. Somewhat anxiously we boarded the flight and then spent the next few hours gripping the arms of our seats while our laughing pilot kept diving the plane under the clouds to see where he was going. I remember looking around at various points in the flight and seeing all these giant rugby men stunned into ashen-faced silence. I also recall that at one point, adding a slightly surreal air to the proceedings, someone came round offering us little fairy cakes.

We survived the flight, we survived the match – a narrow victory – and soon after our return I found myself walking into the elegant surroundings of the Grosvenor House Hotel on London's Park Lane for a meeting with Leicester supremo Peter Wheeler. The deal he offered me was slightly more than I was making in my City job, so that evening I called Dad for his advice and he told me to add my bank salary to their offer and see what they said. An hour after proposing my terms, Peter Wheeler called back and said, 'Fine, welcome aboard.' That was it. In a matter of minutes I had doubled my salary and joined one of the most powerful clubs in Northern Hemisphere rugby.

Leicester had a reputation for playing 'boring' 10-man rugby at this time and I had heard all the old jokes, particularly popular in the Bath area, before getting into my car and heading up the M1 to the city which would be my home for the next four years: 'Leicester backs spend the morning in the gym and the afternoon in the job centre . . . Leicester's idea of expansive rugby is to give the ball to the fly-half occasionally but only for him to kick penalties . . .' etc., etc.

Leicester, quite simply, is a great club, whatever style of rugby they were perceived to be playing at that time, and I didn't need to do much soul-searching before signing for them. But there were a number of other smaller factors which persuaded me that I was making a sound career move. Firstly, Austin Healey had also arrived that summer from Orrell, which I took to be a powerful indication that Leicester intended to play a bit of rugby. You don't buy Austin Healey unless you plan to throw the ball around and mix it up a bit in the backs.

Perhaps I am biased because he is a great friend – and I also love attacking rugby – but Austin is without question one of the most intelligent, creative and versatile footballers I have ever seen. I don't think it would be an exaggeration to say that he is one of the few backs in recent times to have the spark of genius in him. (I can't believe I just wrote that, but, as Austin rarely reads books without pictures or pop-up animals in them, he'll probably be none the wiser.)

Furthermore, as a back who loves going forward with the ball in hand, I took one look at the names in the Leicester pack and thought that if I didn't get the ball from time to time playing behind that lot then I was never going to get it. If any forwards in Britain were going to give you an armchair ride in the backs, it was the Leicester mob. The front row was the famous ABC club of Rowntree, Cockerill and Garforth and behind them were three more English heavyweights in the form of Martin Johnson, Dean Richards and Neil Back. There was one further element behind my decision, too – I was only twenty-three years old and didn't know how far I could go in the game. At Leicester, the most hard-nosed, unforgiving club in England, there could be no hiding place and I would soon find out if I had it in me to perform at the very highest level. I didn't want to get to the end of a reasonably successful career ten years down the line and be left wondering whether I could have moved up to a higher level, if only I had had the courage or the confidence. I had to go to Leicester to find out.

The former Wallabies coach Bob Dwyer arrived at the Tigers that same summer and, on paper at least, the big, mustachioed Aussie seemed like the perfect man for the job: a hard man with a simple view of the game in charge of . . . well, a hard team with a simple view of the game. Leicester, it seemed, was a team made in his own image. Like many new coaches in sport, Bob wanted to stamp his identity and authority on the team early and he soon dispensed with the services of Rory Underwood and Dean Richards, two of the club's longest serving members and icons for the Welford Road faithful. It was a bold move but it certainly ruffled a few feathers at a club that prides itself on the tightness and loyalty of its family.

At Quins just two months earlier, rugby had been an amateur game and we used to train two evenings a week after work and have a runabout on the Saturday. Combined with a job and other commitments it was a taxing schedule, but the training itself was powder-puff stuff compared to what I was about to experience. At Leicester I trained every day – and in a way I had never done before. I was never the most committed trainer and was generally happy enough to let my friends in the forwards spill all the claret and the sweat. Then suddenly I was tossed into this utterly alien, ultra-competitive environment in which your own team-mates were trying to kick the shit out of you on a daily basis. It was a major culture shock. The rucking session on Tuesday and the defence session on Wednesday were particularly brutal and when we played ten-against-ten games we competed as if our very futures depended upon it. There was an almost diabolical intensity to the atmosphere on the training ground at Leicester. It wasn't so much a winning mentality as a bloody-minded, stubborn one. If Leicester had a club motto it would be whatever the Latin is for 'Over My Dead Body'. In hindsight it was not at all difficult to see why they went on to win four league championships and two European Cups over the coming years.

I had to get my head down in those early months and show my new team-mates that I was worth a place at their club. In order to be accepted at Welford Road you have to prove yourself in battle and cop a few stitches at the bottom of a ruck. Until you are seen a few times emerging from the bottom of a pile of bodies streaming with blood, you haven't truly arrived at Leicester Tigers. They cared nothing for reputations, only for actions. I was amazed by how regularly the Leicester boys fought among themselves on the training ground and was even more astounded to see them laughing about it just minutes later back in the changing room.

At least once a week there would be a brawl in training, and it was generally among the forwards and usually one on one (unless Austin was involved when it would be about fifteen on one. When they could catch him, the forwards liked nothing better than giving him a clip around the ear). Most of the fights took place in the touch rugby or semi-opposed sessions, and only rarely in full contact contests where satisfaction can be had by clattering someone in the tackle. It's when you can't get your hands on the bloke who's been winding you up that feelings tend to boil over. I've only had one fight in training and that was with Austin during an England training session at the Bank of England ground in the build-up to the 1999 World Cup finals. As fights go it wasn't very impressive I'm afraid. One of us had caught the other with an elbow and the next moment we're standing off against each other, grabbing each other by the shirts and saying 'Come on then . . .' 'No, you come on then.' We might as well have been in an arts and crafts boutique arguing over what knitted tea cosy to buy. Our forwards would have been ashamed if they had seen us.

Another new face to appear in the Leicester senior squad that summer was a young, grinning blond lad called Lewis Moody. The first time I saw him climb out of his orange Beetle in the club car park, I thought he must have got lost and had come to ask directions. He looked so skinny I thought there was no conceivable way he could be a rugby player, let alone a back row forward at Leicester Tigers. Then he tackled me and I knew why. God it hurt. A great player and a great bloke that Moody, but mad as a hatter on the pitch. With the possible exception of Neil Back, I have never come across a man with so little regard for his own safety. I have spent many an afternoon watching in amazement from the relative safety of the midfield as this madman has happily thrown himself into the path of as many swinging boots and knees as a person can find in eighty minutes. Not for nothing does he go by the nickname of Mongo, the character in the film *Blazing Saddles* who punches horses. I have a theory that it was Mongo who won the World Cup for England, but more of that later.

Another new player to arrive that season was a big, fast, raw back called Leon Lloyd, a nineteen-year-old with a big, bold hair-do and an attitude to match. He had come from Barkers Butt, Backy's old club up the road in Coventry, effectively as a replacement for the great Rory Underwood. Others may have been daunted by the prospect of living up to the standards set by England's most prolific try scorer, but not Leon. One of the nicest lads you could ever hope to meet off the pitch, Leon is one of those sportsmen with a touch of the Jekyll and Hyde about him, and he likes to play his rugby like a foam-flecked maniac bent on terrorising anyone who crosses his path. Forever taunting opponents on the pitch, and no stranger to a scrap, Leon used to give the impression that there was a very angry man somewhere inside him. Great player, too. Jon Callard, the Bath and England full-back, was a similar character, softly spoken off the pitch but spitting fury on it and, whenever Leicester and Bath clashed, the two of them used to spend most of the match hurling insults at each other.

For my first two months at Leicester I lived in a Holiday Inn, together with Austin and the Scotsman Craig Joiner, another summer recruit. It was located in the middle of a roundabout just around the corner from Welford Road and, although it might not have been the most exotic setting, it boasted a fine carvery that fed half of the Leicester squad after training for several weeks until the club saw our room bill and made some enquiries. Why, they wanted to know, were the three of us eating nineteen roast beef dinners a day?

I made my league debut in a 28-25 home win over arch rivals Bath which was sealed with a late penalty try – to the delight of the Welford Road crowd who had seen one awarded to Bath just a few months earlier in the Pilkington Cup final in highly controversial circumstances. The try had been given in the final minute at Twickenham, handing Bath victory, and it so incensed Neil Back that he pushed over referee Stephen Lander and was later banned for six months. (The disciplinary panel was not convinced by Neil's defence that he thought the older looking man in the funny coloured shirt with the whistle in his mouth was Bath player Andy Robinson, now the England head coach.)

I played reasonably well that day but it was only when

Backy returned to the side later in the season that I began to make a consistently significant impression. Linking up with him gave my career a great impetus for which I will always be grateful. Suddenly every time I went into a contact situation, I would look around and see this little blond bloke at my shoulder and I would be able to offload the ball to him and thus maintain the continuity that was quickly becoming such an important part of the modern game. One of the qualities that I have tried to develop over the years is the ability to stay up in the tackle and use my long arms and handling skills to keep the ball alive. With Neil at my shoulder I started to look very adept at recycling and it was probably beneficial for him too that he now had a centre thinking along the same lines as himself.

Another game which stands out in the memory from those early days at Leicester was my first one back at Harlequins since leaving the club. You always want to do well against your old club but perhaps there was also a small part of me that wanted to show Dick Best I was worth a few quid more than the derisory offer he had put on the negotiating table in the summer. We won the match 34–18 and I remember scoring a try when I managed to step out of a tackle by Gary Connolly, the former Great Britain rugby league captain, and then hold off Will Carling to score. I had started to receive some half-decent notices in the press by this time and there were some louder calls for me to be called into the

England team. But there was still one person I had yet to win over, it seemed: Bob Dwyer. After that match he publicly admitted that when he first saw me play he thought I was 'grossly overrated' but that now he was starting to think I was 'pretty good'. A few weeks earlier he had exploded on the training ground and shouted at me: 'Mate, are you really a second row forward in disguise because most centres I know can pass and handle the ball?' As passing and handling were meant to be two of the stronger facets of my game, you can imagine how I felt as his taunts rained down on me. I also had to cop a lot of highly unamusing abuse from my team-mates on the subject in the weeks that followed Bob's blast.

My relationship with Bob was a generally happy one and if angry words ever passed between us, they usually travelled back in exactly the same direction. I have never seen anyone benefit from insulting his coach and so I have tended to bite my tongue on the occasions when I have received an earful, warranted or otherwise. In a quieter moment I will argue my case, but I never let rip in the heat of the moment. As I knew him then, Bob Dwyer lived, breathed and ate rugby, and, for all I know, probably passed it on the toilet, too. I remember his wife, a 'rugby widow' if ever there was one, telling us she would go downstairs at three in the morning and he would be sitting there analysing rugby matches he had videoed before heading off to work at six. He was completely obsessive and there were moments when we genuinely worried about his health and thought he might collapse in the changing room, his blood pressure was so high. He was a great storyteller with a very colourful turn of phrase and an active imagination, and he was generally at his best when he was away from the pitch and allowed himself a moment or two of not thinking about rugby. Some of his team talks and expressions are still recalled with amused fondness today: 'One day I was out walking with the wife and we were feeding the ducks and then suddenly this pike came up from the bottom and said: "Whammo – that's my piece of bread!"' he explained on one occasion, wildly snapping his hands together in imitation of his pike. 'That's the kind of enthusiasm I want you guys to have when you go hunting for the ball. Whammo!' On another occasion: 'You've gotta run like there's a dog chasing you . . . No, f**k it! Like there's a tiger chasing you . . . No, f**k it! Like there's a man with a knife chasing you . . .'

I don't think I would be revealing one of rugby's longest and best kept secrets if I said that Bob could also be quite angry when we lost. People talk about Sir Alex Ferguson's so-called 'hair-dryer treatment' at Manchester United but I'd be willing to wager that they are mere tearoom tiffs compared to Bob's. Bob Dwyer goes purple. There was one occasion towards the end of his time with Leicester when we were convinced he was going to have a coronary. It was half-time in a match against London Irish, we were 9-3 up but should have been out of sight, and Bob went absolutely berserk. It got to the point where we all began looking at each other and thinking 'he's going to keel over if he carries on like this'.

On another occasion we had just snatched a draw at Sale at the end of an ultimately disappointing season (1996/7) to clinch a place in Europe and Bob was giving an interview to a television crew when some bloke walked past and shouted, 'Leicester cheats!' Bob swivelled around and grabbed his abuser and said, 'F★★k off, mate! Can't you see I'm doing a f★★★ing interview?' and then resumed his normal talking voice and carried on as if nothing had happened.

By the time Bob came to leave Leicester I like to think that he had more respect for me as a player than he had when he first arrived and regarded me as some kind of a lumbering, cack-handed lock who had somehow got lost in the midfield and never found his way back to the scrum. He also made a key decision which had an enormous impact on my career and I'll always owe him one for that. It seems so obvious now that I cannot think why I had never thought of it myself, or why other coaches had not suggested it: he moved me to inside centre. Realising that I lacked the raw pace needed for outside centre and recognising that what skills I did have were better suited to the tighter role at inside, he simply switched me and Stuart Potter around. (Stuart fulfilled a role on the pitch and the clubhouse afterwards similar to that performed by my fellow England centre Mike Tindall today. He could run through and destroy brick walls at an incredible pace and then, if there was no big match on the immediate horizon and we could celebrate, he would proceed to drink the forwards under the table.) Bob's decision to make the switch was the second major turning point in my playing career after my old friend Benny Fennell at Durham casually suggested that I might be better off in the centres than at fly-half or full-back. Both moves paid instant dividends and on this occasion I scored five tries in my first run-out in my new position against Cambridge University in December.

We almost had a disaster later that month, however, when we played so-called minnows Newbury in the cup at Welford Road and made the cardinal sporting error of underestimating the opposition. Our second rower, Matt Poole, was hosting a fancy-dress party that night, and we all took our outfits into the changing room before the match and it quickly came to resemble the costume department of a Hollywood studio with Batman capes and togas hanging off the pegs. We were perhaps guilty of thinking more about nightclubs than rugby that afternoon because we were a long way from being the crack professional outfit we were meant to be when we ran out on to the pitch and were pushed to the very limit by our visitors. I managed to score a try in the last couple of minutes to secure us a narrow win and it was with our tails firmly between our legs that we scraped into the next round. (One vivid image of the party that night sticks in my head as bright as a light bulb to this day: the sight of Austin Healey and his wife Louise – then his girlfriend – having an argument and going toe to toe outside a nightclub, Oz dressed as a gorilla and Louise as a polar bear.)

Joel Stransky, the man whose drop goal had won South Africa the World Cup two years earlier, in 1995, had joined Leicester that month and our performance that day must have given him every reason to believe he had signed for a team of Disney characters. Joel was unavailable to play in the European Cup, but he would have been far more impressed by our display against a highly regarded Toulouse side just into the New Year. Austin was on fire at scrum-half as we hammered them 37–11 to reach the final. Although the Welford Road ground was frozen pretty hard and the French didn't seem to fancy it that much in the cold, it was still a very impressive all-round display by us and helped to erase some of the embarrassment of the Cup debacle. I had one of my better games that day and the following morning's press was full of calls for me to be called into the England team at the next opportunity. One journalist, who had obviously drunk too much, said I had 'the sharpest brain in English rugby' and in his column Bob Dwyer even admitted he had been wrong in his original assessment of me, saying I had the 'catch-and-pass skills to play at any level'!

In January, I was invited to a thirty-five-man England get-together before the 1997 Five Nations Championships. In those days, whenever I found myself in a new environment, it was my approach to stay in the shadows and just keep my head down and so my memories of that first call-up are dim. One incident, though, stands out very vividly and I still occasionally find myself chuckling at the recollection of it today. Jack Rowell was giving some kind of lecture using an overhead projector and about halfway through a fly settled on his illuminated notes, sending a giant shadow across the screen on the wall. It was one of those silly mistakes any of us can make when our mind is concentrated on something else, but rather than brush the fly off the projector Rowell went over to the screen and started flailing at the insect's shadow. There followed some low sniggering throughout the room, which quickly turned to nervous guffaws when the hooker Mark 'Ronnie' Regan, shouted out 'Village!' – as in village idiot. Effectively calling the man who might launch your international career an imbecile may not appear the most obvious route to the top, but then Ronnie has never let his career get in the way of a good joke. I never called Jack Rowell a village idiot, but he still never gave me a cap and I continued to play for the 'A' team that season.

One paper claimed that I had put on 3 stone since joining Leicester, adding power to my alleged 'guile'. This was utter rubbish. If I sat in front of the television for five years eating nothing but chocolate eclairs, crisps and pizza I'd be lucky if I put on 2 stone at the most. It has been with good reason that I have been known throughout my life variously as Cheesewire, Shaggy, Pepperami Legs, Rodney (Trotter), Beanpole and so on . . . When the drugs guys come round to test us, they take one look at me and think, 'Well, whatever he's on sure isn't working.' It was true that when I came to Leicester I set myself the goal of becoming about a stone and a half heavier and a yard and a half faster and I got close to fulfilling both those aims that season. But 3 stone? It's simply not possible to double your weight in six months!

The European final that year was at the end of January and we headed to Cardiff Arms Park to face a Brive side that we were expected to pulverise with the same ruthlessness with which we had dispatched their French brothers at Toulouse three weeks earlier. I wasn't quite so sure about that and looking at the team sheets now you wonder why anyone had us as red-hot favourites in the first place. The two bruising packs were pretty well matched, but in the backs they were exceptionally strong with Christophe Lamaison and David Venditti in the centres as well as Sebastien Viars, Alain Penaud and Philippe Carbonneau. We had Rob

Liley and John Liley, myself, Stuart Potter, Steve Hackney, Leon Lloyd and Austin Healey, which was a fairly good line-up but not in the same class as theirs. It was all going to be decided in the forwards, our monsters against theirs, but in the end theirs played as well as any pack I've ever seen and their blindside flanker, Gregory Kacala, had the game of his life. For the first sixty minutes they absolutely battered us and we barely laid hands on the ball.

It was an incredible performance by a pack without a single French international in it and even Leicester's mighty forwards had to conccde they were well beaten on the day. In 1986 the French had beaten the All Blacks 16-3 in a notoriously violent Test match, known as The Battle of Nantes, during which the great New Zealand number eight Wayne Shelford had his scrotum ripped open and one of his testicles popped out. In the aftermath there were newspaper accusations that some of the French forwards had been on some kind of stimulants. I know the Brive boys weren't on any kind of drugs in the final against us that day but something inside was certainly firing them up. The final score was 28-9 and it was no more than they deserved. The French, I have found throughout my career, have a habit of bringing you down to earth just when you are starting to feel pretty pleased with yourselves.

That first year was a strange and ultimately depressing season for us at Leicester. We had got off to a flying start and as we turned into the New Year we were fighting for honours on all three fronts: the league, the Pilkington Cup and the European Cup. But as our fixture backlog began to mount up and the injuries and fatigue started to take their toll, it all began to fall apart at the seams, starting with that remarkable and painful afternoon in Cardiff. We had one massive last performance left in us and ran out 39-28 winners against Bath in the Pilkington Cup, a match during which I bagged a couple of tries to maintain my weirdly prolific scoring record against them. Our arch rivals, though, exacted a heavy revenge when we met again in the league, hammering us 47-9 as our championship campaign came off the rails in spectacular fashion. Perhaps like the great Leeds United football sides of the late 1960s and early 1970s, Leicester were the victims of their own lofty ambitions that season, setting the pace for the chasing pack only to tire and stumble heading around the final bend. After so much effort and having played so much outstanding rugby, it was dismal to see it all go to pieces.

The backlog of matches was a major factor in our decline. Professional rugby had just kicked off and the people who ran the game were trying to squeeze in as many games as possible to maximise exposure and revenue. In the end, such a saturation policy is probably counterproductive because by the end of the season everyone is shattered or injured and the winners limp rather than sprint over the finishing line. In one of our final matches, against Wasps, I tore my ankle ligaments but, as we already had so many players out injured and there was so much at stake, I was given a series of injections to kill the pain and allow me to keep playing. Seven years later my ankle is still shot to pieces and I cannot do any running on it without strapping it first.

It was a measure of the standards we had set ourselves that winning the Pilkington Cup felt almost like an anti-climax, a feeling compounded by the fact that it was probably the most boring, miserable game of rugby played since records began. We had done all the hard yards just to get there, beating not only Bath but also Newcastle and Gloucester (all away from home), and we edged Sale 9–3 in the final thanks to three Joel Stransky penalties. The scoreline tells you virtually everything you need to know about the match and I remember the biggest cheer of the day came when the Tannoy man announced that Dean Richards was coming on as a substitute. The major incident in the match, from a personal point of view, came with ten minutes to go and the match still in the balance when I felt my hamstring go. I looked over to the bench and was just about to indicate that I would have to go off when Austin turned to me and said: 'Don't even fucking think about it – we need you out here.' And so, with a knackered ankle and a twinged hamstring, I hobbled about until the final whistle, aggravating both injuries with every step.

The final whistle that afternoon sounded especially sweet to my ears, not just because we had hung on to win a bit of silverware at the end of a gruelling season, but because it meant that I would probably still be able to fulfil a dream cherished by every rugby player in the British Isles. Incredibly, I had been chosen in the Lions party to tour South Africa. Although I had yet to be capped, the tour management team of Ian McGeechan, Jim Telfer and Fran Cotton had seen something in my style of play that suited their strategy for the tour. My selection hadn't come as a total surprise partly because there had been mounting speculation in the press after I had made the preliminary party of sixty names earlier in the year but also because Dad's old mate Stan Bagshaw, who had been chosen as kitman for the trip, was incapable of keeping a secret and gave us a strong hint or two that I was definitely in the running.

I have to admit that after a fairly decent season for Leicester I was only too happy to believe the hype and that, had I not been chosen for the final party, I would have felt mildly disappointed. I was living with Austin by this stage and I am still plotting my revenge on him for the trick he played on me the day the final Lions squad was announced. The post arrived and Austin ran around the house waving his selection letter while offering his commiserations that there had not been a similar one for me. Unlike me, Austin was already involved in the England set-up by then and his inclusion as a player of such versatility was no surprise. So for the next two hours I moped about the house kicking myself for being so stupid as to think that as an uncapped player I had any chance of getting on that flight in the first place. And then Austin pulled out a letter and handed it to me. I suppose I could have punched him there and then, but I prefer my revenge eaten cold and I am taking my opportunities at a leisurely pace and in my own good time. My calculated policy of vengeance got off to a good start early in 2004 when I managed to get the mouthy little sod thrown off *The Weakest Link* in the first round even though he had got all his questions right. And that's just for starters, my little friend.

Making the party was without doubt the high point of my fledgling career, but doing my hamstring in the cup final came close to wrecking the dream. It was only thanks to the common sense and decency of the tour doctor, James Robson, a good man of whom I would get to see far too much in the coming weeks, that I came to be among the thirty-five players to board the flight to Johannesburg that May.

Robbo knew all the hamstring needed was a little time and his fitness test could have been passed by my grandma!

It had been an incredible year for me. I no longer had to get up at 5.30 in the morning to go to an office for ten hours; I was now getting paid good money to run around outside with my mates; I had joined one of the best club sides in the world, played some great rugby with them, found my best position and won my first winners' medal at club level. I had made a number of great new friends along the way and been selected to go on a British Lions tour as a callow, uncapped twenty-four-year-old with my whole career and adult life stretching out before me.

As if that wasn't enough for one young man to enjoy in twelve months, I had also met a gorgeous girl who I had somehow managed to persuade – not without some effort, it should be stressed – that I was that noble knight on the white charger she had been searching for all her life. There certainly hadn't been anything especially chivalrous about my behaviour at our first encounter, I am told. I say 'I am told' because our first meeting allegedly took place when Austin, Craig Joiner and myself were on our first night out since joining Leicester and I don't recall a great deal about it – or anything at all to be perfectly honest. She was apparently very, very unimpressed by my efforts to dance with her.

The next time we met was after a Leicester league match and I was in a far more presentable state when this very attractive, talkative young girl latched on to me as if I was her long lost brother. It was only years later I discovered that her gushing enthusiasm for my company was based on nothing more romantic than her desire to get away from some bloke across the other side of the room. And so it was that I came to fall for my future wife and mother of my children, but over the next few months I had to put in some seriously hard yards on the Training Ground of Romance to pass my fitness test at the end of it. In short, in spite of my best efforts for three or four months, she didn't really want to know. Personally, I blame Austin and here seems as good a place as any to launch the second phase of the long drawn-out vengeance policy I have in my mind for my old housemate.

One evening I asked Caro out for a date and we had a lovely evening at a local Italian restaurant. We had a couple of glasses of wine but no more, and I like to think I had been a charming young suitor when I invited her back to see my house and meet my flatmates. Big mistake. Have you ever seen that advert when a man brings home a girl only to walk in on all his male flatmates all dressed up in tiaras and tutus doing the ironing? Well, this was worse. As I put the key in the latch and pushed open the door I was met with a truly horrifying vision. There, lying on the floor of our sitting room with not a shred of clothing about him and with some exotic French film on the television, was Austin Healey, International Athlete. Without ceremony, I all but shoved Caro back out on to the street and dribbled a lame excuse about a forgotten wallet in the car before we returned two minutes later to find Austin fully clothed and asking if we had had a nice evening! I continued to chase Caro for the rest of the year and she finally held her hands up and admitted defeat in the face of my persistence. If you want to be statistical about these things, we became an official item on the morning of 1 January 1997 – and before you could say 'nice property, reasonable rent' I had moved my bags into her mum's vacant house up the road.

Chapter Three

I HAD GOT TO know Fran Cotton quite well through my northern connections and I knew from past experience that any tour fronted by him didn't only stand a good chance of being successful, but was also likely to be highly enjoyable into the bargain. Not long before, Fran had been in charge of a Northern XV for a match against Samoa at Huddersfield and we had warmed up for it in traditionally amateur fashion by spending the Sunday evening in a pub called the Windmill. Some of the squad woke up in the hotel reception at 7.30 the following morning still in their going-out clothes, but we actually managed to hammer the Samoans on the Tuesday night (to be fair to them, the freezing hail and biting wind were hardly Pacific island conditions!). We all bonded well that night and what we might have lost in the physical department we more than made up for in terms of unity and camaraderie. You can train your socks off until you reach Olympic athlete standards, but in rugby it counts for very little unless you have a bunch of players willing to spill blood for each other on the pitch. Today, we do most of our bonding on the training ground, but back then the pub was where it all happened.

Sure enough, Fran deployed a similar strategy on the day the Lions squad congregated at Oatlands Park Hotel in Weybridge, to the south-west of London. That evening we were dropped off at a pub called the White Swan in Walton-on-Thames, Fran put an open-ended tab behind the bar and just told us to get on with it. Dieticians and physical fitness instructors would probably release an inward scream at the very thought of this get-together, but personally I thought it was a masterstroke. There were thirty-five players in total in a tour party of forty-seven, from four different countries and a dozen or so different clubs. The fact that all of us knew a handful of others was a danger rather than an advantage because it ran the risk of cliques being formed. The only time we had come into contact with each other in the past was when we tried to take lumps out of each other in international and club matches. By shoving us in a room together and breaking the ice with a few trays of beers, any pre-match tensions and divisions were swept away at a stroke.

That 1997 Lions' was the last of the old-style tours. The game had just turned professional but that two-month trip represented a final hurrah for the amateur era. It was a very tight squad, with a great relationship between the midweek and Saturday teams. No one gave us a prayer against the reigning world champions, who were five-to-one ON with the bookmakers to take the series, and that made us even tighter. The main criticisms of the squad were that we were not big enough, our captain Martin Johnson was an inexperienced liability, some of us were too old and some of us were too young. The one accusation that no one could throw at the selectors was that their party was safe and predictable.

The day before we left, all our girlfriends and wives and children came down to the hotel to say goodbye. While the young, single blokes in the party can't wait to get on the plane, for the older guys with families these meetings are often tinged with sadness. For me, with my dodgy hamstring, I just wanted to put my feet on South African soil and pull a Lions shirt over my head before anyone noticed that I only had one operational leg. By the time I reached South Africa, however, Dr Robson had worked his magic and I was fighting fit. We had booked the business section of a Virgin Atlantic flight and during the ten-hour journey we had plenty of time to focus on the challenges that lay ahead. For my part, I simply had no idea what to expect and I could only guess what lay in store. I had never played a full international for England, let alone represented the mighty Lions, and I had never been to South Africa. What I did know was that we would be up against some of the hardest rugby players on the planet who yield not an inch to anyone, especially when defending their own backyard. New Zealand, who have produced some of the great Test sides of all time, had only won one Test series there prior to 1997. The England tour of 1994 had involved a lot of fighting, I had heard, and although there were cameras everywhere now and it was more difficult to get away with the sly shots, it would still be brutal. Hard is the only way the South Africans can play rugby.

I was as naïve as I was uncapped at the start of that tour but thus far in my career I had always delivered the goods when asked to move up a level. I had been chosen, I was told, partly because of my ability to create space for others, to hold the ball up in the tackle and produce something unexpected, but I had no illusions that I was there in anything other than a supporting role to the more senior centres, Jerry Guscott, Alan Bateman, Alan Tait and Scott Gibbs.

As a squad of players we were certainly in very capable hands. The tour manager, Fran Cotton, was a Lions legend himself and commanded instant respect, while our two Scottish coaches, Ian McGeechan and Jim Telfer, the good and bad cop respectively, were both inspirational men in their own different ways. The one characteristic they both shared in abundance was their intelligence. McGeechan might wear his brain-power more visibly, but behind Telfer's bluff hard-man demeanour lay an equally sharp rugby brain.

The pair of them had spent ten months drawing up a strategy for beating South Africa and they had worked out fairly early on that you don't go to South Africa and bully them. You stand up to them, certainly, but you are better off trying to run around them rather than through them. Cunning, guile, mobility and surprise were the Lions' best hopes. Aware of the physical superiority of the Boks, the coaches devised a game plan to move the ball around as quickly and as far as possible in order to drag their big, powerful forwards from one side of the pitch to the other, not just to tire them out but also to remove them from the action as much as possible. What they didn't want was for us to get bogged down in a set-piece battle and they chose a squad to execute that plan accordingly. The Boks were the best defensive team in the world at the time and the plan was to pull them out wide where their back row couldn't reach us.

Appointing Martin Johnson as captain was another inspired decision despite the fact that he had only skippered his club side half a dozen or so times. The critics said he lacked experience and media skills and that he was a disciplinary time bomb, liable to lamp someone in the heat of the battle and get himself sent off. The Leicester boys knew better, though, and by the end of that tour you wouldn't find a man in the British Isles who still questioned his appointment. You can't help respecting Johnno – it's like gravity: you can't resist it. One of the main reasons they chose Johnno as captain was because they wanted a physically intimidating presence, a scary looking character who took a backward step before no one. As Fran said at the time: 'I do like the thought of a 6-foot 8-inch, 18-stone captain knocking on the opposition dressing-room door as opposed to a sylph-like winger. It does make a very strong statement.'

On the eve of our opening match against Eastern Province Invitational XV in Port Elizabeth, McGeechan addressed the whole squad and put the challenge ahead of us into perspective when he described it as 'three World Cup finals and ten Five Nations matches in the space of eight weeks'. I had been called into the side at the last minute after Scott Gibbs failed to recover from a bruised thigh. Although this curtain raiser was by no means the most intimidating fixture on our itinerary the management had wanted to field a strong side in order to make a bit of a statement to our hosts.

It was an odd sensation pulling on the red shirt of the Lions before I had been given the honour of doing the same with the white of England, but whatever worries I may have been feeling in that dressing room were as nothing compared to the emotions that seemed to be convulsing our Welsh full-back, Neil Jenkins. Jenks was one of the most experienced players in our squad, having made his international debut six years earlier. He was also one of the greatest goal-kickers the game has ever seen, as cool and metronomic as you like even in the most intense atmospheres. I imagined therefore that he would be one of those nerveless buggers in the build-up to a match and it was quite a shock to see him pacing around the dressing room and retching his guts out, sounding for all the world like a walrus humping his way up the beach in search of a mate.

Richard Cockerill, the Leicester and England hooker, is another retcher but each player has his own way of dealing with pre-match tension. Many of the forwards I have known like to take themselves off to the showers where they beat each other up a bit in order to get themselves pumped up and primed for the real fight ahead. Personally, I always look for humour as a valve to release some of the mounting pressure. In my position at inside centre, you want to have as cool a head as possible as you need to make quick judgements and have a clear vision of what is going on around you. Shouting at toilets, smacking my best mate in the mouth and making jungle noises in the showers is not the best mental preparation for me, I find. I do my job best when I can keep a lid on all those primeval passions and my way of doing that is looking around for something to divert or amuse me. I don't actually crack jokes in the dressing room before a match for the simple reason that I'd get thumped by a load of 18-stone forwards if I did. Apart from anything else, I wouldn't want to under-mine the controlled fury and focus that is necessary for the forwards to do their job properly. Certainly, in those final minutes before we got the knock on the changing-room door in Port Elizabeth, it would have been very unwise indeed if I, the uncapped one, had proceeded to treat the lads to a selection of my favourite Tommy Cooper gags.

It's strange what your mind chooses to remember of these occasions. That day was one of the most momentous events in my young life and yet it wasn't the inspirational pre-match talk from Jason Leonard, our captain for the game, nor the spectacle and sound of a South African rugby crowd that stand out most in my mind. It was the sight of Dorian West as I emerged from the tunnel. And quite a sight – and smell – it was, too. I always like to be the last out on to the pitch and as I looked up to take in the atmosphere on what was for me an historic occasion all I got was a faceful of the Leicester hooker. It was right in front of me, in all its bright red horror, eyes popping out of its sockets as it screamed 'COME ON THE LASSO!!! GIVE 'EM A HIDING!!!' ('Lasso', as in a long piece of rope, was another of the nicknames inspired by my apparently hilarious physique). My old chum Dorian, it turned out, was in the middle of a rugby and boozing tour with the British Police and I can report that our country's finest coppers stank like a pub carpet after a Glasgow wedding reception as they all craned over the wall to cheer us out.

God knows what kind of a state they were in by the final whistle, but the match passed in something of a blur for me, too. It was vital that we won the match so as to lay down a marker for the rest of the tour, but for a brief period it was very tight and they actually led us 11-10 at one point. In the end we ran out 39-11 winners and produced some lovely passages of running rugby in a generally satisfying performance. It may have been sheer coincidence but the turning point seemed to come early in the second half when their giant Springbok lock Kobus Wiese emerged from the side of the ruck and was promptly driven back about 5 yards by a hammering tackle from Scott Quinnell.

After a quiet start I grew in confidence and performed reasonably well playing alongside Jerry Guscott for the first time and outside Scotland's Gregor Townsend. Gregor copped a little bit of criticism for his kicking from hand but some of his attacking play was fabulous and he set up four of our five tries that afternoon. He's my kind of player, Gregor, a true footballer capable of magic and a joy to play alongside if you are on his wavelength. He thinks and runs different lines from the vast majority of players but, unless his team-mates are reading him, he can be made to look like a bit of a berk sometimes. It was the same when George Best played for Northern Ireland – he'd slot a string of beautiful passes but most of his team-mates were donkeys and didn't have the vision to run on to them. But it was

Best, and not them, who ended up looking stupid and took the flak afterwards. So, too, with Gregor whenever he played in mediocre teams, but at least out there in South Africa with the Lions his genius stood a chance.

I managed to get on the scoresheet a couple of minutes from time when Gregor burst forward and released Tony Underwood who carried it on for a while before popping it to me to go over under the sticks. Nowadays when I celebrate a score I smile and try and enjoy the occasion, but when I was a youngster I just punched the air and tried to look really hard and scary. That's exactly what I did when I scored my first Lions try but, if I had that moment again, my shirt would have been over my head and I would have been doing cartwheels all the way back to our half.

There was no euphoria after that match, just a sense of having got the tour off to a solid start while showing glimpses of our full potential. One South African journalist described our opponents that day as one of the worst sides in the Southern Hemisphere – but we hadn't heard anyone describe them in that way in the run-up to the match. Funny that. Eastern Province were not a brilliant side by any means but nor were they a rugby version of the Duchess of Norfolk's XI, the cosy team put out against the touring sides in the traditional tea-and-cakes curtain raiser to an Ashes cricket tour in England.

Our performance was generally well received by our

own press and one headline even said 'Greenwood Puts Life Into The Lions', which definitely flattered me a bit. I played pretty well with the ball in hand, particularly in the second half as our forwards got on top, but I look back on that eighty minutes more as a lesson learned than one handed out. I was just a wide-eyed, skinny student of the game with precisely no experience of international rugby and on one occasion I had my shorts sharply pulled down and my backside firmly slapped by a master of his subject. I was playing opposite Hennie le Roux, a member of the World Cup-winning side of 1995, and he taught me a lesson in the art of midfield play that I have been using myself ever since, but which left me smarting and stinging with embarrassment at the time. Early in the second half, with the match still very much in the balance, they were awarded a scrum in an attacking position, and Le Roux, who had just moved to fly-half, set up a try-scoring opportunity simply by attracting my attention.

All he did was turn around and fix his eyes on mine before he began walking away with a look that said: 'Hey, you spotty, naïve youth, come this way with me because I'm about to get the ball and you're meant to be covering me.' Like a zombie I dutifully followed him, not quite with my arms stretched out in front of me but they might just as well have been for all the use I was about to become to the Lions' defensive cover. Before I knew what was happening Le Roux had dragged me right out of position and opened a massive gap between me and Gregor through which winger Deon Kayser was suddenly sprinting through to score. In that one moment I realised that I was standing at the foot of a very steep learning curve and that I had better start scrambling up it quick so that, a) I didn't make a complete tit of myself, and because b) I realised that if I paid attention I could perhaps go home with a box full of new tricks. For someone like me who lacks raw power and sheer pace, or any pace at all come to think of it, it is important to have as many rabbits in the hat as possible. I've used Le Roux's trick a lot ever since and it's amazing how often it works. It's like being sucked into a trance.

Gregor taught me a second ruse that day – the art of using the ball as an extra attacker. It's quite difficult to describe but, in short, you are feinting a move to deceive your opposite man. When the ball is being passed towards you, you adjust your line of running as if to attack it and then fade off it at the last moment. Your movement towards the ball has effectively become a kind of extra man as you hope to succeed in drawing in your man before disappearing at another angle.

Fran Cotton told reporters after the match that I had played myself into contention for a place in the Test team. I have no idea whether that was the case or not but, either way, it was a very clever bit of management and kidology. In one stroke he boosted my confidence while throwing down a warning to the more senior players that no one could take anything for granted on this tour.

I didn't take any part in our next match, a midweek clash against Border in East London which was played in a mudbath and ended in a narrow 18-14 victory. Defeat would have been a blow to morale but such were the conditions that it was difficult to read a great deal of significance into events on the day. I was back in action four days later when I was thrown on with ten minutes to go against Western Province in Cape Town in an altogether more interesting contest. Three incidents from that match remain particularly clear in my memory to this day, two of which manage to raise a wry smile and one which still makes me shudder with fury at the very thought of it. If, in thirty or forty years' time, you see a tall, skinny old man hobbling down the road cursing to himself and kicking a can along the pavement, that will be me in all probability, as I recall the moment with undiminished annoyance. There we were at Newlands Stadium, one of the great fortresses of South African rugby and the scene of any number of historic encounters, and I had only been on the field for about five minutes when I was presented with a bomb-proof opportunity to carve out the most glorious moment in my career to date.

I completely and utterly screwed up.

There were two minutes to go and, with the score

38-21, we knew we had the game won. The action was camped around the halfway mark when Gregor called a move that is as old as the hills and one which most international teams have in the locker: the fly-half has the ball, the inside centre drifts wide, the full-back and outside centre come up the middle to attract the opposition centres but the fly-half misses them out and slides the ball to the inside centre who, if all goes to plan, should have a big hole to run through. And it did all go to plan in every last detail . . . until the ball reached me. Gregor's pass was absolutely perfect, slap in the bread basket, and as it floated towards me in front of me there lay a gap you could have driven the Chinese Army through. All I had to do was to hold on to it and I was away, hapless South Africans trailing in my wake, on a 50-yard glory run to the line in my Lions shirt where I would swallow-dive under the posts for a picture that would surely be adorning my dining-room wall for the rest of my days. That was my mistake – I was already dreaming. My eye was figuratively and literally off the ball. A split second later it was bouncing around on the turf and I was looking to the heavens with my head in my hands. What an absolute twenty-four-carat prat! I can honestly say that has been the only time I have dropped a try-scoring pass since I was a schoolboy. It's like taking catches off my own bowling – I just don't drop them. I could imagine Bob Dwyer sitting at home in his front room shaking his head and muttering to himself: 'What did I tell you, Greenwood? You're a lumbering, second-row donkey after all.'

I hate to think how I would have felt had my mistake led to the Lions missing out on a victory, but happily that was already comfortably in the bag. One of the other outstanding memories from that encounter was coming off the bench and Jerry Guscott turning to me and saying: 'It's f***ing fantastic, isn't it?'

'What is, Jerry?'

'Just look around the stadium — they're streaming out.'

It was true. There were still ten minutes to go, but the home fans knew they were well beaten and simply couldn't bear to sit out any more embarrassment at the hands of a Lions team which, in the build-up, they had probably fancied outplaying. It was a great sight. These guys were a very good side and we had beaten them convincingly.

The other memory was seeing our winger, Jon 'Bentos' Bentley, hurling his opposite man, James Small, into the advertising hoardings as the pair of them played out a comical running battle which ended with them refusing to shake hands at the final whistle. Small was never one who liked to be too far from the centre of attention, and he had been giving it plenty of chat in the build-up to the match, eager as he was to make an impression and secure a place in the Test side. As for Bentos . . . well, he just likes to make an impression.

Showmen, the pair of them, and when they met head-on in this match it was always going to be pure theatre with a hint of farce. They might just as well have been wearing sequined tailcoats, revolving bow ties and top hats. Much was made of their confrontation, but from where I was sitting, and knowing Bentos for the good-natured show-off that he is, it was clear this was panto-mime handbags for the cameras and fine entertainment it was, too.

Bentos, one of the ex-rugby league lads in the squad, was a good character to have around during those eight weeks, and it's strange to think now, seven years on, that I haven't spoken to him since, just as I had never spoken to him before that day we all met up in Weybridge for our pre-tour preparations. That's one of the extraordinary features of a Lions tour, certainly the ones back then: for two months you live cheek-by-jowl with a lot of strangers, all tight and united in a common cause, spilling blood and sweat for one another. You battle together, eat and drink together, watch television together, celebrate and commiserate with each other, you take the plaudits and the criticism together and then, win or lose, you fly home and you never see half of them again. But there'll always be that bond, that common experience banked away in the back of our minds. In years to come, the Scottish prop Tom Smith, say, might be tramping his way across the Highlands, Keith Wood may be in a pub on the west coast of

Ireland, Scott Gibbs could be somewhere up a Welsh mountain and I could be back in Hurst Green: four men from four different countries and backgrounds but together as one with our scars from and our memories of a Lions tour. Even Austin, working the chip-fryer at his local motorway services, can never have that taken away from him.

We left Cape Town with three wins out of three and headed up to the town of Witbank for our next match against Mpumalanga, formerly South Eastern Province, with our form, confidence and fitness all in reasonably good shape. It was to be our first game at altitude up on the high veld and I was to start the match alongside the Welshman Allan Bateman, a man and a player of whom I cannot speak highly enough. He was another former rugby league player and another character I had not met before the tour, but one I soon got to know very well as we roomed together from day one at Oatlands. He looked after me off the pitch as well as on it and, playing alongside him, I quickly understood how he came to earn the nickname 'the Clamp' when he was at Cronulla Sharks: once he got a hand on you in the tackle, you weren't going anywhere. Even though he didn't get a run-out in the Test side until the final match after Jerry broke his arm, I would say that without question he was one of the best players on that tour. It was just unfortunate for him that Gibbs and Guscott were also out there.

Allan and I combined well that day as we ran in ten tries, some of them absolute beauties, to thrash Mpumalanga 64–14. It was a superb all-round performance but I remember Nick Beal at full-back playing particularly well and Neil Jenkins at fly-half was simply magnificent. Everyone thinks of Jenks as a kicker but what a great distributor he was, too. It was a beautiful day, I remember, but the same surely could not be said of our opponents' conduct that afternoon. They were a nasty bunch of bastards – why bother to pretend otherwise? – and some of the violence was downright savage. Unlike some others – and I may well be wrong – I didn't think the foul play was a premeditated plan to cause physical damage and shake us up mentally ahead of the first Test. It was more that they didn't take to being utterly humiliated, which is exactly what happened to them. At times it was like a game of touch rugby and they could barely lay a legitimate finger on us as we tossed it about and sailed through, over and around them for score after score after score. It was a rout.

Make a fool of a South African rugby player and you'll be doing well to escape with much less than a burst mouth. One of the impressive aspects of that brutal contest, from a Lions' point of view, was the discipline we showed in the face of some seriously violent play. Not that you are ever going to find me squaring up to some hairy, 20-stone farmer who likes to relax away from rugby by tackling wildebeest or punching himself in the face. Their lock Marius Bosman was completely out of control that day and he was very lucky not to have been sent off when he ended Doddie Weir's tour by stamping on his knee and causing severe ligament damage at a ruck early in the second half. Doddie was absolutely heart-broken in the changing room when our doctor, James Robson, gave him the news that his tour was almost certainly over. Earlier, Bosman was throwing punches like a man possessed and he came close to taking out Rob Wainwright's eye when he raked him with his studs at a ruck. It was a strange day for Rob who also scored a hat-trick of tries in nine minutes. As the final whistle blew, having kept our cool and not retaliated in the face of severe provocation, we just walked off the pitch and pointed to the scoreboard.

There were no cosy post-match beers with the South Africans that day. In fact we didn't mix with them at all on that tour . . . or, come to think of it, after any of the England games against them that I've played in. They don't like us and we don't like them. Fact. Full stop. I don't know what it was like in times past, but it is an inescapable fact of modern international rugby that you very rarely socialise with your opponents after the match. Even at the official dinners, players tend to stick to their own (unless of course you happen to be Jason Leonard, the man who knows absolutely everyone and is never happier than when he's pumping flesh, slapping

backs and kissing babies like a US presidential
candidate). There is slightly more mingling among the
Northern Hemisphere countries because many of us
know each other from club rugby. With the French
there is the language problem and you soon recognise
that there is little point in staring at each other and
occasionally grunting something incomprehensible.
The Australians are probably the friendliest of the
Southern Hemisphere sides, and I count the great
Wallabies Danny Herbert and David Wilson amongst
my good mates, but I can honestly say that I have never
had a beer with the South Africans or the New
Zealanders after a match. Their rugby people really
don't like the English at all. I don't think it's a general
national attitude, but a purely rugby phenomenon.

There may have been little love lost between the
players on that 1997 tour, but I was surprised by the
warmth of the reception we received from the South
African people we met. They were truly hospitable and
friendly in my experience. As a great rugby nation,
South Africans understand better than anyone why the
Lions are special and they have bought into the romance
and tradition of it all. If you go over there in an England
shirt you'll often cop a bit of abuse, but the Lions are
treated with greater warmth. Perhaps it's because you
have surrendered your narrow national identity for a
wider, vaguer cause and you are granted some kind of
amnesty off the pitch. It's the same in New Zealand. Go

there with England and you might just as well be an alien or a virus, but with the Lions, I'm told, the reception is more welcoming.

Battered, bruised and short of a couple of players, we headed up to Pretoria to take on Northern Transvaal. I was only a spectator as the Saturday Lions, the unofficial first team, slumped to a 35–30 defeat and the morale of the whole squad crashed to the floor the moment the final whistle sounded. The tour had reached its critical point and it was just a case of whether we folded now or dug very, very deep in order to meet the far stiffer challenges ahead. There was deep-seated gloom in that dressing room afterwards, and an unspoken awareness that everything we had come out for now seemed to hang on our match four days later against Gauteng Lions (formerly Transvaal) at Ellis Park in Johannesburg.

At the venue where South Africa had won the World Cup so dramatically two years earlier and against a very powerful provincial side, the task of reviving party morale fell to a largely second-string Lions team that evening. You only had to run your finger down the names on their team sheet to understand the size of the task before us: Du Toit, Le Roux, Hendricks, Van Rensburg, Swart, Roussow, Dalton, Wiese, Thorne . . . And the reality of the encounter was every bit as tough and fraught as the prospect had promised as both sides hurled themselves at each other from the outset. They recognised our vulnerability, no question, and understood that if they broke us here, they had probably broken us for the Test series. It took an awesome defensive performance by the whole team to hold them and keep us in the game.

Heading into the final quarter of the game we were six points adrift and we faced the very real prospect of becoming the first Lions side to suffer back-to-back defeats in South Africa for seventy years. I'm not claiming all the credit for what happened next, but I'm definitely having a small slice of it, thanks, regardless of the whingeing and protests you might hear from Austin or John Bentley. In fact it was probably my single most important contribution to the Lions' cause over the two tours that I have had the privilege to have been invited on. I found some space and made a break down the right, but that was the easy bit. The difficult part came when all 19-stone of the Gauteng lock Kobus Wiese landed on me. It is one of the immutable laws of physics that when brick outhouses, elephants and South African forwards fall on your back, the centre of the earth exercises an irresistible pull over you. I knew that Austin was steaming up on my inside – he's like a fly around a cow's backside when there's a try in the offing – and I managed to keep my stick insect frame up long enough to pop a pass to him as Wiese drove me into the turf. Austin sped over into the corner and, as he always does after he's had to run 10 yards, promptly had a minor asthma attack. Jenks, choking back the vomit no doubt, slotted the conversion from the touchline to put us in front for the first time in the match.

Under ordinary circumstances, Austin and I would have bagged all the glory in the following day's papers assuming we managed to hang on for victory. As it turned out, John Bentley, the greedy bastard, only went and robbed us of our moment in the sun by producing arguably the greatest solo Lions try in living memory. The big Yorkshireman was about 70 yards from their line when he received the ball and, faced with a wall of Gauteng shirts and with no obvious gaps or hobbling props to run at, there didn't appear to be much on. As he set off and broke to the right, I remember thinking, 'What on earth does he think he's doing?' but he beat two players and I thought, 'Fair enough, now he's going to have to pass it though, surely' but he just kept going. As he approached their twenty-two, he seemed to have run up a blind alley as three defenders waited to cut off his passage to the corner. By now the rest of us were haring after him, screaming at him to offload in order to keep the move going, but he completely ignored us and with a fabulous swerve cut inside and left all three South Africans on their arses before surging under the posts with a couple more of them on his back. It was an absolutely ridiculous try, true rugby league style, and we mobbed him in the knowledge that he had clinched a thunderingly important win.

You often hear or read about opponents being

'stunned' by setbacks in sport, but the Gauteng Lions were well and truly astounded in that instance. They had hammered away at us for over an hour, wave after wave of attacks crashing in on us, and although they breached us a couple of times, they never broke us. If I were in their side, I would have thought it inevitable that the defensive wall would have collapsed under the sheer force and the relentlessness of the pressure heading into that final twenty minutes. Instead, in the space of five minutes, we popped our heads above the parapet, broke out of the siege and crossed *their* line for two excellent tries.

I don't think you can overestimate the importance of that brief passage of play. We hadn't just salvaged our pride and confidence in those moments; we had also inflicted a few blows on the self-belief of the Springboks. Against one of their strongest provincial teams, our shadow Test side had shown we were prepared to scrap for every inch of turf and that, even under the cosh, we still had the wit and balls to try some magic. It was a brilliant feeling walking back into the dressing room where the Saturday team were waiting for us, slapping our backs and cheering us to the rafters. There was already a good camaraderie in the party but in that one moment we took the spirit and the unity to an entirely different level.

I had my one big night out on the town the following evening. I wasn't involved in Saturday's match against

Natal and so it was with a clear conscience that I headed out with Austin and Jerry for what was never intended to be more than a couple of quiet beers. The management had warned us to be careful about going out for a drink while in South Africa. It wasn't so much that they didn't trust us to look after our bodies while we were there, more that they didn't want a front-page newspaper photograph of Britain and Ireland's finest athletes with a bottle of tequila in their mouths. That kind of exposure just ends up distracting everyone involved with the tour, from the journalists to the players. 'Don't do anything daft' was the simple and reasonable advice of the management. So what did I do that Thursday? I went out on the town and got completely off my trolley, ended up shouting the hotel down from the freezing cold swimming pool and got to bed at approximately six in the morning.

I thought nothing of it the next day, largely because I was unconscious in bed nursing one of the great hangovers until six in the evening while the rest of the squad played golf at a beautiful course nearby. I could barely lift my head off the pillow, but finally managed to scrape myself off the mattress to stumble down to the squad dinner. My head was still pounding and I had just sat down when I felt the firm tap of a Fran Cotton finger on my shoulder. 'Can we have a word on the top table, please, William?' My heart froze as I made that 'walk of shame', a latter-day Oliver Twist shuffling up to see the scary beadles at the head of the room. Fran, bless his heart, opened up with the line: 'Ten years ago I'd have been in the pool with you, lad, but the game's pro now, Will. You've got to be careful.' He and Geech then gave me a fine roasting while Jim Telfer, by far the scariest of the trio, just stared at me as if I were a dog turd on the end of his shoe without saying a single word. It wasn't actually a final warning or an ultimatum, but there was no way I was going to repeat that mistake and that was the end of the matter.

On Saturday, twenty-four hours after my disgrace, the probable Test team did us all proud and more than maintained the momentum we had recovered in midweek by annihilating Natal 42-12. Four days later I was back in action at the Boland Stadium in Wellington to face an Emerging Springboks side featuring Kayser, Percy Montgomery, Van Rensburg, Robbie Kempson, Hendricks and Jaco Coetzee. This was almost an unofficial England cap for me as there were twelve of us in the starting line-up that day. I had never played against Montgomery before or, indeed, ever heard of him. I remember thinking he was a pretty decent player for someone so skinny; he made me look like Os du Randt. I was paired alongside Allan Bateman in the centres and once again loved the experience of learning from the old maestro. I enjoyed every moment of the game – bar one – as we humped the next generation of Boks 51-22, with Nick Beal doing his Test chances no harm with a hat-trick of tries. I hadn't been paying too much attention to what was being said in the press about us as a team or me individually, but after my lapse of judgement the week before I felt I had perhaps clawed back some respect when I read in the *Cape Times* that 'the midfield pairing of Allan Bateman and Will Greenwood crushed the opposition. They were a class act, both as a unit and individually.'

I was involved in one very ugly incident late on when I put in Bealer for one of his three tries. I had released the pass about ten minutes earlier, it seemed, and was just minding my own business when Robbie Kempson, the prop who went on to win thirty-seven caps, hit me late with a big tackle. Not content with that, he then spat on me from point-blank range as I stood up. I don't really 'do' angry, especially not with South African props, but I am good at incredulous and I just stared at him in utter disbelief. 'What the hell is this guy doing?' I was thinking. 'Take a look at the scoreboard, my friend, and take it on the chin.'

I think by this stage of the tour the South Africans were just plain furious with us. No one had given us a prayer on our arrival in South Africa, saying we were a bunch of lightweights who would get steamrollered by their big bruiser forwards. But with the exception of that one defeat, we had been running them off their own pitches, match after match, and they didn't like it one little bit. It was especially galling for them when it was our midweek team that gave them a good hiding.

It was with our confidence fully restored that we headed back to Cape Town for the first Test. The moment of reckoning had finally arrived, the first of Geech's 'three World Cup finals' and there were few surprises in our starting line-up. A shoulder injury had ruled out Rob Howley at scrum-half and Matt Dawson was given the nod ahead of Austin for the number nine shirt. The Irish and Leicester back-rower Eric Miller was set to play a central role in the match but he had to be pulled out of the team at the last minute after a terrible drugs cock-up. His dad had come over to see him play and when Eric mentioned that he was feeling a bit poorly he gave him an ordinary over-the-counter cold remedy, neither of them aware that it contained banned substances. If Eric had played and been tested he would have been banned for months, possibly years, so they had no option but to withdraw him. It made you think of that Olympic 400-metre runner who had trained for four years for his big moment and then failed to hear the starting gun in his first heat. And it got worse for Eric. In the second Test he was sent on as a substitute, and he was so pumped up when he sprinted out that he tore his quad muscle and then missed the third Test as a result of the injury. Why do these things only happen to Eric? Great man, great footballer, Eric, and as a former Gaelic footballer, like Geordan Murphy, the best I have ever seen under the high ball, but he is also the only man I know who has spent hours assembling his flatpack bedroom wardrobe *downstairs*.

I watched the match from the stands just behind Geech and Jim Telfer and was so transfixed by the contest that I haven't the faintest idea who I was sitting next to. The stadium was a sea of red Lions shirts and rocked to the sound of our support to the extent that it felt more like a home game. God knows what it felt like to be out there as a player, but it was spine-tingling stuff just watching from the stands. It was just one of those magnificent occasions when you wanted to be out there getting a piece of it. I remember in particular Tim Rodber putting in a massive hit on Henry Honnibal.

It was a predictably brutal contest up front but our monsters, led by Johnno, were magnificent and they were starting to take control of the game when Matt Dawson dummied half the Springbok team and went over in the right corner. Cue red bedlam in the stands. Then Alan Tait popped over on the left and did his little gun-slinging salute and the game was all but ours. Cue absolute chaos among Lions fans. On Monday, Tait, a top man after my own heart, was back in the gym doing some gentle weights and tending to his imaginary calf injury. It's not often you'll meet a worse trainer than me but Alan, canny lad, is up there with some of the greatest malingerers of them all. As far as I could work out he always had an injury on Monday and it continued to trouble him all week until it miraculously cleared up on Saturday morning.

When the Lions beat the world champions that day they confounded the expectations of virtually everyone in world rugby, and you certainly couldn't describe it as a freak result. In football, a team can spend a whole match on the back foot frantically clearing their lines and then nick a goal in the last minute for victory, but it doesn't often happen like that in rugby. If your forwards take a pasting for most of the match, you will lose ninety-nine times out of a hundred. Scorelines in rugby are generally more accurate reflections of the balance of play than they are in football and the Lions' 25-16 win was an appropriate return for what the two sides had put in.

As you may imagine the dressing room was a riotous place that evening and the whole squad then went out to celebrate at a bar called the Green Man where we hammered out increasingly discordant versions of Oasis' 'Wonderwall', which was well established as our unofficial tour song by then. It was mainly the midweek boys punishing the beers, however, as the Test team were out on their feet after their heroics and they also had the second Test in just seven days to concentrate the mind. (But even we were pretty level-headed that night, to be honest.) I have learned through a handful of painful experiences down the years that you have to be very careful about how you treat your body in the aftermath of a hard game. The body pain doesn't hit you for about forty-eight hours, and if in the meantime you fill your boots with lager, you are going to feel doubly sore when it comes. In those days, as a twenty-four-year-old, I could shake the booze off quite easily and train the following day without any obvious difficulty. But I simply haven't been able to do that since . . . well, since that Lions tour in all truth; hangovers absolutely kill me and unless I have just won the World Cup, like most players now I do my utmost to avoid getting involved in an old-style session of twenty pints and a bottle of aftershave. I have tried to be honest about the rugby drinking culture back then, partly because I'm just telling it the way it was, but also to show quite how far the game has come since then in terms of preparation, fitness, diet and general lifestyle. Only a few years separate then and now but the difference between how players from the two eras look after themselves is absolutely enormous.

It is no coincidence that in the mid-1990s England could only hope to beat Southern Hemisphere opposition on the odd occasion, but that in the four years from 2000 they didn't lose a single game to any of the Tri-Nations sides. That is not something you achieve by drinking snakebite and smoking fags. I can't recall precisely what my thoughts were on the subject during that tour to South Africa, but I suspect that at the back of all our minds we were dimly aware that we had probably downed our final bottle of the proverbial aftershave. Rugby was getting serious and you realised that if you could beat the mighty Boks in their own backyard, when in all honesty you were only truly professional in the sense that you were being paid money, then you could achieve anything in the game if you really knuckled down.

Four days after that historic win in Cape Town, the midweek side flew up to Bloemfontein to play the Free State Cheetahs (formerly Orange Free State) in the biggest match of the tour without Test status. We were in the heart of Afrikaans country, where hairy props and wildebeest roam the land virtually indistinguishable from one another, and it was with good reason that the clash had been dubbed the 'unofficial fourth Test'. They were one hell of a good side and, after that first Test 'upset', they were going to be an angry mob, too. South Africans don't like losing under any circumstances, least of all to beardless, lightweight wimps from the British Isles. Under normal circumstances the whole squad would have travelled up together in a show of solidarity but on this occasion fourteen of those who were set to be involved the following Saturday stayed in Durban to rest.

I was especially pumped up for this match because Mum and Dad had just arrived in South Africa to see out the last few weeks of the tour and I wanted to put on a good show for them. It was great to see them on the afternoon of the match and I still have a lovely photograph of the three of us outside the team hotel, me in my Lions shirt and them looking very proud. I suppose there must have been some danger that, after the glory of the first Test triumph, some complacency or even arrogance might have crept into our attitude, but if any of us had been thinking along those lines, it was most emphatically knocked out of us in Jim Telfer's pep talk in the dressing room before we ran out. I can't for the life of me remember his exact words, but I know that by the time he had finished I felt like I could run through a brick wall and then beat up the whole of South Africa when I got to the other side.

The Bath lock Nigel Redman, a replacement for Doddie Weir, was our captain and when we ran out behind him you just had that feeling that there was no chance of us losing that day. It may sound like a load of mystical nonsense, but there are occasions when you just know, as surely as night follows day and popes kiss runways, that you are going to win – and 23 June 1997 in Bloemfontein was one of those occasions for me. We were outstanding in the first half and completely ran them off the park. Everything we tried came off, with bells on, and you felt that you could toss the ball anywhere you liked, safe in the knowledge that someone in a red shirt would be there to grab hold of it. I've always searched for the 100 per cent game, and of course there is no such thing, but those first forty minutes were the best I have ever played, without a shadow of a doubt.

Then it all went black.

What I am about to describe comes not from the deep recesses of my own memory, but partly from video footage, partly from newspaper reports and partly from what I have learned from Mum and Dad, players, doctors and the other witnesses who were there to see me cheat death by, I'm told, a very fine margin. One moment it was a few seconds before half-time and I was taking a pass from Mike Catt and the next I was waking up in a strange bed, the light streaming in through the window, still in my full Lions kit with my gumshield tucked into my sock. I'm dreaming here, I thought. I felt slightly woozy and my shoulder was killing me. 'What am I doing in Lions kit when I haven't even played for England yet? Why's everyone talking in a South African accent? Someone's spiked my drink with hallucinogenic drugs.' It took me two or three unnerving minutes to get a handle on what on earth was going on and how I came to be there.

When I said I played almost the flawless game that evening I neglected to mention two major errors I committed. Error One: I didn't perform my customary pre-match ritual of cutting off the sleeves of my shirt. Allan Bateman said he thought the ground would be dewy and suggested leaving the sleeves on so it would be easier to hold on to the ball. Error Two: I wore the wrong shirt number. Normally I wear thirteen despite being an inside centre, but that night I wore twelve because there had been a cock-up with the kit, the numbers got mixed up and I couldn't swap with Allan because we are completely different builds. (I am a bit weird and superstitious like that. As well as being the last player out of the tunnel, I wear lucky socks under my outer pair and then ceremoniously burn them once they have been reduced to stinking rags.)

I received the ball from Cattie and then, so I'm told, got thumped in a massive tackle by their number eight Jaco Coetzee. Not long before I remember reflecting on how the bone-hard pitch was playing to our advantage because we really didn't want to get bogged down in a set-piece battle with that bunch. On the video you see me getting tipped upside down and then my head landing at right angles to my neck before my gangling legs flop limply to the ground. My sleeve was being held in the tackle so I couldn't put my arm out to break my fall and protect myself. I was completely unconscious and everyone, except my old mate Neil Back, seemed to recognise that something serious was afoot. You could hear the thud of my head on the ground from some distance. Backie apparently leaned over me and made a joke to the effect that I was a greedy beggar and that would teach me to pass the ball in the future. He had been on my inside shoulder, as ever, and wanted me to offload to him. I'm sure it was highly amusing – I just wish I'd been there.

Austin was one of the first to react and he ran over, put me on my side, ripped my gumshield out so that I didn't swallow my tongue and tucked it neatly into my sock. It's a difficult call for people in these situations if you are dealing with someone with a serious neck injury, because any movement can cause major damage. Rob Wainwright, our Scots flanker, was an army doctor and he too realised something was amiss and immediately raised the alarm. At this point in the episode I owe a vote of thanks to Jason Leonard. My poor old mum, as you can imagine, was in a highly agitated state at the side of the pitch and was trying to get on to the field to start hand-bagging the Free State players, saying over and over, 'What have you done to him?' Jase, thank heavens, managed to restrain her and sweet-talk her into staying away. People have since expressed sympathy to me over this whole episode but to be honest it doesn't even register as a bad experience for the simple reason that I cannot remember a blind detail about it. I was just lying there catching up on some kip. The ones I feel sorry for are my parents – and the doctor, James Robson, who came within seconds of cutting open my throat.

I was still completely unconscious when I was strapped tight to the stretcher and carried off the field, getting on for about ten minutes later. Anxiety was fast turning to alarm bordering on panic by the time they got me into the dressing room and laid me down on the table. I have seen it on the *Living With Lions* video just the once – it's not my favourite film – and it struck me that it must have been a very difficult decision for whoever was holding the camera at that point as to whether he should carry on filming. For all he knew I could have been dead or dying. Mum and Dad had followed me into the room and there was still no reaction when they shone a torch into my eyes. They were increasingly desperate to get some kind of response because, with every minute that ticked by, the closer my brain came to dying. Robbo, our doctor, was almost quivering as he took out his scalpel ready to perform an emergency tracheotomy to clear my airwaves. Mum, at this point is leaning over me and saying, 'Come on, Will . . . Don't worry, he's going to be all right . . . Come on, Will love . . .' And then after about fifteen minutes I stirred, lifted my head and whispered: 'Mum, f**k off and leave me alone, will you?!'

I still have no recollection of this, of course, but Dad tells me that in the ambulance on the way to Bloemfontein Hospital I kept sitting up, despite the paramedics' efforts to keep me flat on my back, saying: 'Psst! Dad, tell them it's my hamstring, tell them it's my hamstring, tell them it's not concussion!' My old man had always told me never to admit to concussion because you face a mandatory three weeks on the sidelines. At the hospital I spoke to Caro back in England for about forty-five minutes but had no memory of doing so, and the following day I rang her and apologised for not having called earlier to tell her what had happened.

When my world finally came back into focus early the next morning and I realised that I wasn't in a drug-induced dreamland after all, the first thing I noticed was the searing pain in my left shoulder. 'Relax, Mr Greenwood, you've hurt your head,' the doctor said as I tried to pull myself out of bed. 'Sod the head, my friend, it's the shoulder you should be worrying about,' I replied. An X-ray revealed that it had been pulverised in the fall and that I was certain to be out for several months and would miss the start of the new season.

The mini-drama unfortunately overshadowed one of the great Lions performances which ended in a 52–30 win against one of the strongest sides in world rugby outside internationals. John Bentley had scored a hat-trick before half-time and some still hold that it was the best performance of the whole tour. The knowledge that I was out of the tour was especially hard to accept after being told that there was a strong probability I would have made the bench for the Test side. The disappointment, though, was soon put into perspective when Robbo and I got back to the team hotel and people kept shaking my hand and saying: 'It's good to see you are still alive.' I owe the doctor an enormous debt of gratitude for everything he did for me during that episode – not that he would accept any, of course.

At the time, I asked him if there was anything I could do for him by way of thanks and, after a long pause, he said, 'Just say hello to my wife and daughters when you're next being interviewed on Sky Sports.'

At the start of the next season there was plenty of chat about the 'psychological' impact of my heavy concussion when, in fact, it was my mutilated shoulder that slowed my return to form. How, I kept asking the armchair psychiatrists, can I possibly be traumatised or disturbed by an experience of which I have not the slightest recollection? An assassin's bullet could miss your head by an inch but, none the wiser, you continue merrily on your way.

Besides, a few days later, it wasn't the state of *my* consciousness that people should have been fretting about – it was the whole squad's as we celebrated an historic series triumph over South Africa with an 18-15 win in Durban. A few images amid the mayhem of the match stand out in my mind. In the pre-match huddle I remember seeing the stocky figure of Scott Gibbs, as wide as he was tall, gesturing with his hands as if to say to the rest of the lads, 'Our performances so far have been this high, now let's move up a level.' That sent a shiver of goose pimples down the neck, too. Like everyone else who saw it, I'll also never forget the sight of Gibbs sending 20-stone Os du Randt crashing to the floor with another bullocking run. To be fair to the big prop, he was dead on his feet by this stage, having been pulled all over the park by our more mobile forwards. If you're carrying that much beef, it's not the running you want, it's settling down for a nice muddy 'skrum' and squeezing some 16-stone lightweight somewhere into the stratosphere. Watching Gibbs smashing everything in his path like a stampeding rhino you might imagine that he was some kind of a meathead without a brain cell in his skull. But it's quite the opposite, in fact. You almost do a double take when you see him shortly after the match putting on his little round rimless glasses, sparking a fag and then talking to you in a very quiet, thoughtful voice.

It was Jerry Guscott's famous drop goal, followed by five minutes of desperate defending, that sealed a heart-stopping 18-15 win that afternoon. At the start of the tour the critics had queued up to criticise the decision to play Jenks, a fly-half, at full-back, but in that decisive Test, in what turned out to be a ground-breaking moment for Northern and Southern Hemisphere rugby, they scored three tries to nil and we still won. They didn't have a recognised kicker and missed a total of fifteen points in penalties and conversions. We had Jenks, bless his vomit.

After a night celebrating I decided to fly home as I didn't want to be a hanger-on, but I slightly regret it now because the rest of the boys had a fabulous week. (There was no need for a full-scale investigation into what went wrong in our 35-16 defeat in the third Test

in Johannesburg. The barman told them everything.)
Bizarrely, as I flew north my sister Emma and cousin
Amy were flying south to see the last leg of the tour and
it was strange to think that we were only a few miles
apart when we crossed somewhere near the equator.
Apart from anything else, though, flying back early
meant I blew the chance to see something of South
Africa – a country, I have been reliably informed,
among the most beautiful and interesting on earth
where, away from the rugby pitch, you generally get a
slap on the back rather than in the face. One of the few
downsides of touring is that you find yourself in some of
the most exotic locations on the planet and yet you
might just as well be in my hometown of Blackburn for
all the sights you get to see. Hotel lifts and lobbies,
training grounds, changing rooms, tunnels, a prop's arse
at the bottom of a ruck, the inside of a bus, the back of
Keith Wood's head, Jason Leonard's jockstrap, the odd
golf course or restaurant, perhaps the glimpse of a distant
mountain if you are lucky – and then you fly home.

I certainly had plenty to reflect on during that long
flight back over the equator and home. Pride in having
played a part in a monumental Lions triumph was
slightly dented by the throbbing pain in my shoulder
which I knew would jeopardise my chances of receiving
an England call for the autumn internationals. At the
end of a long domestic season, it had been a brutal,
gruelling tour with a casualty list that accounted for

almost half the party by its close: Ieuan Evans (groin), Paul Grayson (groin), Doddie Weir (knee), Scott Quinnell (groin), Rob Howley (shoulder), me (head and shoulder), Keith Wood (groin), Alan Tait (groin), Eric Miller (thigh), Jason Leonard (thigh), Kyran Bracken (shoulder), Gregor Townsend (thigh), Jerry Guscott (arm) and Tony Underwood (hip). The fact that we emerged triumphant said a lot about our strength in depth, but even more about the unity and spirit of everyone involved. I will always remember that group of lads as among the tightest I have had the pleasure of touring with. I honestly can't recall a single instance of a player talking out of line or sniping at some aspect of what was a meticulously planned and magnificently organised tour. And although I missed out on becoming only the third uncapped Englishman to win a Lions cap, at least I would have another chance in Australia in four years' time.

And I was still alive.

Chapter Four

'YOU SHOULD GO and get your brain tested, mate. That might help.' Bob Dwyer was by no means the first person to question my state of mind since my return to action after the Bloemfontein incident two or three months earlier, and, like others with more than a passing concern for my career and wellbeing, I know he had my best interests at heart. But if I did have any psychological problems in the early weeks of the 1997/8 season they had absolutely nothing whatsoever to do with getting a bang on the head in a rugby match – about which I can remember nothing anyway – and everything to do with half the world, his wife and their Yorkshire terrier queuing up to ask me: 'Are you all right, mate? . . . How's the head? . . . It must really prey on your mind . . . No wonder you're slightly off your game – who wouldn't be after an experience like that . . .'

When it gets to the point when otherwise intelligent people start telling you that it's time you went and got your head read, then it is that, if anything, which will drive a man mad. If there is one thing certain to send you fleeing into the arms of your local sports psychologist, it is the drip-drip torture of being asked about your state of mental health. In hindsight, I should have worn a T-shirt throughout this period which read: 'No, I'm not soft in the head, I've just got quite a sore shoulder actually, but thanks for asking.' Or perhaps I should have given in and gone the other way, shaved half my head, donned a turquoise silk gown, announced I was the Messiah and put in a specific transfer request to spend the rest of my career with Newport down at Rodney Parade.

I could barely pick up the sports section of a newspaper without reading: 'Will Greenwood, who almost died in South Africa, made a half-break, etc. . . .' Where once no journalist could refer to me without adding the sub-clause that I was 'son of former England captain and coach Dick', now I could not read about my efforts in a match report without being reminded that I had almost died in Bloemfontein and that, quite under-standably, I was now a total basket case as a consequence. I suppose I could have stood in the fountains in Trafalgar Square and spent a morning shouting: 'It's my shoulder! It's my shoulder! Is anyone listening?!?' But then I guess everyone would have shrugged their shoulders and said: 'See, what did I tell you? It's *really* affected the poor lad, that whole South African near-death experience. Shame, because he had a bit of potential, I thought. His dad'll be devastated . . .'

The simple truth of the matter was that my shoulder had been absolutely mangled in that tackle against Free State Cheetahs and, when I returned to club rugby, there was still some tenderness and pain as I hadn't had enough recovery time, and perhaps I was not hurling myself into contact situations with the same gusto. While my mind was saying 'yes' to taking on defences or going into the tackle at full pelt, my shoulder was saying 'no', and you only need to fall slightly off your game for it to start eating away at your confidence. Though I didn't know it at the time, thank heavens, that latest in a long series of shoulder problems was the start of a two-year injury nightmare, which almost led to me giving up the game altogether and going back into the City or finding some other line of work. It was only when, as a last resort and thanks to my manager Nick, I flew to Munich, showed my groin to half of Germany's female population and then allowed a total stranger to inject me with a witch's potion of shark's fin, cockerel skin, beeswax and God only knows what else, that my body recovered and thus my rugby career with it.

Almost every player will go through a tough injury period and there is no telling if it will come at the beginning, middle or end of their careers. By the age of twenty-one I had already dislocated my shoulder five times, broken my collarbone and had major shoulder reconstruction, but, other than straining my ankle ligaments before the Lions tour, I had been largely free of injury for about four years. It was those two years leading up to the 1999 World Cup finals that were to prove to be the most frustrating and depressing of my career. If you are a professional sportsman, serious injury is exasperating. All you can do is sit about or hobble around and wait for it to heal while your career slips slowly by in front of you and your team-mates pass you in the clubhouse like semi-strangers. Then, once your body gives you permission, you begin a long, lonely training programme before you are ready to rejoin the fray.

With so much free time on your hands when you are injured, you can end up going to places and doing things that you might not consider under ordinary circumstances. Like going to watch a local boxing match between Leicester and Peterborough and getting tear-gassed, for instance. How I ended up spending an evening sitting in the middle of several hundred hard nuts straining at the gold chains around their necks to beat the living hell out of each other, I'm still not entirely sure.

I'd never been to a fight night and I had only taken a passing interest in boxing until the injury lay-off that autumn. Austin had also had a shoulder operation and as part of our recovery programme we did some boxing training at a place called Braunston Working Men's

Club, where we became friendly with a promising young light-heavyweight called Neil Linford. The training was an eye-opener, literally and figuratively, and it was excellent for helping to rebuild the strength in our damaged shoulders. Neil, who fought for Leicester, invited us to come along to the match at arch rivals Peterborough one Friday evening and, never having seen a live fight, I had no hesitation in agreeing. Frank Maloney, Lennox Lewis's former manager, was travelling up from London to see the bouts but he was almost three hours late and the fans started boozing heavily during the delay. By the time the first fight finally got underway the whole place was absolutely steaming.

Unaware that the crowd splits along strictly partisan lines on such occasions, Austin, myself and Craig Joiner had sat down among the plastic seats on one side of the hall when everyone around us started singing 'Pe-ter-borough! Pe-ter-borough! Pe-ter-borough!!' They didn't seem all that well disposed towards those across the other side of the room who were chanting 'Leicester! Leicester! Leicester!' I think it was when the Leicester lads started pointing at us and running their fingers under their throats that we realised our evening of local light entertainment was going to turn out a little differently from what we had imagined. By the third bout, some of the Leicester fans had come round to our side and, with accompanying hand gestures, were openly asking the Peterborough lot out: 'Come on then . . . Is that all you've got? . . . Do you want a piece of this? . . .'

The fourth fight featured the Peterborough favourite, an Asian lad so skinny he made me look like Les Dawson, and when he came out strutting his stuff the home support erupted, thinking that this was the moment when they were going to put one over the visitors. Out of the Leicester corner, however, came what can only be described as a human pit bull and within thirty seconds of the opening bell the Peterborough lad was lying on the floor being counted out. That, it seemed, was the final straw for the guy sitting in front of us. Taking off his inch-thick gold necklace from around his 2-foot-thick neck, he handed it to the woman on his right and said: 'Hold this, Mum.' Long before we had reached this moment in the evening's fun, I had clocked every single exit in the hall and, being the girl in the backs that I am, I had planned the speediest and safest deliverance from the hell that was inevitably going to break loose.

Austin's wife Louise was a police officer at the time and she was later able to confirm that the ugly little ginger pug who finally kicked off the battle was well known to the local constabulary. Strutting over to where we were sitting, ugly-ginger-man said to man-with-tree-trunk-neck-and-all-over-body-tattoo-on-quiet-night-out-with-Mum: 'How do you fancy a bit of this?' and promptly sprayed a can of CS gas in his face. Sitting behind him, we got a full blast of the anti-riot gas and, as we clutched our faces, pandemonium broke out all around. In the mêlée (caused by us running away and everyone else looking for someone to fight) we somehow managed to lose Austin so we had to go back to find him and just pray that he wasn't lying at the bottom of a pile of furious skinheads punching his lights out. It would have been just like any other training session with the Leicester forwards for Austin, but Craig and I generally preferred to leave the head-butting and eye-gouging to the experts and luckily we managed to find him amid the flying chairs and fists and pull him outside.

The CS gas, though, had given Austin an asthma attack and he was scrambling around for his inhaler and puffing away as we jumped into his embarrassingly posh Range Rover and sped away. Barely had the words 'If I ever see that f***ing ginger bastard again then I'm going to f***ing kill him' left Austin's mouth when, right there, walking over the pedestrian crossing in front of us, was said ginger bastard himself, spurting blood, it seemed, from about half a dozen points over his body. Austin's better judgement won the argument, though, and he contented himself with a sudden, loud revving of the engine to hurry our friend along his way before we bombed back to Leicester, grateful that we were able to earn our livings as sportsmen in a cissy sport like rugby union.

It was not long after our Fright Night in Peterborough that I was given the all-clear to resume playing again and I was named in the Leicester side to face arch rivals Bath at Welford Road. Clive Woodward had recently been appointed England coach in succession to Jack Rowell and he was there in the crowd to cast his eye over England's two most powerful clubs at that time ahead of what promised to be the most ambitious and punishing schedule of autumn internationals England had ever undertaken: two Tests against New Zealand and one apiece against South Africa and Australia, all in the space of four weeks. Clive was something of an unknown quantity to most of us at this stage, but we knew that he was likely to shake things up in the England camp, stamp his own identity on the squad and bring in some new faces to replace some of the veterans who had served the country so superbly in the nineties. The World Cup finals were two years away and it was with that in my mind, we figured, that he would start blooding and grooming some youngsters. If you wanted to make an impression on the new coach, what better time to do it and what better opposition to do it against than the three giants of world rugby at that time? I wanted to be in Clive Woodward's first squad.

I don't know what it is about Bath but throughout my career I have had more good games against them than bad and, if you look at the stats, you'll see that I have also managed to score a lot of tries against them, too. Perhaps it was because I knew Bath to be such a good side that I again raised my game against them that afternoon at Welford Road; or maybe it was because I was fed up with all the frustrations of that early season, but I definitely played one of my more impressive games for Leicester since joining them fifteen months earlier. We won the match and I got on the scoresheet with a 'chip-and-gather' try to cap a performance that did my confidence a world of good. It may have helped that the press raved about my try in the papers the following morning, but I was just delighted that all my enthusiasm and rhythm came flooding back in a matter of minutes. There is no rhyme or reason to confidence in sport, I have found – it's either there or it isn't and often you simply don't know why you lose it or regain it. In rugby, it might just take one little break, one dummy or one great pass and suddenly you are thinking, 'Hey, maybe I'm not so bad after all.' Equally, you might score a great try, but still not feel 100 per cent buoyant after celebrating it. The match against Bath ended a fallow period for me which I could trace right back to the split second in Bloemfontein when I put out my hands to take that fateful pass from Mike Catt and got wiped out by Jaco Coetzee. Suddenly I wanted the ball in my hands once again and I was hunting gaps and putting my shoulder into contact situations without any fear.

Bath were still very much the team to beat in those days and victory over them was always followed by some long, hard celebrations in the clubhouse. Around two weeks later we had celebrated again after a good win in Europe and I was lying in bed with my hangover at around six in the morning, holding out hope somewhere in the depths of my blackout that no-one would call me before about midday. But then I had yet to meet Clive Woodward who, I would soon discover, though not quite an insomniac, was someone who believed that the working day began when the sun rose in the east and ended when it set in the west. Although he might not quite be in Maggie Thatcher's league, Clive Woodward is someone who sees his own sleep as an optional extra, a luxury rather than a necessity. He was, and still is, a man on a mission.

So there he was on the end of my telephone at daybreak that autumn morning as I lifted my head barely an inch off my pillow. 'Will? It's Clive Woodward. I have chosen you to play for England against Australia at Twickenham. Congratulations.' Like all young sportsmen I had dreamed of playing for my country since my early school days at St Mary's Hall, and now, when the great moment finally came, all I could do was go blank for about five seconds and whisper 'Great, thanks' — and then I rolled over and went straight back to sleep. I almost heard myself say: 'Hey, Clive, is it important — can I call you later, mate?' but I didn't have the energy, thank heavens. When I finally emerged from my pit several hours later, I shuffled downstairs, drank four glasses of water and it must have been a good quarter of an hour before I was dimly aware of having spoken to Clive Woodward. But it was true – Ceefax confirmed it – I was to be an England player!

England would have been ranked around fifth in the world at this point and, regardless of what any of us said at the time, we north of the equator all knew in the back of our minds that there was plenty to do in order to start matching the big three teams from the Southern Hemisphere on a regular basis. Now they were all here in our own backyard, queuing up and eager as ever to give the mother country of rugby a nice bloody nose and a kick up the shorts. Back-to-back Tests were not as common then as they are today and even in the Tri-Nations and Six (then Five) Nations you had a two-week gap between clashes. But there was no such luxury that autumn as we strapped in, gripped the armrests and braced ourselves for a month of collisions with the best rugby players on the planet. Somehow this felt far more daunting than going to South Africa with the Lions. Nobody had paid me a great deal of attention out there as I was not at the centre of the Test match action and there were far bigger names and reputations than mine on which the media and public could focus.

But now I had been chosen as a potential heir to the great Will Carling, probably the most high-profile England player of all time, and in the build-up to my debut I found myself engulfed in a maelstrom of press conferences, television interviews, meetings with sponsors and RFU officials in between all the training sessions and team talks. It was all quite daunting for someone whose media exposure up until then had involved little more than giving a couple of quotes to the odd reporter in the car park at Welford Road or down at The Stoop. Most players are likely to be shoehorned into their international career against say, Romania, or on a summer tour to Canada, or they might get thrown on for the last ten minutes against Scotland or Wales in the Five Nations if the result was in the bag. They slowly gain some experience of the Test arena, on and off the pitch, and, before they know it, they have matured into their roles and have become part of the furniture. That's not quite how it happened for many of us that autumn as Clive Woodward launched his first bold version of the England team he wanted to mould for World Cup glory over the coming years. From the moment you saw his first squad announcement you realised that Clive Woodward wasn't going to mess about with his team rebuilding; there were going to be no parachutes or soft landings for the detachment of new recruits he called up, that was for sure. If we wanted to be part of England's future, we just had to hit the ground running and get on with it.

Dad is one of the world's great fax senders and on that

mid-November morning of my debut, the hotel receptionist handed me the first of what would be many messages of pre-match encouragement from him over the coming years. 'You passed the theory test years ago, now go out and pass the practical!' He's not known as 'the Riddler' in rugby circles for nothing. Over breakfast I read in the newspapers that I was the eleventh man to follow his father into an England shirt, the thirtieth Sedbergh old boy to wear one and that I was the tallest centre ever to play for England. 'Brilliant,' I thought as I munched on my Corn Flakes, 'I may fluff a hat-trick of try-scoring passes, miss ten tackles and get sent off, but at least I'm 6 foot 5 inches. They could never stop me being lanky.'

Although it is easy to remember remarkable incidents and powerful images from the day of a match played several years earlier, it's very difficult to recall your actual feelings. I'm sure I must have been aquiver with a whole range of strong emotions that day, but because I didn't vomit, faint, bash my head against a wall or have to be restrained from trying to fight all the Australians all at once in the tunnel, those feelings have long since floated away on a stream of subsequent experiences. I do remember arriving at the West car park about an hour and a half before kickoff and feeling the buzz as I walked through a tunnel of supporters on the way into Twickenham. I also recall looking around the changing room and thinking how it all looked much like any other with its bare painted breezeblock walls and wooden benches. (Clive soon saw to a major overhaul of that room, complete with personalised individual locker areas and soundbite slogans on the wall designed to inspire us during the build-up. Not a single detail was omitted from his masterplan to transform us into the best team in the world.) I also recall glancing around shortly before heading out down the tunnel and inwardly remarking what a green, spotty-faced bunch of youngsters many of us were. England had a new captain in Lawrence Dallaglio, only four of the starting fifteen had featured in the line-up for the Five Nations match against Wales back in March and five of us were pulling on the shirt for the first time: Matt Perry, David Rees, Andy Long, Will Green and myself. There we were, a bunch of virtual strangers, all a-huddle in the dressing room, united by the red rose, about to go into battle for each other against the mighty Wallabies.

Jerry Guscott was injured and had dropped out, and so it was alongside the former skipper Phil de Glanville that I lined up against Tim Horan and Pat Howard, in my book two of the greatest centres of the modern era. Mum and Dad were there somewhere in the crowd and so too was Caro, busy drying her eyes and recomposing herself after an eventful journey getting to the ground. Unable to find a parking space anywhere near the team hotel in Richmond, she had to pay someone a tenner to leave her car outside their house, but by the time she had organised that, the last courtesy buses had left the hotel. There were no taxis around and so Caro climbed on to a local bus, by now in floods of tears, thinking she was going to miss the match. An elderly lady asked her what was wrong and Caro explained that she was trying, without much success, to get to Twickenham. 'Gosh, you must really like your rugby,' the old lady replied, looking a little nonplussed. When Caro explained that her boyfriend was winning his first cap and that the match was just about to start, the woman promptly got up and told the driver of Caro's predicament, and he immediately took a detour from his scheduled route (the bus was otherwise empty) and dropped her right outside the Twickenham gates. Whoever said chivalry and London Transport died in the Middle Ages?

Running down the tunnel and on to the pitch to the roar of 75,000 fans was a sensational experience for me, but, in all truth, that's pretty well where the excitement stopped for all concerned that afternoon. The build-up to the match, sadly, was far more exciting than the match itself which was killed as a spectacle by incessant rain. Rain is the worst case scenario for me as an inside centre, because much of my attacking game is built around my handling and passing skills. Passing is meant to be my great forte and you don't have to have watched rugby more than a couple of times to understand that dry conditions are better for throwing it around a bit and trying to play an expansive game. We should all be able to catch and make a simple pass when it's wet, but even at international level slinging out a looping 20- or 30-yard effort to the wing or the full-back becomes an activity fraught with risk in the rain. Against a team as good as the Wallabies, you want to make as few errors as possible, especially if you're making your debut, and you're keener than ever not to make a total arse of yourself in front of all your family and friends and a television audience running into tens of millions. The sound of 75,000 people groaning and tutting after you have made a cock-up is never music to the ears, but when you are a youngster fresh to the strange world of international sport, it's almost shocking.

Luckily, I had a reasonably solid game in a scrappy match that ended in a creditable 15-15 draw. My defence was pretty sound, I didn't make any dreadful blunders going forward, and nobody booed or threw things at me when I walked back down the tunnel at the final whistle. It was not a day for trying anything too fancy and when going forward I had spent most of the afternoon operating as a battering ram which, with my frame, I hear you snigger, must have been a bit like laying siege to a medieval castle with a fishing rod. Granted, it doesn't exactly prompt defenders to run up the white flag in immediate surrender, but I have always been fairly good at spotting and making the most of any gaps and design faults in the wall ahead of me. Once into the breach, my peculiar build for a centre, all long arms

Ready for training.
Aged 3, with
Emma in Rome.

Might have tried
Formula One!
Aged 6 in Rome.

Sports family of the Year BBC *Grandstand* 1978.

A young Harlequin.

Running the 800 metres in the
National Prep Schools Heats, 1983.

Winning the school Victor
Ludorum, aged 12.

Family golf practice.
Mum, Emma, Tom
and I in the Lake
District, 1981.

Playing at
St Mary's Hall
1st XV, 1984.

The Sedbergh
Run, aged 16.

At Stonyhurst with Dad and Tom, aged 18.

Durham University back line, March 1993. (l–r) Coults, Hodgey, Chinny, Smiler, me, Dooney and Stimmo.

UAU final, Durham vs. Loughborough 1991.
Ben Fennell can be seen just behind my left shoulder wearing black tape.

England Under 21's, Ballymore, Australia, 1993.
Spot the four World Cup winners!

England Under 21's, Sydney, Australia, 1993.
Oz, Biff Hanley and me celebrating England beating Australia 22–12.

1997 South Africa
Lions Tour. Daws,
Jenks, Tony and me.

The uncapped Lion –
my all time favourite
photo! June 1997.

Post playing Transvaal
at Ellis Park.
Backy, Oz and me,
1997 Lions Tour.

and legs, has its advantages because it means I can perhaps remain on my feet for a little longer than others, and win a few crucial moments before reinforcements arrive and I can pass the attack to them.

But by far my greatest achievement that day came after the final whistle when I managed to avoid the traditional post-match drinking ritual inflicted on players who had just won their first England cap. After seeing what had happened to Austin following his debut against Ireland in February, I had serious doubts about whether the glory of representing fifty million English souls on a rugby pitch for the first time was worth the post-match hell you were forced to endure back then when the sun was still setting on rugby's Palaeolithic era. As a youngster working my way up the representative ranks I had heard all the horror stories about fresh-faced lads up from the shires being forced to down buckets of bitter and pints of Pernod by their bigger, hairier, more experienced peers, but it was only when I saw Austin crawl back through the door of the Leicester house we shared that the full horror of it all struck me.

You could take eighty massive hits out on the field on your debut and you could be stamped on, raked, gouged, bitten and kicked for the eighty minutes, but I can assure that you would not look more battered and desperate than Austin the day after making his international bow. I am not exaggerating here, but that drinking binge nearly killed him. All the blood vessels in his eyes had exploded and they were so red I thought he was going to start bleeding out of them. It took him almost three weeks to recover and, in hindsight, I think it was partly as a result of his experience that the age-old tradition of death-by-beer for the debut boy disappeared very, very quickly at around this time.

What saved me that day, though, was more the fact that Clive had put us under strict orders not to drink at all during those autumn internationals when our bodies were already under enough pressure to recover for the next weekly challenge. 'Lads, I don't want any binges over the next month, even to celebrate a victory,' he announced and I could have got up and kissed the man there and then – and to hell with what the forwards thought. From the stories I have recounted about the drinking fun we had in the amateur days, I may have given you the impression that I was some kind of champion of the beer tankard, an Olympic standard ale-quaffer capable of drinking a whole pack of forwards under the table. But I have to come clean and admit the sad truth that I'm an absolute lightweight. You need only pop out for a couple of quiet ones with, say, Jason Leonard or any given Leicester forward of the nineties, to realise that in drinking, just as in sport, there is a premier league and there is non-league. I am distinctly non-league, with no hope of promotion and the threat of insolvency hanging over me. However, it didn't get me out of the other England ritual whereby new caps are called to the front of the team bus, one at a time, and made to sing a song. I chose *The Jungle Book*'s 'I'm The King Of The Swingers' and barely had the first bars left my mouth when, like all debut-makers before, I was roundly booed and told to sit down.

During that autumn series of internationals, Clive began the process of overhauling the backroom staff and bringing in a host of specialists to concentrate on various aspects of our game, on and off the field. Former All Black (and their future coach) John Mitchell came in as forwards coach with a reputation as a seriously hard-nosed trainer, but after a year at Leicester I was well prepared for some of the severe rucking sessions he put us all through. Leicester provided as good a grounding in hard training as anywhere in those days, and it was no coincidence that half the England team of that period were plucked from the club.

Dave Alred was brought in as the kicking specialist and former Great Britain rugby league coach Phil Larder was drafted in as defensive coach. Both of them were still with the England set-up seven years later – a testament not just to their own skills and contribution, but also to Clive Woodward's nose for picking out the best people in the business to fulfil narrow and specific roles within the set-up. The fitness experts, nutritionists and vision coaches would follow later but already the basis of a formidable support staff was starting to take shape.

For me the most exciting arrival in the England camp was that of Brian Ashton as backs coach. As Brian is a great family friend who used to live a few doors down from us on Smithy Row in Hurst Green, I suppose I am duty bound to say that he possesses one of the best brains in rugby football – but it happens to be true. He is one of the most inspiring and enlightening coaches I have ever worked with. Fact. There are moves with Brian Ashton's thumbprint on them that we were still using with England at the 2003 World Cup. I don't *mind* the rucking and the mauling, the tackling, the kicking from hand, and so on, because they are all vital parts of the game I love playing. Sometimes I even enjoy them – but the main reason I play rugby is to have that feeling of attacking with the ball in hand and trying to use some cunning and guile to beat opposition, to do something spontaneous and instinctive from phase one which the men opposite just can't defend. Brian Ashton sings from the same song sheet.

While these new faces on the coaching staff set about establishing their plans to help build a new England, we the players were preparing ourselves to take on one of the great All Black teams of the modern era. When you look at the names in the starting line-up that day – Christian Cullen, Jeff Wilson, Frank Bunce, Jonah Lomu, Andrew Mehrtens, Craig Dowd, Norm Hewitt, Olo Brown, Ian Jones, Zinzan and Robin Brooke, Josh Kronfeld and Taine Randell – you wonder quite how it was they never managed to win the World Cup. It was a team of incredible pace and skill, it was very well drilled and it was extremely experienced. And they were playing us. It was the All Blacks against the greenhorns.

The atmosphere at Twickenham a week earlier had been fairly muted as the prospects of a great spectacle were washed away by the hammering rain, but at Old Trafford there was a tremendous buzz about the stadium. The place was absolutely jumping and you got goose pimples and the shivers down the neck long before that shrill blast of the opening whistle. There is some fabulous rugby support up north, based around old clubs like Sale, Orrell, Waterloo as well as all the Yorkshire, Durham and Cumbria mobs, and, knowing that world as I do, I'm sure the sixty-thousand-odd tickets could have been sold several times over for that match.

In the dressing room, Lol Dallaglio was extremely pumped up and he strode around with fists clenched and jaw set, shouting at his fellow forwards in that slightly scary London gangster-style twang of his to take the fight to the All Blacks from the first whistle. By contrast, Phil de Glanville, the unofficial leader of the backs, was counselling calm among us, stressing the importance of thinking and seeing clearly and not allowing our judgement to be clouded by the passions of the moment. I have to admit that I was as nervous that afternoon as

I have ever been before a match and I was grateful for Phil's calming influence. Often on these occasions you can feel like a passenger in a car being driven by someone else and that's how it was for me right then as I tapped my studs on the changing-room floor and waited impatiently for the knock on the door to tell us it was time. Before I knew what I was doing, I was sprinting down the tunnel and running out into a barrage of northern noise and colour and, as soon as I was out on the pitch, the nerves quickly converted themselves into pure excitement and a sharp focus on what I had to do. The crowd sang 'Land Of Hope And Glory' that day and if there is one tune that stirs the soul and stiffens the upper lip for me, it is Edward Elgar's classic. No disrespect to Her Majesty but I wish we could have it before every match.

After the anthems, the All Blacks performed their customary *haka* and as they slapped their thighs, puffed out their chests and sang the Maori for 'I die! I die! / I live! I live! / For this is the hairy man who fetched the sun and caused it to shine again . . .' Richard Cockerill, the Leicester hooker, broke from the long white line we had formed to face their traditional challenge and headed off to confront his opposite number, Norm Hewitt. If you want proof that backs and forwards come from different planets, you need look no further than this little episode. It made for a great spectacle and it perfectly captured the terrific tension that had been mounting in the build-up to the game, particularly once we had all arrived inside Old Trafford. But not for all the tries and all the trophies in Christendom would you ever find me seeking out my opposite man in the All Blacks and going nose to nose with him while he tried to execute his ancient tribal war dance. I have always loved the *haka*. I find it spectacular and stirring and, long after my playing career is over, I will still get a shiver of excitement when I see it being performed.

I certainly didn't make a fool of myself that afternoon and I even managed to punch a few holes past the great Frank Bunce and Alama Ieremia, playing in the All Black centres, to earn myself a slap on the back in the following day's papers. I also came close to scoring my first international try, only to be beaten to it by Phil, and I have a great picture of the two of us enjoying the moment; it is still on my wall at home today. No one has ever accused either Phil or me of being the fastest men on the planet, but there we are celebrating the try, while standing nearby are the unfocused but distinctly unimpressed figures of Lomu, Cullen and Wilson, collectively among the great back threes of all time.

England played very well that afternoon but still lost 25-8. The All Blacks always seemed to have another gear and their finishing was ruthlessly clinical, scoring three tries through Jones, Randell and Wilson against the run of play. What they showed us that day was that you can have all the possession you like but it's not worth tuppence ha'penny if you don't do anything with it. One moment we were in the game and it felt like we were dominating it, and then you looked up at the scoreboard and saw that we were about twelve points adrift. The general consensus was that this youthful England team was going to get stuffed out of sight but after giving a good account of ourselves, the banner headlines the following morning were bursting with praise for our efforts. Honour in defeat seemed to be the general feeling about our performance, but there was an ugly aftermath to the contest which served to stoke the fires ahead of our next encounter with John Hart's team two weeks later. Hart was upset by what he called the 'outright thuggery' of England's forwards and he was probably referring specifically to an incident in which Martin Johnson gave their scrum-half Justin Marshall a less than playful slap off the ball. The incident was missed by the referee Peter Marshall but Johnno was later cited and banned for the match against South Africa the following weekend. There were all manner of dark arts being performed in the shadows of the rucks, mauls and scrums but neither Martin nor England as a whole could have had much cause for complaint.

But there was one other controversy which still rankles a little today when I think about it; the accusation by the New Zealanders that England went on a 'lap of honour' after the match. We were walking back down the tunnel when one of the RFU officials stopped and said he thought it would be a nice touch if we went back to thank the fans because we didn't get to play up north very often and they had given us some of the best support I have ever had at a rugby match. So we ran back and clapped the crowd as we jogged around the pitch and the stadium DJ cranked out 'Land Of Hope And Glory'. This seemed to upset the All Blacks who were convinced we were trying to steal their glory and make the implicit claim that we were the true winners of the contest.

You can call the England team what you like – go on, most people have – but we are not stupid. As far as I understand how laps of honour work, one of their prerequisites is that you actually have to win the game to earn the honour to run the lap. Perhaps we should have issued a press release before we returned to the pitch explaining that we were about to embark on a 'lap of thanks' so that everybody understood exactly what was happening and there would have been no diplomatic fallout: 'We, the England team, would like to apologise unreservedly in advance for any offence we are about to give to anyone who might interpret our act of thanking the locals for their support as an act of grotesque and insulting arrogance to anyone born south of the equator and specifically to anyone on two islands in the South Pacific Ocean with the geographic coordinates 41 00 S 174 00 E . . .'

But it was too late, and the following morning we

woke up to discover that we were all a bunch of arrogant bastards. Another day, another 'England are arrogant' claim. God, it's so boring. No one could rightly accuse us of being overconfident back in 1997. We were a new team starting out. We had won nothing. We were more in awe than contempt of our Southern Hemisphere opponents. We would look at the opposition team sheet and say, 'Holy Moly, look who we're playing against today!' and as a youngster in my second international it was a daunting honour to be on the same pitch as guys like Lomu, Cullen and Wilson. If anything we showed too much respect to Southern Hemisphere opposition in those days. So the claim that it was a lap of honour we did that afternoon was highly mischievous, unadulterated rubbish and, unless I have lost my marbles, it was also totally nonsensical. It's never exactly hands-across-the-ocean stuff with New Zealand at the best of times, especially if the people they are reaching out to happen to be the English, but that accusation was particularly out of order.

It was a dreadful PR day for me personally as well, as I succeeded in upsetting virtually everybody connected with the England camp with a series of Chaplinesque gaffes. During a live television interview after the match I announced that we hadn't drunk a single can of the two cases of beer left in the dressing room, at a stroke infuriating one of our main sponsors who had provided them. I then accidentally plugged the main rivals of our energy drink sponsors after mixing up their names in my head. The day before I had said to the press that Phil Larder had instructed us to turn the match into a street fight, meaning that we were to mess up the contact area, and that came out in the papers as 'England Want To Scrap The All Blacks'. By the time we returned to the team hotel I am surprised that no one handed me a walking cane and a bowler hat, thanked me for all my efforts and gave me a gentle push in the direction of the nearest music hall.

If it is true that you learn from your mistakes, I had just graduated from my PR, marketing and media course with first class honours in the space of twenty-four hours. Most of us are a little more surefooted at dealing with the media these days and are less likely to be caught off guard by a cleverly couched question. To help us avoid the type of gaffes I made during that period, our media people in the RFU give us all a list of fifty possible questions with various possible answers. We are not meant just to trot them out verbatim like robots but the idea is to give a steer to those players who feel uncomfortable under inquisition. Although I like to speak my mind and talk openly during interview I do go through the list because when you are tired and you can't think straight after a long round of interviews, it's good to have a couple of stock answers to wheel out. In my experience, the rugby press, almost to a man, has been pretty honest and straight-dealing with the England players and although they generally don't try to catch us out, we can all say stupid things from time to time – as I proved so handsomely at the time of that All Blacks match.

The third leg of our autumn challenge pitched us against a powerful South Africa side bent on revenge for their humiliation at the hands of an England-dominated Lions squad a few months earlier. It turned out to be a tortuous afternoon for us all as we slumped to a 29–13 defeat, England's heaviest ever at Twickenham. We were missing Johnno through suspension and a string of others through injury, but there were no excuses afterwards because we had been well beaten by a far better team on the day. I have played South Africa so many times in my career that my memory of this first encounter with them is fairly dim. The mind has a habit of automatically deleting or suppressing bad experiences and perhaps I have blanked out most of the details from that day. I didn't play particularly poorly and nor did the team; it was more a case that the Boks played very well. If you have been beaten by the South Africans, it generally means you have been beaten up by them too (legitimately in most, though not all, instances!). I recently saw some press pictures from that match and there were a handful of us all standing beneath the posts waiting for the conversion looking run well and truly ragged.

I don't know whether the stats bear out my impression, or whether I just imagined it, but I remember thinking how much bigger and more powerful than us the South Africans seemed that day. Perhaps it's a trick your mind plays on you when you are being beaten, but it certainly felt a little like boys against men out there. Clive's bold move to throw us in against the best teams in the world over that period was made in the hope that we might sneak a win or two, but more in the expectation that we would learn an awful lot about top-level rugby very quickly. And if we gained anything that afternoon, it was the realisation that we had a vast amount of work to do if we were going to turn the tables on the Southern Hemisphere and start bullying them.

Opposite me in the centres that day was a player called Dicky Muir, a cracking footballer in the Paddy Howard mould who uses his brain as much as his brawn and of whom you never quite know what he will try next. For me the easiest style of centre to play against is the 6-foot 2-inch, 110 kilo muscle-monster who sticks it under his arm and runs in a straight line right at me with a face which says 'I'm going to beat you up'. Fine. I just assume the crash position, get him on the deck and watch Neil Back or Richard Hill fly in and nick the ball. The most difficult opponents for me are the artful, canny beggars like Howard and Muir, who are about half my height, and I end up like the cartoon beanpole farmer, in all but dungarees, running around his farmyard trying to lay his hands on an elusive chicken.

If the match against the Boks had been a painful education for us, our second clash with New Zealand was a classic, one many claimed was the best game Twickenham had ever staged. Certainly no one could have predicted the final 26-26 scoreline, nor guessed that we would have even got close to beating a team of such calibre and experience who had won their previous eleven Tests. The controversies at Old Trafford had given an extra edge to the contest while the All Blacks were keen to give Zinzan Brooke, one of the greatest players the game has ever seen, a fittingly triumphant send-off in his fifty-eighth and last Test.

I don't think I have ever been involved in a start to a game quite like the one in this match where we raced into a 20-3 lead inside sixteen minutes with tries from David Rees, Richard Hill and Lawrence Dallaglio, who played absolutely magnificently throughout. Rees had all his front teeth smashed out when he dived over in the corner under a pile of black shirts having chipped the ball over Jonah Lomu for our first try. I then set up Hill's try with a break down the left-hand side, which I can still picture as if it were yesterday. The All Blacks must have looked at me and thought there was no way this gangly slowcoach was ever going to score and went to pick up the fast guys outside me. I could have sold them corner-shop dummies all day long, it seemed, but when I got to within 5 yards of the line and thought I couldn't fail to score my first try for England, little Justin Marshall, fair play to him, stuck out his arm as I stepped inside him. I staggered and I knew he had got me so I turned round and saw Phil de Glanville screaming like fury for me to pass the ball to him but I slipped it to Richard Hill instead (Hilly and I have the same manager in Nick Keller. Sorry Phil) and he fell over the line. When Lol Dallaglio powered over a few minutes later, we were slapping ourselves in the face to see if we were dreaming.

Andrew Mehrtens has never been the most popular man in the English camp, least of all after his daft comment a few years ago that 'England were pricks to lose to' (or 'prucks', as he pronounced it). 'Daft' because none of us could remember any specific incident after a match which might have given him cause to feel offended and dafter still because he had never actually been on a losing side against England at that point. Perhaps he was referring to the famous lap of honour that never was. I have not the faintest idea of what he is like as a character; for all I know he could be the most charming man on the planet. But whatever we might think of his diplomatic skills you have to say he was a simply magnificent rugby player in his prime and he was immense at Twickenham that December afternoon in 1997 as he orchestrated an awesome fightback by the All Blacks, scoring a total of twenty-one points, including a try, in the process.

The pleasing aspect from our point of view was that, though we let slip a seventeen-point lead, we were actually losing with five minutes to go but came back to snatch a draw with a penalty when we could easily have folded completely under the All Black onslaught. There is always fight in the England team, as there is in most sides representing their country, but on that day we saw the first glimmers of something completely different: self-belief. It was a great game to be involved in, and it was probably my best game out of the four that autumn, and the press were virtually wetting themselves with excitement afterwards. There was silence in our dressing room at the end because we had just played against one of *the* great rugby teams and come within a whisker of turning them over.

Our back row that day was Hill, Back and Dallaglio, a combination that would remain England's first choice for the next six years, and they were absolutely out-standing. Nobody, though, played poorly and the general consensus was that Clive Woodward had shown he was on the right track with his vision of fifteen-man, all-running, multi-skilled rugby – a concept that had been ridiculed in a number of quarters, not least from within the RFU itself, when Clive first made his ambitions clear. It was a milestone game for him, not just in terms of the result and the self-belief it engendered, but also because he tried a different game plan in which my old Waterloo chum Paul Grayson –

fly-half that day – and myself played flat rather than very deep like England midfields in the past. The idea was to get us to probe and test the opposition from close quarters, and it seemed to work very well.

'That's the best I've ever seen England play and that's because they've never played that way before,' the New Zealand coach John Hart said and he was absolutely spot-on. It certainly felt as if we had contributed to something pretty special in England's 126-year rugby history. Those four weeks were some learning curve and the following day I went out with a couple of old mates to a pub on the Fulham Road for my first beer in over a month, still trying to take in all that had happened. I certainly hadn't let myself down and Brian Moore, I read in the paper that day, even said I had been England's best back throughout the series. But there was never any chance that I might start getting a bit full of myself – not with Bob Dwyer around at any rate. He called from Leicester to congratulate me before adding: 'Will, mate, I've got a bag off nails up here just in case your feet are not back on the ground yet.'

There was actually no need for Bob to bring me back down to earth because Jason Keyter of Harlequins did it for him in our first domestic game after the internationals. Jason hit me with a late tackle and my troublesome shoulder popped out of its socket as I hit the ground. It was not especially painful because of all the adrenalin coursing through me at the time and when

I shook my arm it just suction-pumped back into the socket. I had to go straight off, though, because I knew that in order for it to have come out, the ball of the arm would have had to burst its way through the ligaments. In the event I was out of action for four weeks, which was a hard blow to withstand as it had taken me so long to recover my form and fitness after smashing the same shoulder in South Africa six months earlier. I am no Steve Redgrave when it comes to training, as I have explained earlier, but I have always worked hard to recover from injury, and I was back, slightly ahead of schedule, two weeks before the start of the Five Nations. The speed and timing of my recovery was not to everyone's satisfaction, however, and I copped a bit of abuse from a small handful in Leicester circles who thought I was only interested in playing for England. Whatever.

When we travelled to Paris for the championship opener against the French, the pundits and bookmakers had us firmly installed as favourites for the Grand Slam. The predictions were based purely on that one performance against the All Blacks and the fact that the French had been massacred 52-10 by the Springboks not long before. The French, though, had made eight changes since then and they have an historical tendency to rebound sharply from setbacks. Is there any other team in the world that can be so dreadful one day and so majestic the next? Admittedly on this occasion we helped their return to form with a pretty average first-half performance before going down 24-17. We were more impressive in the second half but, despite all the autumn euphoria in the press, the truth was that we had now gone six games without a win.

To lose to France in France may be a disappointment but it is certainly never a disgrace and it was a little confusing reading some of the newspapers which were full of so much doom and gloom the following day. You draw at home to New Zealand and you are the best team in the world; then you lose to France away and you're the worst. What's that all about? If you were being kind and positive you'd say it was that people were so desperate for us to do well they were just venting their frustration on us. If you were being unkind you'd say there was no balanced perspective in the media. What sells papers are extremes: extremely good news or extremely bad news. It's either black or white, never grey. Perhaps they felt silly for talking us up too much after the New Zealand game.

Dad was enraged by the negativity of reporting after the game and sent a letter to Clive Woodward offering his support. He reminded Clive that as his coach twenty years earlier he had told all the England players to find a smile after a similar defeat in Paris and asked him to repeat the favour. We didn't quite go through the rest of the championship with a perma-grin on our faces because there is something particularly deflating about losing the opening game and having the Holy Grail of a Grand Slam snatched away from the off, but we did at least manage to beat Wales, Scotland and Ireland without a great deal of difficulty. There is, though, only so much satisfaction to be had from winning the Triple Crown and I imagine that the other three countries would agree. When someone else is picking up the main prize, you don't exactly bounce up and down in the changing room, spray each other with champagne, shed tears of joy and shout: 'Hurrah! Hurrah! We're the second best team in Europe!' As one former player wrote at the time: 'England clinched the Triple Crown yesterday, but does anyone really give a damn?'

Our best performance of the Five Nations in 1998 came in our second match against Wales at Twickenham where we played them off the park for a 60-26 victory. There was a feeling before the game that England had reached a critical point under Clive Woodward and he was even handed the dreaded vote of confidence a few days earlier. 'Clive Woodward has the full backing of the RFU . . .' translates roughly as 'One more defeat and that clown's out of the door'. But there were no mutterings in the corridors after we ran in eight tries to demolish the Welsh and woke up the following morning to read that we were not a bunch of useless losers after all, but were in fact the most exciting team on the planet who could probably beat Brazil at football, too, if we really put our minds to it. Clive had also undergone a remarkable transformation from muppet to maestro in the space of a fortnight. It was an especially memorable day for the Greenwoods as we ended a thirty-year, eleven-match wait for a win in an England shirt. England had lost four and drawn one of the five games Dad had played for England between 1966 and 1969 and my record was lost three and drawn two. At this stage, the Greenwoods were hardly going down as the greatest father-son combo in rugby history. I also managed to score a try to cap an unforgettable day and when Dad, ever the perfectionist, sent me his customary in-depth analysis of my game, he pointed out that there was actually very little difference between that performance and the one against the French for which I had received a bit of flak.

After beating Scotland 34-20 at Murrayfield for a ninth consecutive win over them, we overcame wooden-spooners Ireland 35-17 in a slightly bad-tempered occasion at Twickenham to finish the tournament with a record points aggregate and a feeling that Clive's vision of total rugby was starting to come into focus. In those days, Clive's philosophy was to go out and entertain, to play attacking rugby, rather than just grind out results in games that most people would have forgotten about a few weeks after they had been played. He wanted to get the England fans excited by being ambitious and making a statement and I think he succeeded in doing that over those six months.

Although we later added some streetwise, hard-nosed efficiency to the desire to entertain, Clive never lost that desire to inspire the crowd.

If the international campaign had finished on a small high, the same could not be said of our season at Leicester which ended with Bob Dwyer being shown the door. If there was any consolation for Bob at the end of a season in which we failed to mount a serious challenge for honours, it was that he did not have a coronary. By our final game, his face was so purple he looked like a plum with a moustache, or one of the Mr Men characters. I wasn't there when he was told his services were no longer required, but his face, I imagine, would have been a perfect study in rage. The irony would not have been lost on him either that the man chosen to replace him was Dean Richards, the Leicester favourite he dropped from the team not long after his arrival.

Newcastle, under player-manager Rob Andrew, won the league that year – and I for one certainly wasn't sending them a telegram to pass on my heartfelt congratulations. For the first and only time in my career I was sent off for allegedly head-butting Andrew during a 27-10 defeat. The match was more of a brawl than a sporting contest and, after a series of running scraps, it erupted into a free-for-all shortly before the final whistle. Normally, on these occasions you will find me frantically looking around for someone equally soft, a like-minded soul I could snarl at and push about while, under my breath, complimenting him on his new haircut and asking after his wife and kids. There are always a dangerous few moments before the ref arrives on the scene when I fear I might actually have to lamp someone or be lamped, but once he's there I can safely go into a full theatrical mode, grab my opponent by the throat and roar: 'You don't know who you're messing with, you big fat girl of a prop! I'm from Blackburn, me. Do yourself a favour and step away . . . Don't make me knock you out, lardie boy . . . Go on, then, I'll give you the first five punches . . .' And then I walk away eyeballing everyone and trying to look like Chuck Norris. You can do that safe in the knowledge that unless your opponent is either incredibly stupid or incredibly French, he's not going to punch or butt you right under the nose of the referee.

Unfortunately, on this occasion I found myself on the deck with Rob Andrew on top of me rubbing his elbow around my eye socket. It was a distinctly odd moment. Rob Andrew used to be one of my boyhood heroes and I remember the thrill as an awestruck twelve-year-old when I was allowed to sit next to him on the England team coach after an international during Dad's spell as coach between 1983 and 1985. Now there he was, the squeaky clean former England fly-half, apparently trying to dig my eyeball out with his elbow and I'm saying, 'What on earth are you effing doing, you big twat?' But he just carried on and with referee Ed Morrison standing about a foot away I did my hardman bit as it broke up and placed my forehead to Andrew's face in my 'Don't-mess-with-me-I'm-from-Blackburn' mode. Perhaps my performance was just a little too convincing – Morrison was certainly taken in as he showed me the red card and ordered me off. Even Andrew himself afterwards had the good grace to admit that it was 'more of a kiss than a head butt'.

My dismissal brought with it the risk of a sixty-day suspension which would have meant me missing the summer tour to New Zealand, Australia and South Africa, but it was irrelevant in the event because I was forced to undergo a second shoulder reconstruction that summer. The Tour of Hell went without me.

Chapter Five

MATT DAWSON REMARKED not long ago
that he had only to utter the phrase 'Tour of Hell'
and half the regular England squad will immediately rip
off their shirts or shorts, point to a variety of scars and
lesions and express their sincere regret at missing what
turned out to be the most disastrous overseas trip in the
team's history. There were seventeen uncapped players
in the thirty-seven-man squad that set out for a gruelling
and humiliating tour of New Zealand, Australia and
South Africa. Only five of the team which had played a
part in that epic draw with the All Blacks seven months
earlier were on board the plane: Austin Healey, Matt
Perry, Richard Cockerill, Garath Archer and Neil Back.
The inexperience of the squad prompted the then
chairman of the Australian Rugby Union to make one
of the sillier comparisons you will hear when he
described the party as 'the greatest English sellout since
Gallipoli. I think the English will have their own fatal
landings in Australia and New Zealand.' The majority
of the players on that tour later disappeared from the

international scene without trace, and the only positive to be drawn from the four heavy defeats they suffered was the rise to prominence of Jonny Wilkinson and Josh Lewsey.

It must have been a pretty dismal experience for all connected with the tour and it was bad enough just watching it from home 12,000 miles away. By then my arm was back in a sling after I had undergone a second major shoulder operation to tighten the socket with laser technology to stop it from popping out again. I needed four months to recover from the surgery which meant missing out on pre-season training with the rest of the Leicester boys. You won't normally find me complaining about missing training, but you do want to be involved in those hard few weeks before the season starts because there is a lot of bonding which sets the tone for the rest of the year. There is a strong sense that you are all setting out on a mission or adventure as one tight, united group and you end up feeling like some kind of interloper when it gets to October and you slip back into the changing room, clear your throat and sheepishly announce that you're raring to go again.

As it was, I 'rared' for no more than a few weeks before succumbing to a separate injury that condemned me to nine months of hobbling about on the sidelines, rubbing my groin and cursing anyone connected with the medical profession. In the brief action I saw in the 1998/9 season, I managed to maintain my curiously successful record against our friends from Bath by scoring a couple of tries in a massive league win over them. I also featured in England's World Cup qualifiers against Holland, an embarrassing and joyless 110-0 romp, and against Italy – an altogether more nerve-shredding affair which brought us a 23-15 win and an avalanche of ridicule in the press. 'Win A World Cup? This Lot Couldn't Win A Raffle' ran one of the headlines, but I was amused to read that I had saved England's blushes with a 'superb solo effort' in which I chipped over four defenders, scooped up the ball on the bounce and powered over the line like an unstoppable force of nature. The truth was that I had no real idea what to do and when I tried to kick the ball I succeeded only in shin-boning it in the one direction I hadn't intended it to go. This completely foxed the Italian defence, who were clearly unfamiliar with my out-rageous improvisational skills; as they went one way, I went the other and I was then pleasantly surprised to find the ball bouncing back into my arms. Before you could say 'Will Greenwood is an athletic genius' I was swallow-diving between the posts and lapping up the praise of my team-mates and the crowd.

But the joy was short-lived because, as I left the field, a slight twinge I had felt in the Holland game had become a sharp stabbing pain on my pubic bone with every other step I took. I spent four days sitting in giant buckets of ice but it was no good, and the day before the

England match against Australia at Twickenham I pulled up in training, lame once again. It's enough to make you start howling at the moon when you know that you are going to be out of action for an indeterminate period of time – especially when you have just returned from injury anyway – and there is not a damned thing you can do about it.

I loved my time at Leicester and I'd never carp about anything that happened to me there – even when I was dropped for the better part of a whole season the following year – but I'd be lying if I said I didn't feel some bitterness about the way the club went about treating that groin injury. I believe I was let down by a medical staff who didn't seem to me to make even the slightest effort to find out what might be the best way forward. Nothing was ever diagnosed and they did little more than pat me on the back and tell me everything would be better soon. 'Relax, it just needs a bit of rest, Will,' they told me day after day after day, week after interminable week. Every day for six months I turned up at the club for my 'treatment', if that's the correct scientific word for sitting around, reading magazines, drinking tea and lying under a machine that looked like – and probably was – one of those old-style, helmet hair-dryers as favoured by blue-rinse grandmothers.

My wife Caro will tell you that I was not the most cheerful of companions over the months that followed as I moped about feeling sorry for myself, wondering when or if I would ever play another rugby game. The longer you are away from the game, the more the demons of doubt start to swarm and torment you. Sitting at home on the sofa that autumn and winter, watching on television as my team-mates lined up against, first, Australia and South Africa, and then Scotland, France, Ireland and Wales was cruel torture. Even when England ended the Boks' record-equalling run of seventeen victories with a 13-7 win at Twickenham, feelings of happiness for my team-mates were mixed with frustration that I was not there with them to celebrate. Equally, when England lost 31-32 to Wales after a late try by Scott Gibbs and saw the Grand Slam elude them once again, I wanted to be in that dressing room to commiserate.

By the end of that awful season there was a very real possibility not only that I would miss out on selection for the World Cup finals later in the year, but that my career was petering out altogether. When thirty-six other England players flew out for a month's training session at the Couran Cove resort off the Queensland coast, I was left in England holding my wretched groin having been told that I had until 26 July to prove my fitness, or be ruled out of World Cup contention.

It was especially frustrating because there was no visible evidence that there was anything wrong with me: no crutches, no slings, no arrow through a bandaged head, not even so much as a limp. I could walk but I couldn't run. For several months I woke up each morning and, feeling no pain, I'd slip into my running gear, open up the front door and head out for a jog, only to be doubled up in agony by the time I reached the gate a few yards away. The only decent exercise I could do was swimming and I spent so much time in the pool in my increasingly frantic efforts to get fit that, come the summer, I had virtually sprouted fins and scales and was walking around with my mouth open looking really thick and swallowing imaginary plankton. I wished at the time that I had smashed my leg instead; at least then my injury would have been obvious and tangible and I would not have had to spend nine months of my life saying through gritted teeth: 'No one seems entirely sure but it's a problem with my groin, I believe' in answer to the eternal question, 'So what *is actually* wrong with you, Will?'

At the beginning of June, I found myself in a small room in Munich for the better part of a week with my trousers and pants around my ankle while a steady parade of German nurses and specialists came in to stare at my nether regions and say: 'Ja, for sure, zat is wery intewesting, Herr Gweenvood. Herr Wolfhart vill be most fascinated by zis.' Herr Wolfhart is a pioneering German homeopathic doctor and it was to his clinic in Bavaria that I headed more in desperation than serious hope of being cured of my chronic groin condition. I was sceptical at first but my manager Nick Keller virtually dragged me on to the plane, saying, quite rightly: 'What the hell have you got to lose?' If I had known then what I was going to be in for that week I probably would have replied: 'Lose? How about, the last vestiges of my dignity, all control over my sphincter and probably about £5,000.' But all I knew was that the good doctor had allegedly managed to cure a whole string of international athletes, including Michael Owen, Jürgen Klinsmann, Boris Becker and the Spanish golfer José Maria Olazabal, who had seemed certain never to play again until he headed to the Munich clinic.

This was the lowest point in my playing career and my gloom deepened with the news that dear old grandma Haworth had passed away a few days before I was due to fly out. After long deliberation Mum, Dad and I agreed that it would be better if I missed the funeral in order to press on and get myself fixed up in time for the World Cup, but it was with a heavy heart that I boarded the flight and set off for one final stab at ending my injury nightmare.

'OK, Villiam, let's have a little look zen, ja? Drop ze trousers.' Under different circumstances, being asked to unzip for a host of beautiful young women might be quite appealing but after several days of exposing the crown jewels for the rest of the world's curiosity and amusement, I began to wonder quite what I was doing there. Before my critical meeting with Dr Wolfhart I was sitting outside his room waiting to be summoned for an audience when through the door hobbled the Bayern Munich footballers Stefan Effenberg and Samuel Kuffour, fresh from the Champions League final defeat by Manchester United in Barcelona and looking even more miserable and bad-tempered than me. As an ardent Manchester City fan I had more sympathy for them than they might have guessed but I thought it best to leave the pleasantries to an exchange of nods and a solemn frown.

'I can feel ze pain. You vill never sprint again . . .' the doctor said as he pressed his hand to my groin a few minutes later.

'You bleeding what?' I shrieked.

'. . . unless you have an operation.'

It was a Monday and the plan, which Dr Wolfhart spelt out with total conviction, was that I would have a hernia operation on my right side on Tuesday, one on my left on Thursday, and on Friday he would inject me with his concoction of heaven knows what before I boarded a flight home that night. By this stage I was almost beyond caring what he injected me with. ('Crack cocaine? That sounds fine, doctor. You just press on.') After all the dithering I had experienced at Leicester, it was reassuring to have my groin – in a manner of speaking – in the hands of someone who seemed to have a firm grip on the situation.

Before the operation I had to clear my bowel system and I was given a suppository to that end, but there was a minor language problem at the handover and I didn't quite understand the bit about the seven-second activation period. I was only about 8 yards away from the toilet in my room at the Four Seasons Hotel when I did what you do with suppositories, but it was about a yard too far in the event and I almost suffered a further injury blow as I made a desperate final leap for the seat. After the second operation on Thursday, I was barely able to walk as I shuffled out of the clinic to take a cab back to the hotel. I couldn't find one, ended up having to walk and I was virtually in tears by the time I reached the refuge of the lobby and fell into the lift. The hotel was only about 1,500 yards away from the clinic, but I could proceed no faster than a tortoise and I was in such agony that I had to stop every few seconds and just stand in the middle of the pavement, like a madman having a moment. The pain was so great that I was sweating rivers and whenever I tried to ask passers-by to help hail me a taxi, they just tapped their watches and hurried along their way, glancing at me nervously over their shoulders as they scuttled off.

The following morning I returned to the clinic – by taxi – and after eleven local anaesthetics and about fifty injections of the doctor's special formula I was heading to the airport feeling like a pin cushion but with a faint glimmer of hope that my strange week in Germany would prove to have been one well spent. I still don't know exactly what was in Wolfie's potion, but it certainly worked its magic. When I first walked into his clinic I couldn't even trot or move my leg in anything but a straight line, but within two and a half weeks I was reporting myself fit for World Cup training. I haven't had a groin problem since and as far as I'm concerned Dr Wolfhart is a genius. There were plenty of others who also deserve my great thanks in bringing to an end the most depressing episode of my rugby career. My manager and old friend Nick talked me up throughout the whole saga, and persuaded me, in one of my darker moments, that it was far too early to start thinking about alternative career options.

There had also been a great rumpus over who was going to pay the bill for my Munich miracle cure with both Leicester and the RFU disclaiming any liability for the cost. Leicester said that their health insurance plan did not cover treatment overseas, while the Twickenham people said it was up to the club to cough up. If I ended up paying for it myself, it would have been worth every penny and more, but it seemed incredible that, three or four years into the game's professional era, neither of my employers felt obliged, or even willing, to make some kind of contribution to the expense. It was ridiculous that Ian Stafford, a journalist with the *Daily Mail*, was the man who finally produced the credit card after he and Nick came to an arrangement whereby the paper would pay for the treatment in return for some exclusive interviews.

If that period had been a troubling and dismal one for me, I can only imagine how Lawrence Dallaglio, the England captain of the day, felt when he woke up one Sunday morning that May to discover he had been the victim of an undercover sting operation by the *News of the World*. The paper made all sorts of lurid allegations about his private life, and it was dreadful to see him and his family dragged through the mill over the weeks that followed. He was forced to resign the captaincy and it was a major blow for England to lose such an inspirational leader as we headed towards the World Cup finals in the autumn.

As part of our preparations for the World Cup the coaching staff took us down to Lympstone in Devon for a week of training with the Royal Marines in the hope that we would be hardened and bonded by the experience. It is impossible to quantify how helpful that week was in preparing for the finals, but it certainly felt rewarding at the time and all the boys seemed to enjoy the novelty and challenges of it. I am not entirely sure, however, whether our backs coach Brian Ashton will be volunteering for another stint down in Devon following his experience in the helicopter crash simulator. I was next to him when it began its slow descent to the bottom of the dark pool and then turned over on its back. The idea is that you are meant to keep cool, and, knowing where your exit routes are, calmly unstrap yourself and swim to safety. There was an instructor in there with an oxygen tank and a few of the lads had already turned purple and tried to punch their way through the metal walls before being dragged to the surface. But poor old Brian, who agreed to go through with the experience despite suffering a bit from claustrophobia, had forgotten to undo his seatbelt and was desperately trying to pull himself through one of the windows, thinking that his trousers were caught. He had taken half the skin off his back and I was behind him not knowing what on earth was going on, when one of the marines saw what was happening and released him.

Brian may have different memories of his trip to Devon, but for me it was just great to be involved in the England set-up again. I knew that Clive and Brian both wanted me to play a part in the finals, but I still had to prove my match fitness to them and I managed to do that in our two warm-up games against the United States and Canada. 'Will Tanks The Yanks' said one newspaper headline, which was all well and good, but could we tank New Zealand, South Africa, Australia and France and become the first Northern Hemisphere side to lift the Webb Ellis trophy? We were definitely capable of winning one-offs against the big sides from the south but whether we had it in us to put together a sustained run was a completely different question. We had been drawn in a group alongside New Zealand, Tonga and Italy and it would have been a major shock not to have reached the knockout stages. But we were all aware, whether we said it or not, that the match against the All Blacks, our second, would probably make or break our tournament. In addition to the boost it would give to our self-belief, victory would also mean that if, as expected, we went on to win the group, we would have landed a relatively easy route to the later stages. If the rest of the matches followed the script (as they tend to at the rugby World Cup) the losers would face what amounted to a physical assault course in the form of Fiji and South Africa – and that coming on the back of a pool match with an equally robust side in Tonga. Even if we managed to get through that lot still standing, we would not in all probability have been in the best of shape by the time we lined up for the anthems in the semi-final. You can beat teams like Tonga, Fiji and Italy by fifty points or more sometimes, but you always leave the pitch knowing that you have just been given a serious physical examination, even if the scoreline suggests that you have enjoyed rugby's equivalent of a gentle evening stroll along the promenade.

We certainly weren't favourites to lift the cup, but many had us down as dark horses with a number of unknown quantities in our ranks, not least a brilliant young man from Newcastle by the name of Jonny Wilkinson. Jonny had taken his England bow in the centres during my lay-off, but it was as a fly-half that most people saw him making an impact – and thank the

Lord for that, I say from an entirely selfish career point of view! With Jerry Guscott, Mike Catt and Phil de Glanville all in the squad, competition for the two centre places was tight, but I was chosen to start alongside Phil as we ran out 67-7 winners over Italy at Twickenham. I didn't know whether to laugh or cry when, after thirty-five minutes, I felt my hamstring go and I had to limp off. I knew there and then that it was not a severe problem but coming as it did after my earlier problems, I began to wonder whether someone was trying to tell me something.

I managed to shake off the twinge in time to be named on the bench for our crucial encounter with the All Blacks, but I could only watch as we once again dominated our highly fancied opponents yet still finished on the losing side by some distance. According to the great raft of stats produced afterwards we had enjoyed 65 per cent of the possession, 63 per cent of the territory, made half the number of tackles they had, won seventy-three rucks to their twenty-one, won the ball eighty times to twenty-four in open play and yet still managed to lose the game 30-16. We just couldn't seize the day and once again the New Zealand backs were brilliant and clinical in their finishing. As someone whose big rugby gift is supposed to be sniffing a bit of space in the opposition defence, it was especially frustrating to sit there watching my team-mates struggle in vain to find a way of breaching the line of black shirts that afternoon. I'd be flattering myself to think I would have given England a better chance, but I would dearly love to have had a bash. That's the problem with injuries: once you are out of the side for a long spell, you have no God-given right to walk straight back into the position that was once yours.

Clive Woodward had quite enough selection worries on his mind as it was but he almost found himself without his two first-choice scrum halves after what, in hindsight at least, was a highly comical episode on a golf course in Richmond two days after the New Zealand game. I was paired with Austin against Matt Dawson and Nick Beal in a Leicester v Northampton grudge match and by the time we hit the inward nine holes it had become an extremely ill-tempered and distinctly ungentlemanly contest, to say the least. Nick and I kept well clear of it as the two scrum-halves virtually came to blows by the time we had reached the clubhouse. It began when Austin distracted Matt as he went to putt and some words of an 'industrial' nature were exchanged as we went to move on to the next tee. It was then that Matt chose to accuse Austin of stamping down the sand in the bunker to improve his lie, and barely had golf's most heinous accusation been delivered than Austin's club was boomeranging through the morning air – straight at Matt – and he was racing across the fairway to confront him. 'If you accuse me of being a cheat one more time then I'm going to kick your bloody head in,' Austin informed Matt, their noses almost touching. For several moments I feared the worst as England's two leading scrum-halves squared up and threatened untold damage to each other's good looks, but they finally backed down, order was restored and Austin and I were able to complete what, quite frankly, was an embarrassing rout of our Northampton pals. (For the sake of historical accuracy I must record that we won the contest 5&3.)

The England centres were like a set of revolving doors during that World Cup. I returned to the line-up in place of Jerry Guscott for the Tonga match, but then Phil de Glanville pulled out with bruised ribs and Jerry was brought back in. Former England forward Mick Skinner predicted in his newspaper column that I would not finish the match against the tough Tongans because my injuries had shown that I was too brittle and fragile to survive what was sure to be a brutal encounter. With his colourful waistcoats and strong opinions he's a difficult man to ignore, that Mick the Munch, but it's an effort well worth making, I have found on a handful of occasions.

In the event I defied the big flanker to jog off the pitch in one piece ten minutes from the end in a tactical substitution, but Mick's prediction that the Tongans, aka 'the Friendly Islanders', would try and beat us up was absolutely spot on. We won 101-10 but there was no celebrating at the end of an ugly afternoon. The

Tongans quite simply lost their heads and were even more violent than they had been against New Zealand in an earlier pool match. The worst incident came when Matt Perry was upended by Isi Tapueluelu while taking a high ball and he crashed on to his neck with a sickening thud. Phil Vickery, our young prop, piled into the ensuing mêlée and as he did so their prop, Ngalu Taufo'ou, a former policeman, sprinted from 50 yards away and floored flanker Richard Hill, an innocent bystander, with a stiff arm to the back of the head. Phil was shown the yellow card and Taufo'ou was sent off in disgrace. As far as I'm concerned he should never have been allowed to take to a rugby field again. It was a disgustingly premediated and savage act.

According to the record books I scored twice in two minutes early in the second half, but for some reason I have absolutely no recollection of either score. I imagine I just wanted to get to the safety of the deadball area before I got lamped by a 20-stone Tongan and woke up in hospital with my gumshield tucked down my sock again, seeing stars and singing 'Hickory, dickory dock, the mouse ran up the clock . . .'

Next up were Fiji, under former New Zealand prop Brad Johnstone, another highly physical side who also happened to be superb footballers when given the chance to run with the ball in the hand. Johnstone came out with the soundbite of the tournament when he billed the match as 'Fifteen guys with fast cars and laptops against fifteen guys with just rugby balls'. It sounded like something straight from a Hollywood billboard, but the contest was more war film than romantic comedy. By the time the final whistle blew on our 45-24 victory, the Twickenham turf was littered with aching bodies and bloodied faces. I have certainly enjoyed more relaxing birthdays than that but at least I was not one of the seven England players who had to be replaced during a bruising eighty minutes. Jonny Wilkinson was one of the early casualties, felled by a forearm to the head by Fiji captain Greg Smith.

And so to Paris, battered and bruised, to face the world champions. It turned out to be a bad weekend for the tens of thousands of Englishmen who descended on the French capital in the hope of seeing us repeat our victory over Nick Mallett's side at Twickenham almost twelve months earlier. Perhaps this is another occasion where my memory has gone into selective mode and I am in denial about what happened that afternoon, but I can honestly remember very little about the details of the game. It is all an unhappy blur now. The bare facts are that we were hammered 44-29 – the most points England have ever conceded against South Africa – and their fly-half Jannie de Beer, apparently inspired by God, struck five drop goals in succession. De Beer grabbed all the headlines and his was a truly remarkable and weird feat. But the truth was that we were well beaten by them and it wasn't the freak occurrence that many wanted to believe.

The turning point came just before the break when their scrum-half Joost van der Westhuizen went over for a try to put them in front for the first time. I remember him getting to his feet, leaning over Martin Johnson and taunting him with an earful of abuse, which is not something I recommend you try at home (Johnno has ways of tracking you down). It wasn't the most edifying sight you will see on a rugby field, but whatever you think of Van der Westhuizen – and I don't know him any better than I know the man in the moon – I suggest you put on the video of the 1995 World Cup final where South Africa stopped Lomu in his tracks to pull off that incredible and historic victory over the All Blacks. Keep an eye on Van der Westhuizen throughout the game and at the end you will be able to forgive the man for any amount of minor indiscretions.

There is no other word but 'heroic' to describe his performance – they were all magnificent that day – but Van der Westhuizen stands out for me, hurling himself at the feet of anything in black socks, no matter how big or how fast. Technically his tackling was atrocious, but technique didn't work against the giant Lomu. (I have tackled the man once or twice myself over the years, but never on my own terms. What you do is grab on to one of the garters on his socks and then cling on for dear life as you get carried along horizontally like a man hanging off the wing of an aeroplane.) The only way to stop Lomu back then was to throw something in the way of him, as Van der Westhuizen did, and hope it slowed him down sufficiently for someone else to get hold of another part of him. Van der Westhuizen is a rugby player's rugby player – although any such charitable thoughts were far from my mind when he raced over to score that afternoon.

Quite rightly, I copped an earful from our defensive coach Phil Larder for my part in his try. Paul Grayson, who started ahead of Jonny at fly-half, sliced a kick under pressure, and Phil de Glanville and I were guilty of not reacting fast enough to the danger that followed. Their centres, Fleck and Muller, were much faster out of the blocks than us and within a couple of seconds we were scrambling in their wake and were well off the pace when Van der Westhuizen went over. It was 12-16 to South Africa at half-time and although Jonny was brought on after fifty-six minutes there was little the rising star of English rugby could do to reverse the momentum in our direction, as De Beer slotted his five dropped goals in succession. How do you defend against that? England hung in there at first, but the Boks slowly stretched clear and completed what amounted to a thrashing when Roussow went over in injury time. South Africa were just bigger and better than us and De Beer's goals were no more than a statistical blip diverting attention from the plain fact that we were well beaten on the day. (The Boks, you may recall, went on to lose their semi to eventual winners Australia. For the final the Wallabies beat a French side exhausted by their extraordinary comeback win over the favourites New Zealand at Twickenham in the last four.)

We got hammered a second time that day when we hit the bars of Paris to drown our sorrows and rub our bruises. The booze also helped take the sting out of my shoulder which was still smarting after I took a massive hit from Roussow during the match. I hadn't seen him coming and he absolutely nailed me. The hamstring I tweaked against Italy wasn't feeling 100 per cent either and I returned to Leicester, for what would prove to be the second most depressing season of my career, a hunched and hobbling wreck.

Clive Woodward has a mantra that he has drummed into us over the years – 'Greatness is achieved by the discipline of attending to detail' – and it had a particular resonance as we reflected on what had gone wrong during the tournament. There was essentially nothing wrong with our preparations, but in a sport where the margins can be so fine, all the details didn't quite add up to a glorious end. Everyone seemed to agree afterwards that we had spent too much time together in the build-up and our warm-up games weren't quite hard enough perhaps (four years later we went on a summer tour to New Zealand and Australia and that was followed by a game against Wales and two against France). There were other smaller factors, too, such as not having our own chef cooking the right meals and not having ice baths to boost our physical recovery after a match. In isolation, all these factors may sound trifling, but when you add them all up they can mean the difference between glory and failure – as we showed in 2003.

To his credit Clive fronted up and took the brunt of the inevitable battering as the press grabbed his pre-tournament comment 'Judge me on the World Cup' and gleefully proceeded to bash him over the head with it. It was galling to see our coach take so many hits because it was the players who lost the matches.

The turning point of my career at Leicester came in a European game on a wintry night in Glasgow that December where we played very poorly and were deservedly beaten. We were heavily criticised – the England players were singled out for the harshest treatment – and myself and Martin Corry were among several players to be dropped. I liked to think at the time that I was just being given a kick in the shorts, but the sad truth was that I hardly played for the club again. Knocked out of Europe, Leicester were able to channel all their energies into the league and they put together a storming run right to the end of a season which saw them crowned champions. That was great for Leicester but not for me because, understandably, the coaches saw no reason to change what was proving to be a winning formula. You wouldn't have heard me moan once that year (unless you were bugging my house) because I never did in public. I just had to take it on the chin. But it was still exasperating. I was twenty-eight, an England international and a British Lion, and yet I spent most of that season, what should have been the golden days of my career, sitting on the bench or playing with the second team. This slow-working humiliation gradually ate away at my confidence and I could not help but question my ability and future in the game.

Part of the problem was of my own making. The Leicester people asked me who I would recommend if they were to bring in another centre and I had no hesitation in pressing the case for the Aussie Pat Howard who was then with ACT Brumbies. In doing so I had effectively asked for my P45. Pat has become a close friend and, in my opinion, he is one of the best centres of the modern era, a great creator, improviser and thinker. Short and confrontational, he plays right on the edge of the line and he's a nightmare to get past even though he's not that fast. I've played against a host of world-class centres in my career but by far my most difficult opponent has been Pat Howard. I find it incredible that the Australians have pretty well ignored him down the years, although I understand that that has more to do with rugby politics than with the game itself.

As I wasn't playing for Leicester I couldn't be considered for England and for the second year running

I was forced to watch the Six Nations at home or down the pub with some mates. (It's not quite so much fun to watch when you believe you should be playing!) I received a winner's medal after Leicester landed the championship but in truth I ended the season feeling a little sorry for myself as I feared that my career was starting to drift away. I still had a couple of years left on my contract at Leicester and the prospect of spending them playing with the seconds up at Hartlepool on a wet Wednesday night did not exactly have me shaking with breathless excitement.

If Leicester lost faith in my abilities that season, the same could not be said of Clive Woodward and the England coaching set-up. Even though, quite justifiably, he neglected to play me in the Six Nations, Clive still kept me involved and made me feel that my chance would come again if and when I returned to playing first-team club rugby. Another man to whom I owe a debt of gratitude for his role throughout this soul-destroying episode of my career was my manager Nick. I had begun to give serious consideration to the idea of relaunching my career in the City before I became too old. Nick, though, kept telling me to wait, drumming it into me that I still had a good five or six years at the top left in me and that you don't become a crap player over-night. Without his sound guidance I might well have ended up watching the 2003 World Cup finals from a television screen inside an office in the Square Mile.

I was well settled in Leicester at this stage but Nick persuaded me that it was time to move on and start afresh. To get me out of Leicester, he had to do slow, painstaking business with Dean Richards whose skills as a poker player have helped make him a formidable and obstinate operator at the negotiating table. At the same time, Mark Evans, the director of rugby at Harlequins, was doing a lot of business with Nick as he set about trying to shake up the underachieving London club and turn them into genuine title contenders. When Mark expressed an interest in taking me on, I didn't quite jump into his arms but I needed little persuasion to sign up once Leicester had agreed to release me.

The feeling that my career was getting back on track that summer was compounded when I was selected for England's short two-Test tour of South Africa. My fifteenth and most recent cap had come in the quarter-final defeat against South Africa nine months earlier and I had started only nine games for Leicester the entire season. But back in the land I had left a physically broken man after the Lions tour three years earlier, I had a superb chance to revive a career that had all but ground to a standstill.

I had no illusions that I was anything other than a second-string player when I boarded the plane and I wasn't even on the bench when we lost the first Test in Pretoria in highly controversial circumstances. The first incident of that ill-fated match came when Leon Lloyd, my fiery friend from Leicester, came off the bench and promptly clocked the Springbok centre De Wet Barry right under the nose of the referee in retaliation for an earlier dig. Leon has never taken any crap from anyone in his life and he wasn't going to start then. I didn't hear anyone mention the episode then or later but, reading between the lines a few years on, and knowing how unforgiving of indiscretions the England management became, you cannot help but conclude that Leon got a big black mark against his name that day. The South Africans got three points from the ensuing penalty, and, although it didn't lose England the game, it handed a bit of the initiative back to them in an extremely tight contest. One of the England mantras is TCUP (Think Clearly Under Pressure) and if Leon was observing TCUP at all at that moment he was thinking about how to smash it over Barry's head. That's what I've always liked about Leon: he's not going to pretend to be something he's not. He's instinctive, proud and a total psycho on the pitch.

Austin Healey was an absolute hero that day. Austin is principally a scrum-half or a wing, but he can play virtually anywhere in the backs if you ask him to, and that morning Clive handed him the fly-half role, probably the most important position on the pitch, after Jonny Wilkinson pulled out through illness. It was his superb counterattack from England's own line that led to one of the most controversial moments in recent Test match history. Tim Stimpson was juggling with the ball as he crossed the Bok try line and as he went to touch down he was taken out by Springbok flanker Andre Vos (Andre later became my skipper at Quins and happens to be one of the nicest men you could ever hope to meet). It looked like a clear-cut penalty try but after several minutes' deliberation, to the incredulity of most who saw the incident, the fourth official declared that Stimmo had knocked on. We trailed 15-10 at that stage and the converted try would have put us in front. We lost 18-13.

My chance to make an impression for England came in the third of the five tour matches against Griqualand West, a good side who in recent years had beaten Ireland and drawn with New Zealand and in earlier times had twice beaten Australia. They were, in short, no muppets, but we were far too strong for them on the day and I like to think that I seized my opportunity to shine in a 55-16 win in which we ran in seven tries. Perhaps commentators were looking out for me because I had been out of the limelight for so long, but the papers were full of praise over the coming days. I had not played properly for a couple of years at this point, at first owing to being injured and then to being dropped, but it was amazing how fast my confidence returned, just as it had done a few months into the 1997/8 season.

The second Test took place in Bloemfontein, the scene of my concussion, and I would have loved to have got on to the pitch that day, not so much to exorcise any demons, but to confirm that I was back as a player. Three years earlier I had almost died there, but for the last two years I had been dying as a rugby player and there would have been some curious kind of symbolism, for me at least, if I had run on to that pitch and been able to make a contribution to England's series-levelling 27-22 win. But it was not to be and I had to be content with advancing my claims for a return to the first team in the final match of the tour, a highly incendiary encounter against Gauteng Falcons in Brakpan. We won the game 36-27 but not before both sides had effectively punched and kicked the living daylights out of each other. This was, quite honestly, a disgraceful fight of a game and that was partly down to the fact that there were no video cameras there to capture a litany of indiscretions sufficient to put both sides behind bars for several years. You had the feeling from the outset that Gauteng had taken it upon themselves to exact a brutal revenge on England for daring to beat South Africa in the last Test, but we had some pretty feisty characters of our own in the forwards and they certainly didn't take their punishment lying down. I remember Darren Garforth going off with a particularly grisly head injury at one point, and his bloodied image just about captured the essence of that game.

I had a second half-decent game that day and although I managed to score a try it was my creativity that gave me the most satisfaction. Overall, it had been a good tour from a personal and team point of view but it's interesting and slightly disturbing to reflect that, once again, many of the young players who took part in it have long since disappeared back into the shadows of the international game. Thirlby, Johnston, Hanley, Hepher, Walshe, Sheridan, Volley – all of them are extremely good rugby players but unless you are an assiduous student of club rugby it is unlikely that you would be able to put faces to their names. I, too, had effectively slipped back into those same shadows for the previous two years and the fact that all those excellent players never quite pushed on to the highest level illustrated just how tight the margins at the top of the game had become.

Chapter Six

HARLEQUINS AND I had much in common when I joined up with them at the start of the 2000/2001 season. Their own transformation under then chief executive Mark Evans (now director of rugby) and coaches Zinzan Brooke and Richard Hill (the former England scrum-half, not the current flanker) was mirrored by the upheavals in my own career. Like me, Harlequins were looking for a new start and in that respect they were the perfect club for me at that stage of my career. There was a huge change of playing personnel at The Stoop during this period with Will Carling, Pete Mensah, Chris Sheasby, Gareth Rees and Gareth Llewllyn all heading for the exit, while myself, Australian flanker David Wilson, the Irish trio of Keith Wood, Paul Burke and Niall Woods, as well as Eric Peters, Roy Winters and Mark Mapletoft, were all starting to arrive.

My rehabilitation as a player that season was helped by working with England's conditioning coach, Dave Reddin. My physique and overall fitness began to improve markedly working with Dave, who is now my neighbour in Southfields, but it would take a while before I could force my way back into contention for the full England side. At that time Clive Woodward opted for a centre pairing of the experienced Mike Catt and a young, bullocking bulldozer of a player in Mike Tindall, who was just starting to make a big name for himself. He's an absolutely superb player Tinds, completely different in style from Cattie and myself, and the good news for England is that he should be around for years to come. It was those two who lined up in the first of the three autumn internationals against Australia, the reigning world champions who had arrived fresh from squeezing the life out of France in an 18-13 win in Paris. It was a heart-stopping game to watch and reminded me a little of recent games against New Zealand in which England had failed to convert their dominance into enough points for victory. In this game, England had 70 per cent of the possession and about 60 per cent of the territory, yet we only clinched a 22-19 victory in the eighty-fifth minute when Dan Luger touched down in the corner after a brilliant burst and chip by my old Lancastrian friend Iain Balshaw.

Barely had the match finished when we found ourselves embroiled in England's biggest off-pitch controversy since the game turned professional as the players threatened to go on strike – and not play against Argentina that weekend or South Africa the week after

– following a simmering feud with the RFU. I am not an especially political character and as I was not a senior England player at that time, I just slunk off into the background and let the feistier characters in the squad get on with the scrap. The worst aspect of the whole saga was that it put everyone, not least Clive Woodward, in a very ugly position. For the younger players, and those like myself on the fringes of a regular place, it was especially difficult because on the one hand you didn't want to jeopardise your career, but on the other you wanted to stick by your mates and stand up for what was right. The dreadful fact is that today, four years on, I can barely remember the crux of the argument but fundamentally it was about money and about how much the players were worth in relation to the RFU's income. The players' position was that they weren't going to be pushed around and financially exploited like so many cattle. The whole thing lasted for forty-eight hours and it became slightly heated and unpleasant at various points, but, when it was finally over, everybody put it behind them very quickly. The most vulnerable and emotional person throughout the saga was Clive Woodward but, thank heavens, he came through it and was able to get on with building an England squad capable of launching a genuine challenge for the World Cup.

I remember there being an awful lot of meetings down at Pennyhill Park, England's hotel at Bagshot, and various people made impassioned speeches at different points. It wasn't exactly Lech Walesa, the striking ship-yard workers of Gdansk, Solidarity and the beginning of the end for the Communist bloc, but for men who earn a living chasing after muddy balls and beating each other up for laughs it was about as political as it can get. There were, however, two superb moments of low comedy which broke the tension for a while. One came when we were all sitting in our umpteenth meeting on the final evening, our faces set in solemn contemplation of the important principles at stake, when from the back of the room there floated a large paper aeroplane into the midst of the meeting. Instantly, half of the room was on its feet and a mass paper fight broke out until everyone involved remembered their seriousness of purpose and quickly sat down with furrowed brows looking suitably grave and righteous again.

The other moment came as Clive, who was against the strike, was laying out his case and we were all listening to him intently, when young Mike Tindall, who had started just a handful of Test matches at this stage, interrupted him. Leaning towards his coach, and looking slightly scary, Tinds declared: 'Clive, you are *really*, *really* starting to piss me off now.' I looked at Clive for his reaction and then I looked across at Tinds in wide-eyed amazement, thinking: 'Oh my giddy aunt, what on earth has that big northern monkey gone and said now?' It made me think of the time that Mark

Regan called Jack Rowell a village idiot, but at least, I suppose, Tindall could claim that he had his principles to excuse his frankness. It was a suprising moment at any rate, not least because I didn't even know that Tinds could spell 'principles' let alone come over all Mafia about them with the man holding the power to make or break his international career. Clive, though, reacted with remarkable self-control and Tinds lived to fight another day as an England player.

The threat of a strike hung in the balance for a long time, mainly because the younger players didn't want to be railroaded into a decision that might wreck their fledgling careers. During the meeting I sat at the back of the room, and using some notepaper, I made myself a 'swingometer', along the lines of the one used by Peter Snow on election night. Strangely, I still have that swingometer, together with my scribbled notes from that evening, among my various souvenirs from down the years. I remember that the outcome of the vote swung one way and then the other before it was decided that we would strike and our representatives – Martin Johnson, Lawrence Dallaglio and Matt Dawson – went off to meet the RFU bigwigs. The rest of us headed home, expecting the match to be called off, but, forty-eight hours later, we all received a call to say that the dispute had been resolved.

I have no recollection of the details of the deal thrashed out as I was too busy building up my paper aeroplane collection, but the best legacy of the whole unhappy affair was that it brought the players closer together and made the RFU people realise that we were prepared to give them a bloody nose if we thought they were messing us about. The professional era had only just begun and perhaps it was predictable that the new game would reach a stage where certain issues and relationships had to be thrashed out and clearly defined. So in that respect it was another positive to be drawn from an otherwise nasty little episode that this inevitable confrontation took place a full two and a half years before the World Cup.

The match against Argentina went ahead as scheduled, but it was a fairly laboured and forgettable affair as we ground out a 19-0 win. From a personal point of view, however, it was a more memorable occasion because I came off the bench after an hour to make my first appearance for England in almost a year. I managed to make some kind of an impression during my cameo appearance but that probably had as much to do with the peroxide blond thatch I was sporting then as it did with any remarkable skills I happened to show that afternoon. ('The Bleach Boy Is Back' read one headline the following day.)

I had apparently shown enough in those twenty minutes to prompt a number of calls for my reinstatement in the starting line-up. I wouldn't describe those calls as a deafening clamour and no one was quite marching on Parliament Square to push my case but, after such a long period becalmed in the doldrums of international sport, it was gratifying to know that I now had a fair wind of support behind me. When Mike Catt pulled out of the match with bruised ribs and a stomach bug, Clive Woodward handed me a place in the starting line-up for the next match.

On the coach journey to Twickenham I remember seeing a group of South African supporters carrying a banner saying: 'England aren't worth 15 Boks.' Whoever said South Africans lacked a sense of humour? South Africa, coached by Harry Viljoen, looked as strong as ever on paper with the names of Montgomery, Paulse, Terblanche, Van Straaten, Andrews, Krige, Vos, Venter and my old mate Robbie Kempson in the line-up. Opposite us in the centres that day were Japie Mulder and Robbie Fleck, who had recently been dubbed, 'the Bruise Brothers' because of their relish for the physical stuff.

It turned out to be a brutal but spectacular encounter which we won 25-17 and I did my claims for a regular place in the side no harm with one of the best tries I have ever scored. Even today, I still wonder quite how I managed it. It came about ten minutes before the interval when the forwards won some quick ball, we called one of our oldest moves and Jonny Wilkinson fed me with a great pass and I changed direction as I took it. Seeing that I was heading straight into the thick of all their big hairy forwards I started running for my life, weaving through every gap I could find just to get myself out of there as quickly as possible. I remember getting far too close to Krige and Van Straaten for my liking. I was about 25 yards out and by this stage I should have been in hospital but, amazingly, I wasn't just standing up, but actually steaming (yes, steaming) towards the try line. I can only imagine that the Springboks must have been thinking that there was no conceivable way that gangly Greenwood could possibly go the whole way and that I must have been some kind of dummy runner for England's genuine sprinters. It was one of those days on which Fate, for some reason, decided to blow some sunshine up my backside. Maybe she felt I deserved a bit of a break after all the frustrations I had suffered over the past couple of years.

Anyway, the try still didn't look on when their wing Stefan Terblanche, who is about thirty times faster than me, came haring over from the other side of the field. I presumed he was coming to take me out, as you do, and I was looking about to offload when he ran straight across me as if he was going to say hello to someone in the crowd or desperately needed the loo. I suppose he must have been trying to cover someone on my outside. I remember thinking 'Where the hell's he going? Why doesn't he just tackle me?' Then their fearsome number eight Andre Vos, bless his green cotton socks, unintentionally played a major part in the relaunching of my international career when I was about 5 yards out. Vos should have absolutely buried me but he didn't quite get a handle on me because, in sheer panic at the sight of him, I performed a double sidestep, which I never knew I had in my box of tricks. I tripped myself up in doing so, while wrong-footing Andre before sticking out a long arm to slap the ball down over the line. I then went slightly nutty as two years of frustration were expunged from my system in that one beautiful instant. Matt Dawson actually had to tell me to calm down as I celebrated – which I thought was pretty rich coming from a man whose football-style celebration for the Lions in South Africa had caused a few of the Carling 'old farts' to choke on their claret. Vos is now my club captain at Quins and to this day I continue to thank him for his role in reviving my England career.

From the moment I smashed the ball into the turf that afternoon my international career never stopped going forward until after the 2003 World Cup finals. It's strange how sporting careers can turn on just one passage of play or one curious conspiracy of circum-stances and I suppose I owe virtually the whole of that Springbok side a huge debt of gratitude for their inadvertent generosity that autumn day.

That match was an incredibly ferocious contest even by the high standards of Anglo-Bok in the past and five of our players had to go off at some point to be stitched up or treated: Neil Back, Richard Hill, Phil Greening,

Jonny Wilkinson and Dan Luger. The head wound suffered by Hill was bad enough but the one above Back's eye was so deep that it needed two layers of stitches and when he came back on he had so much bandage wrapped around his head he looked like a maharajah. I had felt sick when I looked at Backie trudging off with blood spouting from his gash, but I felt a great lift when I saw him return to the fray fifteen minutes later. Jonny also had his head swathed in bandages for much of the match, but he was composure itself amid the carnage as he slotted six penalties and a conversion to steer us home.

Afterwards the Boks admitted the match was far more physical than anything they encountered in the south, and it was certainly the hardest match I had ever played in — at least up to that point in my career. All the pictures in the following day's papers were of me scoring the try or celebrating it — that's the magic of peroxide for you — and I'd be lying if I didn't admit to lapping it all up at the time. My confidence had been on the floor for so long that, when this day in the sun came along, I was going to enjoy every last moment of it. There are occasions when you are lying under 120 stone of hairy forward with a mouthful of mud and stud and you wonder quite what you are doing with your life. But when you run through half of South Africa to score a try at Twickenham, roared on by 75,000 of your countrymen, it all makes perfect sense.

The first person I spoke to after the match was Mike Catt whose place I had taken and who had predicted I was going to play a blinder and keep him out of the team for the foreseeable future. He's a top man 'Cattman', we have been great friends and comrades since our U21s tour back in 1993, and he had the good grace to come straight over and congratulate me on my try and performance, swearing at me through the smiles as he did so. That victory was our fourth in a row against Southern Hemisphere opposition – gone were the days of heroic defeats – and Martin Johnson, a man who chooses his words carefully, said in public that this was the best England squad he had ever been a part of.

I scored one other especially memorable try that season and it came early in 2001 when Quins reached the European Shield final with a 20-13 win over Brive in France. In fact it was probably the best I've ever scored at any level and it was unusual for me because I ran virtually the entire length of the pitch against a top-class French back division to touch down – me, the man with the pace of Bernard Manning. It remains a source of immense annoyance to this day that there was not a single video or television camera in the ground to record this epoch-defining moment and every time I try and tell Austin or Ben Cohen or one of the other England boys about it, they just pat me on the back and say: 'Yes, yes, of course you did, Will. Of course you ran ninety-five yards through some of the best backs in

Caro and I.

Being carried off
after my accident,
June 1997.

May 1999, me,
James and Tom watch
Manchester City
in the second division
play-off final – the
greatest day in sport!
Man City won.

(*Below left*)
Fennell and me
golfing! Summer
1998, Spain.
(*Below right*)
The other side of
Ben Fennell and me!

Doing the tourist thing with Keller, at the top of Lion's Head, Cape Town in 1998.

Me and Johnno on holiday in Portugal, summer 2002.

The try that relaunched a career – South Africa, November 2000.

Being congratulated by Oz, Catty and Wilko after scoring my hat-trick against Wales, Six Nations 2001.

Scoring the winning try in the match against South Africa – World Cup 2003.

Celebrating!

The final whistle in the World Cup final…

Celebrating with Wilko.

With Lol on the Victory Bus.

Celebrating with Caro, Wilko, my cousin Diana, Lol, and Mr Blair.

With the family: my Mum, brother Tom, sister Emma and my Dad, Christmas 2003.

Archie's first swim.
Singapore, summer
2004.

Archie at four
months. April
2004.

world rugby to score. You do that all the time. Perhaps you should go and lie down.' And then they raise their eyebrows at each other and walk away, leaving me standing there with my arms outstretched as I re-enact my final glorious dive over the Brive line.

The day after that win Jason Leonard and I had to get up at four in the morning to get to Bordeaux for a flight home so that we could make it back in time for England training ahead of our championship match against Wales, their first ever Six Nations match in the newly built Millennium Stadium, and it was also the occasion of Scott Gibbs' fiftieth cap. I have no idea if it has always been that way, but ever since I've been playing them at any rate they genuinely seem to hate us down in Wales. The fans spit on our team coach and give us the full repertoire of hand gestures, and on the last occasion we went out on the town after a match there, people were flicking lit fags at our backs. It was decided then that a night out in Cardiff after we had just hammered their boys on the rugby field was probably not going to be the most enjoyable social occasion. There are a lot of countries that don't welcome us with open arms but Wales is the most hostile and nowadays we just get on the bus and get out of there, as if Cardiff were Kabul.

I remember there being a fairly intimidating atmosphere at the Arms Park sixteen years earlier when, as a twelve-year-old, I had gone with my uncle Ian to watch Dad's England team. We lost 24-15 and I remember

Jonathan Davies scoring a try on his debut. I was behind the posts when he put up a massive bomb of a kick and the whole place erupting when they scored. But the noise was as nothing compared to that which they generated the day we walked down the tunnel all those years later. It was the most incredible noise I have ever heard in a sports stadium and just as we were about to take the pitch Johnno turned to us and said: 'Hear that? Let's silence it.' My dad had always said that the greatest noise in world rugby is a silent Cardiff and that's exactly what it was that afternoon when we raced about thirty points clear in the first half-hour. During the autumn internationals Clive Woodward had warned that sooner or later we were going to give someone a bloody good hiding, and in the end it was our old rivals the Welsh who took it.

It finished 44–15 and will always remain one of the cherished memories of my career because I became the first Englishman to score a hat-trick in almost 120 years of internationals against Wales. My first two tries came in the first ten minutes and the third a minute into the second half. I'd like to say that for my first I outpaced the cover but, truth be told, there wasn't any cover to outpace; for the second one Balsh, who was on fire that day, had made all the hard running and I just hung on his shoulder and went over from 3 yards out with Gibbs sitting on top of me; and the third one had 'Made in Leicester' stamped all over it. I passed to Austin who ran straight for the gap and sucked in the two defenders before simply lobbing the ball into the space on the outside for me to collect and score. There was not much triumphalism in our celebrations that afternoon and even our fans were pretty quiet because it was so one-sided it was almost embarrassing. Dad, though, who had been on the receiving end of some Welsh beatings down the years, was going absolutely potty in the stands and later wrote a light-hearted open apology to the Welsh in one of the newspapers.

It was the biggest home defeat for Wales since internationals began there in 1882, and while we're on the stats and records I should mention that I became the first English centre to score a hat-trick against any team for eighty-seven years. As it stands at the time of writing, I am the leading try scorer in Anglo-Welsh Tests and that remains one of my proudest achievements. When you think of some of the great players produced by both sides down the years, it makes me feel very tall indeed. The only time that I have failed to score against the Welsh was in the Six Nations match at Twickenham in 2004.

We were cock-a-hoop with our display, as any team would be, but it was even more special because for so many decades Cardiff had proved to be a barren hunting ground for England. To hump them by a record score was deeply satisfying. Not that they enjoyed it much, of course. On the way to the post-match function, some of their fans threw their kebabs at us, many more gobbed on the coach and one bloke even head-butted it and split his head open. I have spent many happy times in North Wales since I was a young boy, and I have a lot of great Welsh mates, but when it comes to playing rugby there is no escaping the fact that they hate us passionately further south.

We hammered Italy 80-23 in our next match, Jonny Wilko slotting thirteen of his fifteen kicks and adding a try to boot. In hindsight the other fourteen of us should have just slipped away for an early shower and just left him to get on with it. Our third Six Nations match was against Scotland at Twickenham and in the build-up to it former British Lion and Scottish captain Finlay Calder slagged off England's back line and expressed the view that I was overrated. I know pundits are paid money to say controversial things and stir up a debate, but Finlay, my friend, please, do me a favour. I am not going to argue about my own qualities as a player, but in rebuttal of the more general comment I'm just going to list the names of the England backs involved in what turned out to be a record 43-3 win over your countrymen: Iain Balshaw, Jason Robinson, Austin Healey, Mike Catt, Ben Cohen, Jonny Wilkinson, Matt Dawson, Kyran Bracken and myself. There is little point in elaborating on that, but I do like to think that in years to come I will be able to look someone in the eye and say that over England's recent 'golden period' our backs contributed as much as our forwards to the success. There is an old maxim in rugby that it is the forwards who decide who's going to win the match, and the backs decide by how much – but like all such aphorisms it is a bit of a simplification and you only have to look at those early matches against New Zealand in the late nineties to understand that sometimes it is patently untrue. Our forwards completely dominated those games, but our backs couldn't deliver, while theirs were brutally clinical on the far fewer occasions they received the ball. England have scored a lot of great, great tries in recent times and in the spring of 2001 that particular back line was so hot it was almost in flames.

What, meanwhile, can I say about Scotland without sounding patronising? Their team has suffered a dip in recent years but you certainly won't find me slagging them off or laughing at them. Equally, I don't want to offer them faint praise because it would sound insincere and condescending. Even though I have never lost to the Scots (I was missing when my old university mate Duncan Hodge put one over us in 2000), I have never walked off the same field as them without feeling as if I have been battered from pillar to post. Whatever is wrong with their game at the minute, it's not a lack of effort. Forget the scoreboard: the Scots will always bring ferocity and pride to the pitch and leave nothing on the training ground. It annoys me when I see press comments or headlines about the Scots lacking passion and so on because nothing could be further from the truth. They lack a few quality players as well as strength in depth at the moment, but don't ever accuse them of lacking fight and commitment. What I will say is that they are a great rugby nation, we miss the rivalry and the sooner they pick themselves off the floor the better for everybody, not just themselves, but for all rugby.

By now it was generally acknowledged throughout the rugby world that England were playing as well as they had done in the modern era and, when we annihilated France 48-19, you were unlikely to have found a man in the country who would have bet against us beating Ireland to take the Grand Slam. Respected pundits and even long-time foes and critics were all talking about that team as standing on the verge of greatness and there was a momentum driving us on in those months which simply smashed everything in its path. But the Ireland game, unfortunately, was postponed until the following autumn due to the foot-and-mouth outbreak. Our day of glory would have to wait.

I managed to score at least one try in all four Six Nations matches that spring to make me the leading try scorer in the championships and it was turning into a great season all round for me as Quins were going superbly, too. We beat the Frenchmen of Narbonne 42-33 in extra time to win the European Shield, and also came agonisingly close to landing the Tetley Cup, too, only for Newcastle to pip us 30-27 with a try and conversion so deep into time added on it was almost the following day.

One other moment from that domestic season sticks out clearly in my mind and it came in a 37-6 thrashing at Leicester in which they avenged a painful defeat by us in the cup a few months earlier. Leicester don't like losing and, if you have beaten them, you can put your house on the fact that on the next occasion you meet you will end up on the receiving end of a mighty great shoeing. So it was that day when Quins ran out on to the pitch at Welford Road and spent the next eighty minutes getting walloped from one side of the pitch to the other. For some reason, my name seemed to be very high up on their hit-list in that match and somehow I ended up getting into a fight with, of all people, Martin Johnson.

I feel I have documented my cowardice on these occasions with great honesty and no little accuracy in these pages and I can only reiterate my advice that fighting Martin Johnson is not normally something I would recommend you try at home. My encounter with England's fabled captain began at a ruck when my old friend Graham 'Wig' Rowntree was happily raking the skin off someone's back, and probably whistling nonchalantly as he did so. You would have thought I had known better by this stage in my career but for some reason I barged in and pushed the big prop out of the way and before you could say 'Come on lads, let's all pile into that poncey centre' the whole of the Leicester pack had reared up like cobras. In the usual run of events I'd be quivering and saying in a very small, squeaky voice, 'Leave me alone, I've done nothing wrong!' But it was then that Johnno, 18 stone of solid granite, unleashed himself from about 5 yards away, and catapulted his fist into my face with every last ounce of effort in his giant Neanderthal body. And you know what? I didn't feel a damned thing.

I actually think he's quite soft, that Johnno. I could have laid him out there and then, I suppose – and the rest of those Leicester tarts while I was about it – but the man was my international captain, a sporting hero to millions and an old friend to boot. Quite honestly, I just couldn't bring myself to humiliate the big girl's blouse and so I just eyeballed him and walked away like real men do. But Johnno knows the truth – that he gave me absolutely everything he had and that I barely even noticed. He may have his own version of events that afternoon, and if he does then we'll let the man dream, but it's my book and I'll write it as I saw it.

In these the twilight years of my playing career, young, up-and-coming rugby players occasionally ask me if I have any special advice or tips to pass on to them. In these moments I tend to narrow my eyes, put on my wise-old-man face, stare into the horizon and say: 'Never, ever play rugby on 23 June.' Most just mutter their thanks and hurry off, but there is actually some sound reasoning, based on painful personal experience, behind my advice. It was on 23 June 1997 when I suffered my brush with death in South Africa and it was on that same fateful day four years later, on the Lions tour of Australia, that Fate delivered me a second brutal blow. That season I had played the best rugby of my career – up till then – and it continued when we arrived in Australia and I featured in three of the first four matches (the one exception to the good form being a 28-25 defeat to Australia 'A' in which the whole team was distinctly average). But it was during the match against New South Wales, a beast of a match as it would turn out, that my chances of a Lions cap against Australia were shredded as comprehensively as the ankle I injured that day. I was in the fly-half position midway through the first half when I received the ball and was tackled by two players at once, went over on my foot and then the whole world landed on top of it in the ensuing ruck. I played on for about ten minutes, hoping to shake off the pain, but when the Aussies threw the ball wide from a lineout and I had to turn sharply, I realised I was well and truly crocked. I signalled to the bench that I had to come off and, as the adrenalin ebbed away, the pain in my ankle turned to agony. If it hadn't been strapped heavily, as it always is, I probably would have dislocated and broken it as well.

I was replaced by the Irishman Ronan O'Gara, but it

wasn't long before he had joined us back on the sidelines, the victim of one of the most brazen and savage assaults I have ever witnessed on a rugby field. Duncan McRae, their fly-half, pinned him to the ground and then proceeded to punch him repeatedly in the face, inflicting a hideous wound near his eye that needed eleven stitches. McRae was sent off, but they should have chucked him in jail as far as we were concerned. It was just utterly barbaric – and cowardly into the bargain as Ronan had no chance of defending himself because he was being held down. Five players went into the sin bin during our 41-24 win that day, and many felt that their violence had been premeditated in an effort to shake us up before the first Test. But if that was the plan, it palpably failed because we hammered the Wallabies 29-13 at the Gabba in one of the greatest ever Lions performances.

My ankle swelled up to the size of a melon and I needed crutches to get about as we set off on a nine-hour drive (I was not allowed to fly) to rejoin the squad after I had undergone an MRI scan to discover the full extent of the injury. I didn't need to be an MRI machine or a ligament specialist, however, to know that I had done some serious damage and that in all probability my tour was over. Of the three ligaments in the ankle, two of mine were totally ruptured and the third was hanging on by a mere thread, which had saved it from being dislocated as well. In South Africa I probably wouldn't have started any of the Tests but as the injuries mounted there was a modest chance I might have got on as a substitute. I cannot say for certain but in Australia it seemed as if I was being lined up to play alongside Brian O'Driscoll in the Tests. Dr Robson, the man who had done so much for me in South Africa, felt that if I started my rehabilitation programme immediately there was an outside chance that I could recover for the tail end of the tour. So it was that within twenty-four hours of suffering the injury I found myself aqua-jogging in the team hotel pool.

Once injured you become something of an outsider, whether it's at your club or on an overseas tour, but this injury lay-off was especially frustrating because I had been playing very well and was tantalisingly close to earning a cap when I pulled up. Even when we won the first Test I wasn't able to take a full part in the celebrations that followed because I had physio early the next morning and hobbled up to bed while the others headed out to party. The first few days of a bad injury are the worst as you struggle to come to terms with the frustration of it, and my gloom was compounded by the death of our kitman and liaison officer, Anton Toia. He had gone whale-watching with some of the lads and had decided to swim back to shore. But he never made it. I wasn't as close to Anton as some, but he was a good man and his sudden death was a horrible shock.

The Lions were smashed 35–14 in the second Test, and our casualty list was assuming ludicrous proportions as one player after another fell by the wayside. The most significant injury of the whole tour, in my judgement at least, was the concussion suffered by flanker Richard Hill when he was taken out off the ball by Nathan Gray in that second Test in Melbourne. Hill is an outstanding player whose best work goes largely unnoticed and his absence was a major blow to our hopes.

After two and a half weeks of working my socks off with Robbo to get fit, he had managed to get me back in training and there was a good chance that I might at least get on for some of the decisive third Test. The ligaments were just about bearing the strain under some very heavy strapping and I came through full training sessions on the Tuesday and Wednesday of the final week. There wasn't a great deal of rest and relaxation for the squad on that tour and on the Thursday they threw in an extra session during which I went to push off at an angle only for my ankle stop me in my tracks. 'Not a prayer, my friend' it was saying to me through the strapping, and I went straight over to our coach Graham Henry and gave him the news. Although we had done superbly to get the ligaments shipshape, what we hadn't been able to account for was the bone bruising. I couldn't feel anything if I ran in a straight line but as soon as I tried to turn I felt an intense stabbing pain. If you have a copy of the match programme for the third test you will see that I had been named as one of the replacements. It was that close.

Robbo had done a remarkable job to get me even close to recovery by the end of that tour, but with the benefit of hindsight I now wish that I had joined my England colleagues Phil Greening, Mike Catt and Dan Luger, three other injury victims, who had hired a camper van and followed the tour around Australia with all the fans and had a great time of it. But I couldn't quite bring myself to pack it in.

In the event it turned out to be a pretty depressing tour all round and we were squeezed out 29-23 in the final Test in Sydney. For me, one gesture in particular went a long way towards lifting the gloom and it came from the Irish centre Rob Henderson. I had roomed with Rob throughout the tour and I soon discovered that he was a human being of the very highest order. He's another of these backs you meet from time to time who can hold their own with the forwards when the beers start to flow. It says something of my affection for the man and my admiration of his other qualities that, in the interests of the truth, I am obliged to record that he is also the worst room-mate, not just in world rugby, but since man first shared a cave. Rob liked to come in at three in the morning, turn on the television, spark up a fag, order room service and then get me out of bed so he could thrash me at cribbage. And he did all this as if it was the most natural way in the world to behave, looking at me as if *I* was completely mad when I said: 'Hendo, what the sodding hell do you think you are doing?'

As you might imagine our changing room in Stadium Australia following that third Test defeat was a pretty cheerless place as we all reflected on what might have been. And it was in this gloomy atmosphere that Rob sought me out, peeled the shirt off his back, handed it to me and said: 'Mate, there's no one more deserving of a Lions Test than you. Have this.' I told him not to be ridiculous, but he insisted, and for me that will always be a moment to cherish when I look back on my playing days in years to come. It was a brilliant gesture that perfectly captured the spirit and tradition of the British and Irish Lions: an Irishman giving the shirt off his back to an Englishman. He had sweated in it, bled in it and it was his to show his grandchildren when he was an old man, but he gave it to me instead because I had missed out on a cap. The shirt was framed as soon as I got back to London and it is now hanging proudly on my wall.

A lot has been said about the spirit of the squad on that tour, and it would be foolish to suggest that the members were all happy campers for its entire duration. I was unaware of most of what was going on as I was injured and wasn't there in the dressing room, on the training pitch or in many of the meetings. It seems to have been widely accepted since by all involved on that tour, however, that were it to take place again, certain aspects of it would be changed. There was definitely a bit of whingeing on that tour and when you hear it, your first thought is, 'Shut up, you're on a Lions tour, for heaven's sake.' There is a big banner you often see at Manchester City games which reads, 'We dream of playing for God's team, now play like we dream.' For me that sentiment applies to the Lions. People dream of pulling on the red shirt, so if you are lucky enough to be given a chance, in my book you should just get your head down, do as you are told and give it your best crack. But if the management team made one major mistake I would say that it was in its handling of the 'midweek team'.

One of the masterstrokes of the 1997 Lions tour lay in the coaches' ploy of giving the impression that every last member of the squad had a chance of making the Test team. That was great for squad morale and it also raised the level of everyone's performance because they believed they had a sniff of a Test cap. Four years later, it was pretty damned obvious when we boarded the flight from London what the Test team was going to be, so from the outset a division opened up right down the middle of the squad. One example illustrates the point and if it doesn't actually excuse some of the carping, it will at least go some way to explaining it. There was a training session ahead of the midweek team's game, and ideally and under normal circumstances the practice would be based around them and not the Test team. But on this occasion it was clearly for the benefit of the Test team and the midweek team had to play as if they were Australia, compounding the suspicion that they had been brought on tour as mere cannon fodder.

It is a difficult challenge for a Lions coach in any circumstances, as he works out how to get the best out of thirty-odd players from four different countries at the end of a hard domestic season, and it is probably even more difficult if you are a Kiwi like Graham Henry, the former Wales coach who went on to coach the All Blacks. He made an unfortunate speech, which was well intentioned but came out all wrong and ended up upsetting some of the players. It has been well documented since and it went something along the lines of 'They don't respect you down here, they think you're crap and I know because I'm one of them'. What he meant was that he was a Southern Hemisphere person, not that he thought we were crap. Some took it the wrong way, though, and left the meeting thinking: 'Great, thanks very much, Graham. That's made us all feel terrific.' It reminded me of a story Dad tells about when he took an England team to South Africa in the early 1980s and John Scott, the England captain, gave a 'pep' talk to Huw Davies, the fly-half, in which he told him he was the worst fly-half he had ever had the misfortune of playing with. Huw was not the worst number ten he had ever played with, of course, and it was all just an exercise in reverse psychology, but minutes before a match was probably not the best time to test out the brittleness of a man's confidence.

After emerging from my injury hell the previous summer, I missed just three weeks over the subsequent twelve months but, Sod's law, they just happened to be the three weeks of the Lions Test series. The bone bruising took a long time to heal fully and I probably wasn't running at 100 per cent in the first few weeks of the 2001/2 season before we headed out to Dublin to tackle the unfinished business of the Six Nations. Despite the absence of several key players, including Johnno, we were outright favourites to win the match and clinch our first Grand Slam under Clive. Nobody gave Ireland a prayer, which is just as they would have wanted it as they could go into heroic underdog mode. The match took place on my twenty-ninth birthday, but I was certainly in no mood to celebrate anything by the time the final whistle sounded and Lansdowne Road erupted in happy, emerald uproar. We lost 20-14 and deservedly so. Ireland played quite magnificently, led superbly by Keith Wood, aka 'the Mad Potato', a man so Irish that if you cut him in half all you would find is green and a pint or two of Guinness.

Through subsequent events I have come to learn the true meaning of the word 'distress' and it is not a word I would use to describe my feelings following the loss of a sporting contest. But that defeat in Dublin was about as disappointing as it gets in sport. We had been in unstoppable form six months earlier and I do not think it would be an idle and empty boast to claim that we probably would have steamrollered the Irish, or any other team for that matter, had we met when originally scheduled. My mum said afterwards: 'Life would be incredibly dull if you won all the time. Where's the fun in that?' She's quite right, of course, but any such rational thoughts were swamped by the raw despair of feeling that we had thrown away our best chance of landing the ultimate prize in Northern Hemisphere rugby. For me the turning point of the game came about fifteen minutes into the second half and we were trailing 14–9 when Dan Luger made a superb break deep into their twenty-two, only to be tap-tackled a few yards from the line by Peter Stringer. The Irish then defended like heroes and we just couldn't quite breach their lines. Even though we had lost the match, we were still crowned champions, but there was not one smile to be seen in our changing room afterwards. The atmosphere in there was about as flat as I have experienced with England over the years, but with Australia and South Africa on their way over for the autumn internationals, there was no time to feel sorry for ourselves.

It has been one of the outstanding characteristics of the England team under Clive Woodward that the players have always reacted well to defeats. Far from leading to a loss of form and a softening of our confidence, we have tended to come back hardened by a setback, more focused and more ruthless than we were before. That's exactly what happened that autumn as we set about our visitors with a controlled fury in an attempt to prove to ourselves, if to no one else, that we were in fact a very good team which had just had one poor day in Dublin.

Australia were beaten 21-15 and although all the points came from the boot of Jonny Wilkinson, it was an impressive team performance against the world champions and our defence was awesome at times. The game was as tight and finely balanced as the scoreline suggests, but the same could not be said of our next match against Romania which finished 134-0, the biggest victory in international history. We ran in a record twenty tries, but there reached a stage when every time we crossed the line the game became less and less enjoyable. God knows how the Romanians felt, but I couldn't wait for the final whistle. The collapse of Romanian rugby has been astonishing and sad in equal measure and after annihilating them that year it seemed almost incredible that just a decade or so earlier they had been celebrating victories over France, Scotland and Wales. They were emerging as a significant force in international rugby when the Ceauşescu regime was overthrown in 1989 and the country was convulsed by social upheaval. Back then, there were 11,000 registered rugby players in Romania, but there were just 4,000 in the autumn of 2001, of which only 1,000 of them were senior players. The saddest aspect of that afternoon was that they ran themselves into the ground to make an impression, only to be brushed aside in such a brutal fashion.

While Romania plumbed new depths, England were going from strength to strength and we headed into the Christmas period being hailed as the best team in the world on current form after dispatching South Africa 29–9 at Twickenham. As always, it was a very bruising contest up front but once our forwards began to take control, Jonny nailed them into submission with another flawless kicking display. It says something about the standards he sets himself that, when he walked off the pitch with another twenty-one international points to his name, he looked the picture of misery. In the last act of the game his attempted conversion of Dan Luger's breakaway try had rebounded off the post, and it seemed to take the gloss off his day.

The England management had by now introduced a new piece of technology called Prozone which monitors the performances of individuals in a match, recording, among other data, how much ground you have covered in the eighty minutes. As the type of player who tends to float in games and wait for opportunities to exploit, Prozone does me no favours at all.

Neil Back, by contrast, hits the jackpot with Prozone because, unlike me, he prefers to spend his afternoons bounding across every blade of grass like a demented rabbit. When you read the Prozone results after the match, you could be excused for thinking that I had spent the entire afternoon stretched out on a picnic rug staring at the sky with a blade of grass in my mouth. So when Danny Luger scorched clear from our own line in that final minute it was an opportunity not to be missed and you would have seen me haring after him, virtually waving at the Prozone camera as I went, in a pathetic effort to boost my ratings. I was later criticised by some of rugby's Luddites for my 'football–style' celebration of Danny's try when I jumped on his back and held one arm aloft. It was nothing more than an expression of joy at the end of what had been another extremely tough encounter with a highly physical Springbok side. If I had cleared one of my nostrils as the camera homed in on me, taunted some South African fans in the crowd and refused to shake hands with my opponents after the match, then I would accept that my behaviour might have been unsporting. But if you can't enjoy yourself at the end of England's biggest win over South Africa, when can you?

The autumn series of internationals have become a fabulous challenge in recent years with at least two of the big Southern Hemisphere teams providing the opposition. When I first started playing international rugby, you felt you had only a reasonable chance against these teams, providing all the areas of our game were functioning smoothly. But from that autumn onwards the expectation grew that we would win all our matches against them – at home at least. Just four or five years earlier we were very much the underdogs, the wide-eyed amateurs trying to come to terms with the professional game. That's some transformation.

Since the controversial 18-13 defeat to South Africa eighteen months earlier, England had won the follow-ing three encounters with the Springboks as well as seen off Australia twice, but once again we came up short in the Six Nations, losing 20-15 to France in our third match. The championship had started positively enough with a 29-3 win over Scotland at Murrayfield and a 45-11 massacre of Ireland which took our winning streak at home to thirteen matches and went some way to avenging our defeat by the Irish six months earlier. I scored two of the six tries that day, but the whole team was immense. We ended the campaign with thumping wins over Wales (50-10) and Italy (45-9), but once again we were left with a feeling of profound disap-pointment and a nagging doubt in the back of our minds. We were a very good team – even our harshest critics and fiercest rivals seemed to be agreed on that. But we had no right to consider ourselves to be a great side worthy and capable of winning the World Cup, rugby's ultimate prize, if, year on year, we seemed incapable of going that extra yard to win what the Southern Hemisphere teams back then would have considered to be no more than a local squabble. If we couldn't land the Six Nations, what chance the World Cup? We had one more opportunity to get ourselves right before we could launch our World Cup in the knowledge that we could dig that little bit deeper when we had to.

Chapter Seven

IT WAS THE spring of 2002 and I was having the time of my life. I was an international athlete, I was fit and healthy and I was engaged to be married to the girl of my dreams. Could life get any better, I wondered. In this instance it could – Caro was pregnant.

I'd like to tell you it all unfolded like a good Mills & Boon story, but that wouldn't be entirely accurate. I'd fallen head over heels for Caro from the outset, but perhaps like most young men in a hurry to get nowhere in particular I shied away from that final act of commitment for a long time. I had enjoyed a very happy childhood and had always wanted to start my own family – and yet I still couldn't quite bring myself to go and get the engagement ring. We split up twice in the first five years as a result of my commitment-dodging and on each occasion, curiously, the break happened not long after getting back from a Lions tour. When you are away for long periods of time it is easy to become a little estranged from your partner and you adapt to your new circumstances to cope with the change of scene.

On tours, you spend all your time in the company of other young men: training, playing, eating and socialising together. That world becomes your natural habitat and when you finally return home it takes time to get back into the normal routine. After the Lions tour of 2001 we broke up for seven weeks and, just as had happened four years earlier, it was me who went crawling back to Caro with my tail between my legs. I realised how much I missed her when I woke up one Sunday morning after my umpteenth night out with the lads and thought: 'Who the hell do you think you are, Will Greenwood? Peter bloody Pan?'

We decided to try for a baby in April and hit the jackpot at the first time of asking (more evidence, as if I needed any more at this time, that life was increasingly a breeze). The due date for the birth of our baby was 23 January 2003 and with that fixed I thought it was now the appropriate time to propose. I had always imagined that when I finally got round to proposing to Caro I would take her to Paris in the springtime and by the banks of the Seine I would get down on one knee, sword at my side, and ask for her hand. At which point she would hurl herself into my arms and I would spin her around as the blossom tumbled around us in the morning sunshine. But it didn't quite happen like that. She was actually lying on a bed in Southfields asking for a bucket to be sick into when I popped the question. We had been out to dinner up the road in Wimbledon, and I had been about to start my romantic address when Caro, suffering from morning sickness, announced that she felt tired and ill and wanted to go home. I was a man on a mission, though, and once I had decided that I was going to make the momentous gesture, nothing, not even a severe bout of morning sickness, was going to stop me. I hadn't bought a ring because Caro had never trusted my taste in jewellery and I had decided to let her choose her own. So it was without so much as a Hula-Hoop to offer that, ignoring her groans, I leaned through the gloom, tapped her on the shoulder and said: 'Er, Caro, I've got something to ask you . . .' Happily – and perhaps surprisingly given the circumstances – Caro accepted and we decided to have the big day after the birth of our child as Caro didn't want to walk up the aisle looking huge.

It was an exciting time that summer as we prepared for our new life and when Caro's twelve-week scan at the Chelsea & Westminster Hospital on the Fulham Road revealed that the baby was in good health we were able to tell everyone the good news. When I began pre-season training that year I felt invincible, as if everything in my life had just fallen beautifully into place.

Fate, however, was just setting us up for a very nasty fall.

One Saturday in mid-September, Quins were playing Leeds at home and Caro had decided to go and stay with her mum – Mrs Tasker or Mrs T to me – up in Norfolk. As soon as the match was over, I received a call from Caro to tell me she had woken up to discover that her waters had sprung a leak, the bed was wet through and she had been to hospital to get checked out. In my ignorance of these matters, I said I was sure everything would be fine and that I would see her back in London on Sunday night. 'This is pretty serious, Will,' she said, but, as ever, didn't make a drama out of the situation. I still didn't quite get it and, almost just to keep her happy, I said I would come up in the morning instead. I can't believe how naïve I was. Caro had been told everything was in good order after her twenty-week scan and I assumed it would be plain sailing through to the birth. Perhaps I was in denial and didn't want to admit that anything could be seriously wrong with the pregnancy. If I had had any real understanding of the gravity of the situation I would have been in my car and up the M11 in a flash. I still kick myself today over my stupidity in this episode.

That night I went out to a friend's birthday party on the King's Road and I was still not remotely worried about my earlier conversation with Caro. It was only when I rolled up at the hospital at King's Lynn the following day that I realised something serious was afoot. The staff there told us to get back to London and see our doctor as soon as possible for advice on the best course of action as they had been unable to establish the exact cause of the leakage. Caro was being immensely composed and strong, but I was now feeling very uncomfortable and I wanted to kick myself for my earlier complacency.

The following morning our local GP sent us straight up to the Chelsea & Westminster Hospital where they discovered that the membrane around the baby had ruptured. Originally they put Caro in a maternity ward surrounded by women who were either just about to give birth or had just had their babies, which made her feel even more miserable. In the great swirl of emotions that attend these occasions, Caro had started to feel inadequate in some way. Watching happy families with their newborn babies is not the best environment for a mother who was at risk of losing hers. I had to get her out of there and after I kicked up a big fuss they eventually found her a room of her own.

The baby was just over twenty-one weeks at this stage and he or she would stand no chance of surviving for longer than a few minutes if Caro's waters broke completely. The doctors told us frankly that we faced a very difficult period, but there was an outside chance everything would be OK so long as Caro stayed confined to her bed for the next four or five months. There was a glimmer of hope and we seized it. The human spirit is extraordinary in the way it refuses to give up hope even when the rational mind knows there are virtually no grounds for optimism. For the next three days, while Caro was confined to her hospital bed, I went off to training and each time I came back I could see that she was growing increasingly anxious, even though she was doing a great job in trying to disguise it. I had never heard of 'Braxton Hicks' contractions before but I knew all about them by that Tuesday evening. Named after a Victorian doctor, they are, if you like, a trial run of the real thing and they can start as early as fourteen weeks. Caro, however, knew that what she was feeling were not Braxton Hicks contractions. The simple, brutal truth was that the baby was coming and he or she wasn't going to live for long. All we could do was wait for our tragedy to unfold. I felt sick in the pit of my stomach.

Freddie's day was Thursday 19 September 2002.

I knew Chelsea were playing at home in the UEFA Cup at Stamford Bridge that evening and so to avoid the traffic I shot home after kickoff to get some much-needed rest before swapping shifts with Mrs T at Caro's bedside. The football was on the television in the background when the phone rang and Caro said: 'Will, get here as quick as you can.' I knew what the call meant and there was no use trying to convince myself otherwise. I slumped into the car and everything went into slow motion as I drove back to the Fulham Road. I could feel the emotions rising and stirring inside as the last drops of optimism began to seep away. I tried to stay calm and focused. I had to, for Caro's sake.

We were going to lose the baby. I knew that. Still, though, a tiny part of me was holding out for the miracle, an inextinguishable atom of hope that no amount of hard, brutal facts could kill off. There's always hope, I heard myself say. I parked the car in the same space I had been using over the past three days and I sprinted upstairs and into our room. I could tell Caro had hung on for me. Within moments of my arrival she let out a head-splitting scream of pain – her body wasn't ready for birth – and before I knew what was happening she was on a trolley being wheeled through by Dr Martin Lupton to the delivery room. It's strange what images your mind chooses to record in these desperate moments when everything is a nauseating, panic-fuelled blur, but I remember a kindly Mediterranean-looking lady beaming a lovely joyful smile at us as we passed, obviously thinking: 'Bless them, a little life on the way for them to cherish!'

My head was swimming. I was holding Caro's hand. I wanted to be sick. Heaven only knows how she must have been feeling at that precise moment. Dr Lupton said, 'You have to be aware that there is nothing we can do . . . the baby is just too young . . . he or she almost certainly won't make it . . .' Or words to that effect. I wasn't really listening to him. I still had a little voice inside me saying, 'There's still some hope, don't give up yet.'

I was so ignorant of childbirth that I had given no

thought to what the baby would look like. Does a twenty-two-week-old baby actually look like a person? I simply had no idea. I was looking away, sick with nerves, when I heard a massive whooshing sound as if a water balloon had just burst. Caro is bleeding to death, I thought. Then I looked up and Dr Lupton was holding my boy. It was a wonderful shock. This was no indeterminate mass of human cells; this was a living, breathing, perfectly formed absolute beauty of a little babe. My son, Freddie! I could see his little chest moving up and down.

Caro was in a state of shock, but she hadn't taken any painkilling drugs, thank heavens, and so she was able to appreciate every moment. She held him first and then passed the tiny bundle to me. My mother-in-law, Mrs T, kissed him and I remember her lilac lipstick on his head. The lovely Ghanaian midwife took some photographs of him and made impressions of his feet and hands on some paper. We knew Freddie was going to die at any moment. The clock was ticking in our minds and you could hear every bloody, painful tick of it.

After forty-five minutes Freddie passed away in Caro's arms. It was 10.18 in the evening and our lives imploded.

I didn't really know what I was doing. I went out to call a couple of people. Isn't that what you are meant to do when your child is born? You call people up and tell them the news. So I found myself out in the corridor, shaking as I took out my mobile phone. I called my best mate Ben Fennell, who was now living in Singapore, and as soon as he answered I fell apart. I had tried to be strong for Caro but now I just collapsed into a thousand pieces. 'They've taken him away, Benny' was all I could say.

At about 11.30 the hospital vicar came up and blessed Frederick George Arthur and we then spent some more time with our amazing little boy before Mrs T and the vicar took him away to the Chapel of Rest. We spent an awful, tearful, sleepless night and in the morning we just wanted to get out of there, but Caro was told she had to undergo a series of tests. There was a locum midwife on duty that morning – a sweet woman – but as she didn't work there she didn't have a clue what the procedure was or where anything was kept. Frustration and impatience piled on top of misery.

We got home at about midday and went straight to bed and we wept some more. I wanted to stay there forever, with the curtains drawn. The following morning I answered the door and Ben was standing on my doorstep. After my phone call to him on Thursday night he had cancelled all his work appointments and boarded the first plane back to London. He later told me it was the scariest thing he had ever seen, me staring out of the doorway a haunted, gaunt, wreck of a man. Thank goodness Ben and Mrs T were there that first week. I don't think we could have coped without them. I wanted the world to end. My son had died and something had died inside me, too. Thank goodness, too, for my family as well as our other close friends.

Austin Healey was a rock. I have made a load of jokes at his expense in these pages, but they are made in the confidence of a great friendship. It's difficult for people to know how to react in these situations, but Austin got it absolutely right by saying virtually nothing and just listening. The majority of people, in their kindness, ring up and try to give advice. You know they mean well, but nothing they say is going to help. I didn't listen to a blind word they said. I had the feeling that no one really wanted to listen to what had happened. One or two people, acquaintances rather than friends, said some downright daft and insensitive things. One said: 'Don't worry, you can always have another!' while another said: 'Well, if it's any consolation you can come and babysit ours.' Incredible. What do you say?

For most friends and family it's all just too painful and they want everyone to move on from the whole agonising episode as quickly as possible. They don't want to see you suffer. But there was no way we could move on then, nor for a good while. We were rooted in our grief and there wasn't a damned thing we could have done about it. All we wanted to do was tell people about Freddie's forty-five minutes on this earth; by doing that we felt as if we were giving meaning to his brief life.

I was meant to be playing for Quins against London Irish that very day but I telephoned to explain what had happened. Mike Scott, the team manager, later rang back and asked if it would be all right if they held a minute's silence down at The Stoop and if all the lads wore black armbands during the game. It was a lovely gesture and when the minute began Mike called me again so that I could hear it for myself. What an incredibly powerful moment that was, holding that phone to my ear in Southfields and listening to the sound of silence a few miles up the road, knowing that thousands of people, many of them friends, all had Freddie and us in their thoughts at that moment. Quins had lost the first three games of the season but they hammered Irish that afternoon and Mark Evans, Quins' head coach, later told me that he had never seen the lads play with such fury as they did that day. It's moments like that which help pick you up and pull you through and make you realise it is worth carrying on after all.

We wanted to go back to the hospital to see Freddie over the weekend, but we were told it wasn't possible because the right people weren't there to authorise it. Caro was particularly distraught by this, but Ben got on the phone and sorted it for us. I just didn't have the strength to battle the bureaucracy and spend a morning being put on hold and then transferred from one pen-pushing department to the next. Thanks to Ben we had another special moment holding Freddie, and his grandparents were able to have their pictures taken with him. It may only have lasted for forty-five minutes but his brief appearance in this world had a tremendous impact on us. Looking back on that week now I suppose we did what we did because we knew it was our only chance to do anything for him at all.

We decided to have Freddie cremated near Caro's mum's house in Norfolk because it is a peaceful place and we visited her often. London just didn't seem right. On Tuesday the funeral firm came down to collect Freddie from the hospital and he was placed in a wooden coffin no bigger than a shoebox. Caro sat with the coffin in the front car with Benny and me in the one behind as we set off. This was not a journey a parent should have to make.

I had no idea who, other than family and very close friends, was planning to come to the service which took place just outside King's Lynn, but there were a good sixty people in total from all walks of our life who had dropped what they were doing to come and support us. Many others were unable to come but had the goodness to send us messages. Caro and I carried in the tiny little coffin and it was then that the cruelty and injustice of it really hit me: carrying your kid's coffin is not how it's meant to happen. He should be carrying mine in about forty or fifty years' time.

I wasn't taking much in and the details of the ceremony passed me by in a tearful blur. I read W. H.

Auden's poem 'Funeral Blues' ('Stop all the clocks . . .') and Caro read a bedtime story called *Guess How Much I Love You*. I could barely do it but I'd have hated myself forever if I hadn't been able to find the strength to read a farewell to my son. Just before the end of the ceremony there was a very weird episode. I like to think that it was Freddie having a laugh and trying to inject a bit of humour into an otherwise wretched occasion. There was a power cut just before the coffin was lowered: the process ground to a halt, the lights went out and the organ groaned and faded away. It was a very awkward moment but the day was saved by the congregation who carried on singing. It was still quite a distressing moment for Caro and me because it meant we had to leave without Freddie having been cremated. The vicar, though, assured us that he would not be left alone while the power was being restored.

Our guests came back to a lovely old manor house hotel to have tea and sign a book of condolence. I wasn't too sure about the idea of this gathering at first. A surgeon friend of mine called Harty (short for Hartwright) was telling a story about doing his round on the wards earlier that day when the registrar had asked an elderly patient whether she was being well looked after and received the reply, 'Yes, Dr Halfwit has been tremendous!' At this we all burst into gales of laughter and my first reaction was one of guilt. What am I doing laughing at my son's funeral? I hadn't heard anybody laugh for about ten days at this point, but any negative feelings that consumed me in that one instant quickly evaporated. It was actually a lovely moment because it made me understand that life did go on, just as everyone always says it will and that, amidst all life's tears and despair, there is laughter and love, too.

Caro was especially moved by the gathering and neither of us wanted it to end. We wanted to hang on to the moment forever, but slowly everyone began to melt away. The following day we went to the local garden centre and bought a baby crab apple tree which we planted in Freddie's memory at the end of Mrs T's garden.

On Monday I was back in training with England doing fitness tests. That was a bit surreal. I hadn't wanted to go, but Caro was right to insist I did. It was good to be distracted, to do something physical as well as something reassuring in its familiarity. As I had barely eaten anything for almost a fortnight my tests were the worst on record. Although not much was said, I felt comfortable back in the company of my team-mates, many of whom I had been playing alongside since 1993 in one representative side or other. The odd shake of a hand, a pat on the back and the occasional look here and there was all that was needed to let me know people were looking out for me. Others in the England squad had suffered tragedy, too.

Freddie's death was a dreadful experience for us and I

have never made any attempt to hide the distress it caused. For me, one of the reasons why it was so upsetting was because Freddie died on the outside. He was given a brief sniff of life and then he was spirited away. But his short life has left a number of positive legacies. From a personal point of view I am thankful that he has given my own life the perspective it may previously have lacked. Thanks to Freddie I now understand better what is truly important in life. Furthermore, as a result of the experience, Caro has got heavily involved in the baby charity Tommy's, which aims to research and help prevent miscarriage, stillbirth and premature birth. We have now hosted two sporting balls in memory of Freddie, in conjunction with Tommy's, and managed to raise more than £400,000 for the cause. That's a great gift by anyone's standards. You hear of these tragedies breaking up couples, but Freddie has brought Caro and me even closer together. We thank him for that, too.

While there is breath in our own bodies Freddie will never be forgotten.

Chapter Eight

IT IS DIFFICULT to quantify the exact impact of a traumatic experience on a person, but it was probably just as well for me that I had plenty to occupy and distract me in the months following Freddie's death. He was never far from the forefront of my thoughts, but it certainly helped in those difficult days that my work was all-consuming.

In a way our World Cup campaign began twelve months before the tournament got underway. For any such major championship you have to time your run perfectly so that you are at full throttle when you cross the finishing line. We heard the starting pistol and left the blocks in that autumn of 2002 with three matches in consecutive weeks against New Zealand, Australia and South Africa. When you look at our programme leading up to the World Cup finals, you certainly couldn't accuse our coaches of ducking any challenges. In addition to that autumn series against the cream of the Southern Hemisphere, we then had the Six Nations Championship, a tour to New Zealand and Australia, followed by two Tests against France and one against Wales. It was an intense schedule and we knew that by the time it was completed we would have a very good idea whether or not we were in the right shape and the right state of mind to become the first Northern Hemisphere country to lift the Webb Ellis trophy.

John Mitchell's New Zealanders were our first visitors to Twickenham and, although they had left behind some of their first-choice forwards, their back line promised a formidable challenge with Howlett, Lomu, Umaga, Spencer and Mehrtens in the squad. It turned out to be a belter of a contest which we edged 31-28 after weathering a late storm by the All Blacks who hit back with tries from Lomu (for his second) and substitute Danny Lee. Had it not been for an outstanding cover tackle by Ben Cohen on Ben Blair by the corner flag two minutes from time, it might have been black arms rather than white ones raised in celebration at the end – and who knows quite what a psychological blow that might have struck?

There was little love lost between the two sides in this particular period, and with England very much in the ascendancy as a rugby power you could not help but feel there was some resentment and envy, almost outrage, among the All Blacks that we even dared to assume the mantle of 'world's best team'. I certainly felt the shrill blast of some bitterness on two occasions that afternoon, compounding my impression that New Zealand, beautiful country as it may be, will not be my holiday destination of choice over the coming years.

At one point in the game I chased a chip over the top and was shouldered in the solar plexus, and as I hit the ground I couldn't breathe. As I lay there doubled up in agony gasping for air and waiting for the physio to appear, a handful of All Blacks leaned over me and gave me a tirade of abuse: 'What's wrong with you, you big f***ing p***y. Are you a f***ing little fag or what? . . .'

I had to leave the field at half-time after suffering a dead leg and I was given crutches by the back-up staff in order to keep the weight off it. At the end of the match I walked out of the dressing room and there in the corridor was half the All Black squad looking distinctly under the moon after their defeat. They looked like a poor man's version of *Reservoir Dogs* as they stood there in their suits staring at me and sneering. Then the abuse began again: 'You f***ing w***er . . . Are you a poofter, Greenwood, or what? What's with the crutches, fag?' I couldn't quite believe what I was hearing and I just stood, thinking: a) Do people not get injured in New Zealand? b) Talk about pricks (see Mehrtens, above). c) There is a strong chance here that they are going to start sticking their tongues out at me and say 'Nah-nah-nah-nah-nah'.

It was a very bizarre experience and it was difficult to imagine someone of the stature of, say, Zinzan Brooke or Colin Meads engaging in that kind of childish and pathetic banter. When I was a rugby-mad kid growing up into the 1970s and 1980s, like everyone else of my generation I looked up to the All Blacks in awestruck wonder. I can't say I felt that same degree of respect and admiration when, all those years later, I stood in the Twickenham corridor that evening and copped an earful of abuse for being injured.

It's strange and depressing all at once how your impression of a whole country can be influenced by the behaviour of a dozen or so of its representatives on a rugby field. But it is an inescapable fact that the most graceless and abusive opponents I've come across on a rugby field have been New Zealanders. Perhaps they think they have a divine right to be the best team in the world; perhaps they are victims of their own hype and pressure back home. But just one look in the record books tells its own story: the only World Cup New Zealand have won was the first one in 1987 when we in the north were still warming up for matches with a packet of fags and a few pints. They have had some fantastic players down the years and their ranks have been swelled by plucking the best players from their Pacific Island neighbours. But no one, surely, has the birthright to be best team in the world. You have to go out and earn it.

It turned out to be a bad day all round for the Southern Hemisphere with Ireland beating Australia

18-9 and France beating South Africa 30-10. We played the Australians in our next match and that, too, was a superb spectacle. In its own way, it was one of the most impressive performances I have featured in with England. We looked comfortable enough as we approached half-time 16-6 in front, but not long into the second period we were stunned to find ourselves 28-16 down, following two tries from Elton Flatley and one from Wendell Sailor. In the past England, like many teams, might have pressed the panic button and just thrown themselves forward in a mad frenzy to get back on terms. But this was when the TCUP mantra came to the fore as we slowly clawed back the deficit and then overhauled the Wallabies for a dramatic 31-28 victory. That second-half performance was a highly significant milestone in our development as a team.

A week later we took our winning streak at home to eighteen matches with a victory which, on paper, could give the impression that we enjoyed a very comfortable stroll that afternoon. That, though, could not have been further from the truth. This was the brutal and now infamous encounter when the South Africans completely lost their heads. One of the most extraordinary aspects of their open assault on us was that they launched it, so to speak, in broad daylight. This was no mugging in a provincial game in the backwaters of South Africa far from the prying lenses of television cameras broadcasting live. This all took place at Twickenham under the noses of 78,000 spectators and a massive television audience – although they could see only a fraction of the cheap shots taking place in the shadier regions of the action.

In my experience the South Africans are always as hard as nails but are generally pretty fair, or at least as fair as the next team. They are certainly not an exceptionally dirty team. You'd have to ask their coach Rudolf Straeuli and captain Corne Krige what they were trying to achieve on that particular day because it flew in the face of their traditionally robust but honest approach. Perhaps it was because they had lost to the Scots the week before and, figuring they had no chance against us and with their pride wounded, they decided to have their fun by trying to take as many of us out of the game as possible.

It was one of the ironies of the day that the only man to be dismissed, Jannes Labuschagne, could consider himself a little unlucky. His late tackle on Jonny Wilkinson was more misdemeanour than crime when you set it alongside the other acts committed. Just moments earlier, however, the Boks had been categorically warned by referee Paddy O'Brien about their violent play and he had no option but to carry out his threat of a red card for the next offender.

We won the match 53–3 and in doing so I became the first England player to score twice in a match against South Africa in what was definitely my best performance of the season up to that point. I was now also the third highest try scorer in England's history and I was pleased to be named man of the match for no other reason than that I had not been at my absolute best against Australia. I wasn't bad, but I wasn't brilliant either.

The most satisfying aspect of a very ugly afternoon was that we remained so composed in the face of the worst provocation I have seen, let alone experienced, on an international rugby field. It was a triumph of self-discipline, which is something we had been working on for years. If your penalty count starts running into double figures you're going to struggle to win the game and as a team will always be pulled up for the odd technical offence, it is imperative to cut out the daft mistakes. That is one of the main reasons why Clive Woodward won't have ill-disciplined players in his squad. He has always wanted players like Martin Johnson who plays right on the edge, doesn't take any crap from anyone but rarely steps over the line. Johnno has, however, always had a reputation for foul play, which anyone who has played alongside him will tell you is grossly unfair. Throughout his career there seemed to be one rulebook for him and one for everyone else. He was certainly one of the hardest players I have seen but I have never thought of him as a dirty player. His problem was that he was so high profile that, in club matches especially, journalists and cameramen followed his every move while ignoring the conduct of the less well-known players up and down the country.

I dread to think how Clive Woodward would have reacted had it been us wading into the South Africans. I wouldn't have been at all surprised if he had dropped half the team and banished them into the international wilderness forever. Utterly disgraceful is the only way to describe that South African display. It was tin-hat stuff for eighty minutes as they piled in with knees, kicks, punches, head butts, scratching and gouging. When they walked off the pitch and looked up at the scoreboard, they must have felt totally humiliated.

The worst aspect of the whole performance was that after the match the senior South Africans who spoke to the media gave the impression that *if* anything had gone on out there England had been equally culpable. That was utter nonsense and just added to the embarrassment they heaped upon themselves. If I was a Springbok fan I would have felt degraded as much by the post-match comments as by the rout of a result and the barbaric performance of my team. There was a comical moment when Rudi Straeuli said: 'Look, one of my guys was taken off unconscious. How did that happen? Do you think one of our own guys hit him?' In fact, that's exactly what did happen. Corne Krige was trying to take Matt Dawson's head off, but missed and struck his fly-half Andre Pretorius by mistake. It was at the end of this game that Krige said, 'See you in Perth.' Indeed, Corne, we'd see you there.

Our Six Nations Championship campaign got off to a shocking and depressing start in the New Year with the news that my Harlequins team-mate Nick Duncombe had died on the eve of our opening game against France at Twickenham. Mark Evans, the boss at Quins, turned up at our team hotel at Pennyhill Park in Bagshot and asked to talk to me, Jason Leonard and Danny Luger. We were surprised to see him there and it was a dreadful shock when he told us what had happened. Nick, who was a highly promising scrum-half and had been capped twice by this stage, had gone to the Canary Islands with our Australian team-mate Nathan Williams for a short break. He picked up blood poisoning which was so ferocious that he collapsed and passed away within thirty-six hours. It could have happened to any of us. It was so quick and so random. (Today I like to think that Nick and Freddie have become good friends and that my old Quins mate is keeping an eye out for my little boy.)

Danny Luger was a very big mate of Nicky's and the news of his death affected him as badly as it affected anyone at the club. I thought Dan showed incredible mental strength to come through the match the following day. There was a minute's silence before kickoff, but if there was little joy to be had from our 25-

17 victory, it had nothing to do with our poor second-half performance. Jason won his 100th cap that afternoon, an incredible achievement and it should have been a happy occasion. But no one was celebrating.

In Quins' next match, down at Bristol, we all wore shirts with the name Duncombe printed across our backs. Nathan Williams was a shadow of himself that afternoon and the crowd started giving him some dreadful abuse. I could only assume his hecklers didn't know about Nick's death because I couldn't believe people could be that cruel. I was so incensed that at one point, when the abuse got particularly bad and there was a break in play, I went over to the crowd and told them to give Nathan a break. Nathan had broken down and we had signalled to the bench that he was in no state to continue. 'Why do you think we are wearing this on our back, you idiots?' I shouted pointing over my shoulder.

Nick's passing hung over us throughout the league season at Quins and England's Six Nations campaign that spring. But he would have been delighted by our success as we took apart Wales, Italy and Scotland in our next three outings to set up a Grand Slam decider with the Irish in Dublin. With both sides fancying themselves to walk off with European rugby's biggest trophy, the match was as hyped as any I could remember in Six Nations' history. In most encounters between fairly evenly matched sides you can never safely predict the outcome, but just occasionally you can feel it in your bones. Dublin 2003 was one of those days. Getting on the team coach, there was a strong feeling among the squad that the day would be ours.

There was a highly charged moment before the kickoff which neatly captured the fierce sense of purpose running through the squad that afternoon. After the captains had tossed for ends we lined up for the anthems on the side of the pitch from where we would play the first half, as you always do. Apparently, though, we were on Ireland's 'lucky side' and soon after we took our place a young BBC employee came over and the following exchange took place.

BBC lad: 'Excuse me, Mr Johnson, that's the Irish lucky side. Could you and your team move please?'

Johnno: 'F**k off.'

BBC lad (after scuttling off, then coming back): 'Excuse me, Mr Johnson, you are in the Irish places. Please move your team.'

Johnno: 'F**k off.'

There was no way Johnno was budging an inch – and the referee certainly wasn't going to get involved. Neil Back, meanwhile, was walking up and down the line like a sergeant major at Waterloo, barking: 'No f***er moves. Stand your ground.' In the end the Irish lads filed past us and stood further along from us in the same half and it made for a weird spectacle because the other half was completely empty. Johnno was later criticised for a breach of protocol, which most seemed to feel was a little churlish, but his stubbornness was a powerful and galvanising statement of intent that we weren't going to be pushed around that day.

England were brilliant that afternoon and even our harshest critics could not deny that we deserved our 42-6 victory and the Grand Slam it brought. Playing against an extremely good Irish side, it was pretty tight in the first half as both sets of forwards battled to gain supremacy. For me the turning point came five minutes before half-time when we withstood a furious barrage from them and you could almost feel their self-belief falling away as they failed to find a way through or around us. They didn't manage a single point after the twenty-sixth minute as we ran in four more tries in the second half – two of them by me – to add to Lol Dallaglio's in the first. It was an awesome team performance by anyone's standards, and no individual played poorly. Jonny Wilkinson had a massive game, defensively as well as offensively. He was the best back on the paddock by a country mile and I pity the opposition if he ever has a better game. Afterwards, though, I made a point of seeking out every member of the pack to congratulate them. They were simply immense.

The Irish were very gracious in defeat (just as I like to think we had been eighteen months earlier when they had beaten us on the same ground to deny us the Grand Slam). If I had to lose to one major team in world rugby it would be Ireland. We probably get on better with them than any of the other teams and that evening we all went out and had a superb night on the Dublin tiles. They are just a good bunch of boys who like their rugby and if they do have any issues or axes to grind with England they very rarely show it.

So far, then, so good: three autumn internationals, three wins; five Six Nations games, five wins. When we boarded the plane in the early summer for our one-off Tests against New Zealand and Australia, the England squad was as tight and as confident as I had known it since making my debut almost six years earlier. I had had the privilege of playing in some fabulous teams and alongside some world-class players during that time, but there was something particularly solid and powerful about the team being lined up for the 2003 World Cup finals. We had what was widely regarded as the best pack in the world, one which will surely go down as one of the greatest of all time. Take your pick from Vickery, Thompson, Woodman, Johnson, Kay, Hill, Back, Dallaglio, Leonard, Moody, Worsley, Grewcock, Shaw . . . We had explosive runners in Robinson, Lewsey, Cohen and Tindall. We had myself and two scrum-halves in Kyran Bracken and Matt Dawson who had been around for a while by then and all proved ourselves at the highest level. With a highly talented and experienced second-string team breathing down our necks, we also had great strength in depth and fierce competition for places. And we had Jonny Wilkinson, the best fly-half in the world.

Any sense of satisfaction I might have been feeling about my rugby career and my form, however, was eclipsed in one wonderful moment two days before the New Zealand Test. I was back at the team hotel when Caro rang up to tell me that she was pregnant again. She's a secret poet, my wife, and a very good one, too, and she broke the news to me by reading one of her odes. By the time her final iambic pentameter had bounced off the satellite into my mobile phone, I was almost doing cartwheels around my hotel room. It was simply the best piece of news I had received . . . well, since she had become pregnant with Freddie fifteen months or so earlier.

There is little point in reading the newspapers if you are an Englishman in New Zealand to play a rugby match. The news is always the same: England are rubbish and arrogant; New Zealand are simply marvellous and lovely guys with it. But even if you manage to avoid the crap they write you cannot get away from the impression that there is not a soul in the country who would stop to pee on you if you were on fire. The general feeling abroad in New Zealand before this match was that, as we had had the temerity to beat them at Twickenham eight months earlier, they were going to smash us to pieces with their first-choice XV now that they had us in their own backyard.

Happily, it didn't quite work out like that and we became only the second England team to win on New Zealand soil (the other victory came in 1972). Our 15-13 victory was a truly heroic performance made in the very image of our skipper Johnno. Martin Johnson has produced some soul-stirring displays in his long career with Leicester, England and the Lions but that display in the wind, rain and mud of Wellington must surely rank very high among them. At one point we were down to thirteen men after Neil Back and Lawrence Dallaglio had been sent to the sin bin, but the six forwards who remained, fired up by Johnno, gave not an inch of ground to the All Blacks and at one point drove them halfway up the pitch in a rolling maul. During this period of the game there were also four consecutive 5-metre scrums on our line, but despite there being just six of them in our pack, and conceding 35 stone in weight advantage to the Kiwis, they somehow managed to hold firm. After the match Johnno was asked what had been going through his mind during those scrums, to which he replied: 'My arsehole.'

If you have a video of this match fast forward to a few minutes from time and you will see Mike Tindall and me laughing our heads off. We were on our line trying to catch our breath after some desperate defending when Dave 'Otis' Reddin, our conditioning coach who runs the bench on match days, came bounding along the touchline to give us some urgent advice. The England coaching system has become the most sophisticated in world rugby, and we had been expecting some technical wisdom or tactical insight from Otis when he rushed up and said, . . . 'Lads, lads, tackle! tackle!' Thanks, Otis, you genius. We'd never have thought of that.

It was an incredibly tense finale to the match and I had a dreadful moment seconds from the end when I thought I had blown our hard-fought win. The match officials were using a 'buzzer' whereby, once it sounds, the match is over as soon as the ball goes dead. I haven't had much experience of the buzzer and I picked up the ball deep in our half when it sounded. Immediately, and without thinking, I just ran into touch – and then froze. 'Is that legal?' I wondered as I saw the referee look at his watch and thought he was going to award New Zealand a lineout in a perfect situation for a drop goal. But he blew his whistle, thank heavens, and we were able to celebrate one of our greatest victories.

Once again this was a day to stand back and applaud the piano shifters rather than the piano players, just as it had been in Dublin a few months earlier. 'The white orcs on steroids', as one New Zealand journalist dubbed our forwards the following day, had produced another awesome performance which would have dispirited the All Blacks as much as it had lifted us. We had a couple of quiet beers among ourselves that night but we didn't want to go overboard as we had to catch a flight to Melbourne the following day. We had been abused all week by their press, it was cold, wet and windy and we just wanted to get out of there as soon as possible. Samuel Johnson said that the best thing about Scotland was the road out of it, and after the insults we had taken from the New Zealanders on that trip, and on earlier occasions, I had similar feelings about that aeroplane we boarded the following day.

Like many other outspoken, colourful pundits and former players, David Campese is a man I recommend you go out of your way to avoid or ignore if at all possible, especially if you happen to be a current international and an Englishman to boot. If that means hiding behind walls or running away, just do it. Trust me, it's worth it. 'Campo' has made a second career out of battering the English in the media, but he was not, by any stretch of the imagination, the only Australian to slag us off in the build-up to the Test that summer. You could almost hear the boos and jeers as we stepped off the plane and, if we thought the New Zealand press were one-eyed, the Australian newspapers were even worse. When you read a British rugby correspondent, you will generally find him to be generous and magnanimous towards Southern Hemisphere teams, but Down Under most of the hacks seem to use their columns and match reports as a platform for insulting England. Not that they are very original or creative in their abuse either, and no sooner had we arrived than all the old clichés were being taken out of storage and worn like a pair of comfortable old slippers: 'England are boring . . . England are arrogant . . . Dad's Army is in town . . .' Cue mass yawning in the England camp.

I have always enjoyed beating the Australians, but the 25-14 win over them that summer was, at that stage, comfortably the most satisfying of my career. I'd say our performance for the first hour was the best rugby we've played in seven years under Clive Woodward. I went over from close range in the sixth minute for our first score after we had run through about fifteen phases of play. Tinds powered over not long after to round off another great passage of play which involved some stunning fingertip passing along the line. They had started to creep back into contention when Ben Cohen scored our third with an old favourite. Australia fielded a couple of young centres in Morgan Turinui and Steve Kefu that day and they had Nathan Gray playing at ten in the absence of Elton Flatley who had been suspended for a match after breaking the squad curfew and going out for a beer or two. Jonny and I managed to pull all three of them out of position, allowing Ben, coming short off Wilko's shoulder, to hit the gap and take full-back Chris Latham on the outside to crash over under the posts. Wendell Sailor went over for them late on, but there was no disguising that they had been well and truly stuffed.

One other memory from that match remains vividly

in my mind: Josh Lewsey's immense tackle on Matt Rogers. Josh hit the former rugby league player so hard that one of his ribs popped out and to this day Rogers has been unable to go surfing, his favourite pastime, because he can no longer lie down on the board. I prefer the running to the tackling, but there is something deeply satisfying about a massive tackle and Josh's hit on Rogers was about as massive as they come.

After all the incredibly tedious and unfair criticism from the Australian media we had to put up with in the run-up to the match, it was particularly satisfying to produce a performance of that quality to seal England's first ever win on Aussie soil. What I don't understand is how anyone thinks it serves their cause to slag us off before a match – or slag off any other team for that matter. If it's meant to be 'psychological warfare', do the critics honestly think that we are going to go all introspective and nervous and start thinking: 'Gosh, maybe he's right. Despite the overwhelming weight of evidence to the contrary we are actually total crap'? Secondly, they are going to end up looking like fools after the match when they've lost and/or been completely played off the park, as was the case in Melbourne. I have never seen the sense, let alone the fairness, in wantonly abusing a team before a match.

After the match we flew from Melbourne to Perth where we were going to be based at the start of the World Cup finals later in the year, and at first we privately questioned the wisdom of that leg of the journey. We were all tired and just wanted to get home, but in the event the decision to stop over was an inspired one. For a few days we did nothing but unwind after a tough couple of weeks at the end of a long season, but the main aim was to make us familiar and comfortable with the set-up and surroundings of what would be our home for several weeks in October, and it worked.

It had been a long time since any of us had been out on a bender but we enjoyed a return to our old habits from the amateur days when myself and the Leicester boys spent the day in a vineyard in what was treated as my 'unofficial stag party' ahead of my wedding in about three weeks' time. When our day of wine-tasting got underway at about eleven that morning Graham Rowntree, that well-known connoisseur, bon viveur and future culture attaché no doubt, announced that the rule for the day was that there would be no spitting out of the wines. It turned out to be a great day, not least because I hadn't had a good social session with my old friends at Leicester since leaving the club three years earlier. It wasn't all just mindless boozing and we were given some fascinating insights into wine-making, but my abiding memory of the day was a comment by Rowntree which was as amusing as it was childish. Our guide was talking us through one of the wines, saying: 'You smell the nutty, grass cutting overtones of this little

beauty. A tremendous aroma, I think you'll agree . . .'
At which point Rowntree released a fart so loud and so
long you could almost see the volcanic gases billow
upwards above his head. He followed up his bodily
outburst by saying: 'Pick the f★★★ing grapes out of that
one!' Like naughty schoolboys, we all dissolved into
weeping hysterics. It was pathetic stuff I guess, but being
at the end of a long tour and knowing we soon had to
knuckle down for the World Cup campaign, it was
obvious that we needed to let off some steam (as it
were).

We arrived home in England on Thursday night, and
I had just enough time for a short sleep before I headed
off to Cambridge for my stag weekend. I was feeling
rough enough as it was after a long flight and four days
of fun in Perth, and the idea of another bender filled me
with horror. I'm not going to bore you with the details
of that weekend – and, yes, I do remember them – but
we spent much of it playing different sports as the theme
of the stag was the 'Posh Olympics' and included the
disciplines of real tennis, croquet, golf and racing at
Newmarket. Most of the friends there I had known
from Lancashire, school and university but no stag party
would be complete without the presence of Mike
Tindall and he was there from the kickoff to the final
whistle. (I was actually one of the first to leave. By
Sunday night, being the lightweight that I am, I had had
enough and slipped out of the back door of a pub and

gone off to bed.) It was a great weekend but there was a potentially awkward moment, when after just one hour in the pub on Friday night, my dad decided to pour a pint over Mike Tindall's head. Dad's gesture was completely out of the blue as we were all settling down and just chatting at this point and for one awful moment I thought my England centre partner was going to flatten my old man. Luckily, Tinds is one of the cooler and more laid-back customers you're likely to meet and he just burst out laughing.

Our wedding took place in Norfolk in early July and it was everything we could possibly have imagined and hoped it would be. That two- or three-week period culminating in our wedding was the first time I had had any sustained fun since Freddie had died ten months earlier. The smiles were genuine again. At one stage during the reception it all went very quiet and I went through from the main marquee into a smaller adjoining one to discover a crowd gathered around a table. I craned my neck over the top to see what was going on and there was Austin Healey and my friend Harty, the doctor, arm-wrestling each other, naked apart from ties wrapped around their penises. Harty then spent the next two hours standing at the bar, still completely naked, regaling all-comers with his peculiar brand of humour and storytelling. It was one of those weddings: one happy, funny, slightly mad party.

We spent our honeymoon at the Sandy Lane Hotel

in Barbados courtesy of a very generous friend called Ameel. He had bought the week during the auction at Freddie's Ball and immediately donated it to Caro and me as a gesture of goodwill after everything we had been through. It had been a superb four weeks since the Test against Australia (I also went to Wimbledon and The Open at Sandwich), but it was almost with relief that I handed over my body at Pennyhill Park two days later for several weeks of intense training, thereby swapping one form of physical punishment for another. In spite of all the fun I had during that period, I made an effort to stay in some kind of shape and went to the gym or for a run at least every other day – even on my stag weekend – because we knew we were going to be put through some extremely demanding drills in camp.

For the next two months or so we settled into a regular, almost military routine in which we drove ourselves – or were driven – into the ground in a massive push to make us the fittest team at the World Cup finals. But it was all imaginatively thought out and meticulously organised so that we never grew fed up going through the same regimes day after day. Also we were sent back home at weekends to relax and see our families and so we never went stir crazy, grew sick of each other's company or felt that our personal lives were being overly compromised by our England commitments.

There was a fantastic atmosphere in the camp in those

weeks as the squad was pummelled and honed into shape. Everyone pushed themselves to the limit of their endurance and there were some awesome sights to behold: Johnno and Leonard on a rowing machine or Balshaw pedalling a bike so fast you couldn't see his feet, only a blur of sock and trainer. Probably the most impressive character to watch in training is Jonny Wilkinson, particularly in the endurance tests. Heaven knows what it's doing to his lungs, but it takes the breath away just to watch him.

We barely saw a rugby ball for the first month of camp as we concentrated on getting our bodies into perfect condition. The aim was to put the hard work in the bank at the beginning of our preparations and concentrate on the skills and the tactics later.

The day began with a protein shake at about 6.30 and that was followed by either a session in the gym or a running programme. Breakfast, prepared by our excellent Scottish chef David Campbell, was followed by a session working on tactical organisation, moves and patterns. After lunch we were sent to bed at two o'clock and told not to show our faces for an hour and a half. It was an invitation I had little trouble in accepting. The training was exhausting and our bodies needed all the rest they could get in between. In the afternoon we went to the gym or did running workouts, depending on what we had done that morning. There was little or no socialising while we were in camp and after supper we had a shower or bath and went straight to bed. I roomed with Danny Luger who, like me, loves his kip and our television was always off by 9.30. Under normal circumstances each evening we would meet up for a game of cards or to watch a video, but during those gruelling six weeks the team room sat empty for almost the entire time.

Dave 'Otis' Reddin, my friend and neighbour, was the man responsible for licking us into shape. He has been central to England's success in recent years. When the job of England conditioning coach came up, all the Leicester boys who had been working with him at that time were unanimous in their recommendation: 'Get Otis.' The main thrust of his programme is to get you to go absolutely flat out from the outset. When I was younger we were always told to leave something in the tank so you could finish strongly, but Otis has demolished that idea. He wants you on your knees by the end. He wants you to leave nothing on the pitch when you walk off it. The Duke of Wellington said that the Battle of Waterloo was won on the playing fields of Eton, and in the same vein you could say that our World Cup was won on the playing fields (and gym) of Pennyhill Park, Bagshot. When the final went into extra time, it became as much about fitness as it was about skills and heart.

The organisation of that England camp was an achievement in itself – nothing was left to chance, no detail of our preparations was considered too small or trivial. When we got into full contact training, we were all made to take ice baths afterwards. We were a little suspicious about these baths when they were first introduced – what next, a mud facial and some body brushing? – but we very quickly came to understand their importance to our recovery. Every time you run or lift weights or exert yourself in any way you tear thousands of little fibres and that's the main reason you are stiff after heavy exercise. Ice baths stop the microscopic bleeding and so there is less stiffness, and that increases your capacity to train at maximum intensity. You don't have to wait until the body has healed before you can go at it full pelt again. In January and February, when you have just walked back into the dressing room from the cold, the prospect of an ice bath is not inviting, but that summer it was roasting and we were virtually diving into them, especially the day a record was set for the highest British temperature. Otis, though, is not a stickler for textbook methods and he uses his initiative and imagination to get the most out of us. There were a couple of occasions when it was so hot we were all just about to drop on the training field and Otis suddenly appeared with forty Magnums and Cornettos. They might just as well have been sent from heaven and we tucked into them like kids on a trip to the seaside, as we were on a very strict diet which excluded fat, butter, mayonnaise, chocolates and so on.

I mentioned earlier how I try not to step out of line with a coach out on the training field, preferring instead to address any issues later in the day once tempers have cooled down. But the only time I have broken that habit came at Pennyhill Park on one of the blistering hot days that summer. We were all utterly shattered by our exertions and it was the last session of the day and London Irish had turned up to provide the opposition. The session hadn't gone all that well, and there was a lot of tension and ill-feeling in the air. Dave Alred, the kicking coach, also does a lot of mental work with us, and he called all the backs together at one point and said: 'It's very important for your mental side to kick in and be strong now, lads.' To which I was surprised to hear my voice replying: 'Dave, sometimes your mental shit can just get f***ed.' Everyone looked at me a little pop-eyed and just as Clive Woodward stepped in to tell us all to calm down and behave like grown-ups, we looked over and saw the forwards having a mass brawl with the London Irish lads. Ten minutes later Dave and I were sharing a joke again, but that little episode – my comment and the brawl – give a good insight into the pressures we were putting ourselves under over those few weeks.

By the time we played Wales on 23 August at the Millennium Stadium in the first of three full inter-nationals before heading out to Perth, the squad was in peak condition. The final party had not been picked by this stage and this was seen as a chance for players on the fringes to press their case. Those of us who had toured New Zealand and Australia and played Six Nations were expected to start just one of the games and come on for a brief period in one other. Our second-string team illustrated our great strength in depth when it thrashed the Welsh 43-9 in Cardiff, and then came agonisingly close to pulling off a great win over a full-strength French team in Marseilles, only to be edged out 17-16. The French were lucky, though, because Paul Grayson grazed an upright with a late drop goal attempt and Alex Sanderson crossed the line but failed to touch the ball down properly. A week later our first-choice team hammered the French seconds 45-14, and Clive was finally ready to announce his final squad of thirty.

It's an awful time for some players who have worked flat out for months on end, only to miss out by the finest margin in the final reckoning. On this occasion the unlucky ones included Austin, who had had a tough season with injuries and wasn't considered to be quite ready. In his early days as coach it seemed that Clive liked utility players and there was no better utility player in the land than Austin Healey. But by the time of the 2003 World Cup finals the coach was going for specialists in their positions. For all-round talent and intelligence in reading the game, Austin's up there with any England player of his generation, but if you put him one on one for a specialist position against Cohen,

Robinson, Dawson or Wilkinson, even he would probably admit he came in second. Still, from a personal point of view I felt for him when it was announced and it was sad not to have my old friend on the plane with us. You always need someone to abuse on a long trip, and who better for that purpose than my provocative little friend from Leicester? The other unfortunates to go in the final cull were James Simpson-Daniel, Simon Shaw, Ollie Smith and Graham Rowntree.

Over the next three weeks I thought the management got it right again by heavily scaling back the training and sending us home to be with our families for as much time as possible. The truth is that no matter how strong you are as a squad, there is a limit to how long a group of men can be cooped up together without stresses and tensions starting to emerge. Getting the balance right is vital for a squad's morale and I thought it was spot on to give us time apart, back with our families and friends, for about four or five days a week in that month before we set off. This was also when the decision to make that reconnaissance run to Perth in the summer paid off because it meant that we could delay our departure that little longer. Although we were the last team to arrive in Australia, we settled in as if our Perth hotel was a second home.

As I kissed Caro goodbye and walked out of my front door in Southfields that October morning to meet up with the rest of the squad, her mum was coming in through the gate with her suitcase and I felt a sense of reassurance as I climbed into the back of my taxi. It was an odd cocktail of emotions I experienced at that moment. On the one hand I was nervous about leaving behind my wife, who was now eighteen weeks into her pregnancy; on the other I was thrilled and excited about the biggest adventure of my career – an adventure which I hadn't imagined, around twelve months or so earlier, I'd ever be embarking upon. After Freddie died, for a few weeks I wondered whether I could ever take to a rugby field again. Caro and I have even admitted to each other since that at times we secretly wondered and worried whether the blow of his loss might even tear us apart as a couple. They were dark, dark days during which I had almost lost the will to live. Now, thanks to Caro, my own family, Mrs T, Benny, Austin and all our other friends who helped pick us up, I was back out there again and off to the World Cup finals.

Chapter Nine

O N ENGLAND'S PREVIOUS visit to Perth three months earlier we would have struggled to win a game of crazy golf, never mind the rugby World Cup. After historic wins over the All Blacks and the Wallabies we spent four days relaxing with the same degree of determination, commitment and focus that we had shown on the rugby field during a season of outstanding success. I'm sure Clive Woodward would have been delighted by our continuity, our flexibility and the imagination of our tactics as we switched play from the pub to the casino to the golf course to the vineyard and to the beach. At times, we were breathtaking and I feel honoured to have played my part in what was a fabulous team effort. Phil Larder, our defensive coach, could only have been impressed by the ferocity with which we tackled every pint. Andy Robinson, our forwards coach, could only have stood back and applauded the quality of the scrummaging to get to the bar. Dave Reddin would have been stunned by our fitness levels. If we had had an opposition over that short break, they would have been dragged from pillar to post and then crawled off the pitch shattered by our incredible stamina. I hope I don't sound big-headed here, but quite frankly, we were magnificent that week.

It was all very different when we returned to Perth at the beginning of the October at the start of our campaign to become world beaters of an entirely different nature. We had spent four years battling to establish ourselves as the pre-eminent team of our generation, and it would be a crushing disappointment if we failed to confirm our rise to the top by leaving Sydney seven weeks later without the Webb Ellis trophy tucked away in our hand luggage. All the hard work, all the triumphs, all the great rugby we had played, all the sunshine that had been blown up our backsides – would somehow have felt that little bit less glorious if we proved unable to crown our achievements with the most coveted piece of silverware in rugby's trophy cabinet.

We landed on the Thursday and for the first few days we did precisely nothing as we acclimatised to an entirely different body clock. Training began in earnest on Monday at a very smart private school not far from our hotel and it was as hard as the ground on which it took place. The older guys among us, 'the stiffs' as we called them, spent forty-five minutes every morning loosening up their joints in the swimming pool before the session began.

In the week leading up to our first match against Georgia we were obliged to attend a social function hosted by the mayor of Perth to welcome all the teams in our group. The Uruguayans, the Samoans and the Georgians were all there and so, of course, were our main rivals, the South Africans. I can't say that there was a great deal of mingling or hale-and-hearty backslapping going on between the two teams that evening. ('Oh! Corne and Kobus, old buddies, how tremendous to see you again . . . Might I say how wonderfully fit and well you look. Let me get you another canapé and a glass of wine and we'll catch up on old times . . .') The last time we had been this close to the South Africans they had been punching, gouging and butting us at Twickenham, and eleven months on there was palpable tension as each side studiously avoided the other's company.

Adding a slightly bizarre air to the whole evening, there was a photo shoot at the end in which the whole squad had to pose wearing their World Cup caps, which, quite honestly, were about as silly as headwear gets in these post-medieval days. They were all far too small and we looked like thirty Billy Bunters.

We opened our campaign against Georgia on Sunday and won the match as comfortably as everyone had expected. The final score was 84-6, but we certainly knew that we had been in a game of rugby. The smaller international teams may not have the skills, resources and traditions of the top nations, but you don't have to be especially gifted or funded to be 6 foot 6 inches and 18 stone and to enjoy hurling yourself into opponents. We knew they were going to be tough, but I would go so far as to say that they were as physical a side as any I have ever played against, and they tackled as if their lives depended on it right up to the final whistle. It was perfect preparation for us ahead of what was inevitably going to be a head-on collision with the Boks the following week.

The only blow for England was the loss of our lock Danny Grewcock who broke his toe in the warm-up when Ben Cohen trod on it. (Danny turned out to be the only guy in our squad who had to be replaced in the World Cup, which was a huge testament to our back-up staff.) I scored two tries that evening but almost lost one of my testicles in scoring the second and I had to make a public inspection of my tackle when I got to my feet just to make sure everything was still where it should have been. The Georgian who gave me the pain-ful tug must have misunderstood the instructions from his coach when he was told to try and get hold of the ball in the tackle.

Afterwards the Georgians came into our dressing room and asked to have their pictures taken with us as souvenirs – and that, I can assure you, is the one and only time that has ever happened to me at the end of an international rugby match. It's difficult to imagine, say, the All Black Andrew Mehrtens or South Africa's Joost van der Westhuizen popping their heads round the door and asking for a quick snap with Johnno or Lawrence Dallaglio.

It was the day following the Georgia game when I was playing pool, that Caro called to tell me that she was being admitted to hospital immediately, having gone into pre-labour, just as she had done with Freddie at exactly the same stage of the pregnancy. I plunged once again into a horrible, gut-churning state of anxiety.

Should I stay or should I go? That was the nub of my dilemma. If it meant missing the World Cup, then so be it. I spoke to Clive Woodward that evening and he was magnificent. For him it was a no-brainer. 'Do what you have to do. This is just a World Cup, it's not family,' he said. 'Unless you need to go right now, I'm going to book you on every plane out of here so that you can leave at a moment's notice.' I decided to wait until the morning when I hoped my own mind and the general picture would both be a bit clearer. But it was a further shock to discover that Caro was in intensive care drugged to the eyeballs after undergoing an emergency operation which involved inserting a suture to try and keep the cervix closed. Caro had been administered four different drugs, including antibiotics to kill an infection which had developed, as well as some very powerful anti-contraction drugs which make your heart race and the sweat pour off you in torrents. She was passing in and out of consciousness and had also had a violent reaction to another of the drugs which made her vomit up everything and forced the doctors to ply her with a second round of drugs. She was, in short, not in the best of nick that Tuesday. Her own life was not in danger right then, I was told, but the pregnancy was in serious difficulty.

It was the doctor, Mark Johnson, who informed me of what was going on, and I will remain indebted to him for the rest of my days for the cool-headed, sensible advice that he gave me over that terrible week from 12,000 miles away. Faced with the dilemma of whether I should abandon the World Cup – even temporarily – I needed to know the hard facts so that I could gauge the gravity of the situation and decide whether or when I should fly home. All week he gave me frank and precise updates on the condition of Caro and the baby. Caro's mum, Mrs T, also played a blinder that week. She was completely in control of the situation and it was a great reassurance for me to know that she was at Caro's hospital bedside while I was trying to prepare myself for one of the biggest rugby games in England's history.

I barely spoke to Caro all that week because she was off with the fairies in a drug-induced cloud cuckooland while the babe in her womb was blissfully unaware of the desperate battle to keep him (or her) alive and I was 12,000 miles away wandering around in a bit of a daze myself. The chances of the baby's survival yo-yoed all week but by Thursday everything had stabilised and we took the decision that I would play in Saturday's match and then fly home on Sunday and play it by ear from there. I don't care what Clive Woodward does to me in the future but I owe him a lifetime's thanks for the support he gave me at a time when six years of his hard graft were about to reach an extremely critical point. When I told him I wanted to fly back, there wasn't even a flicker of disappointment on his face. On the contrary. 'If, assuming we get there, we don't see you until the quarter-finals or later, then so be it,' he said. 'There are priorities in life.'

I didn't tell anyone else in the squad about the problems back home, but those who knew me well may have guessed by my unusually quiet and low-key attitude that something unpleasant was brewing. I'm normally fairly vocal out on the training ground and around the camp, but that week I moped about looking a bit haunted. I trained, I ate, I sat by the phone in my room and I slept.

There was, meanwhile, great excitement around the squad as we braced ourselves for the biggest group match of the tournament, a match which had dominated the thoughts of both sides for over a year. 'We'll see you in Perth,' Krige had declared after the Battle of Twickenham, and now the moment had arrived. England had a serious injury problem in the build-up to the match with Richard Hill sidelined with a hamstring pull, scrum-half Matt Dawson ruled out and his two possible replacements, Andy Gomarsall and Kyran Bracken, both struggling to be fit. The Bath number nine Martin Wood flew out as a precaution as did Austin, prompting Clive to quip: 'The bad news is that Austin is flying out, the good news is that he'll probably be flying straight back home again.'

Our training sessions that week were almost savage in their intensity because everyone was keenly aware of the importance of victory. It wouldn't have made the World Cup impossible had we lost and over the previous eighteen months we had shown that we were capable of rising to any challenge, but we would have lost some of the incredible momentum we had built up in that time. In addition, we would have been forced to take the far harder route to the latter stages of the competition, just as we had had to do following our defeat by New Zealand four years earlier. The press were all over us that week, with everyone expecting a bloodbath similar to Twickenham the previous autumn. I did my best to avoid the press that week just in case someone said: 'How's Caro getting on at home?' I'd been trying to keep a lid on my emotions all week, but there was always a chance my anxieties could come flooding out.

I've always found it difficult to eat on the day of a game, which is something you normally do about two and a half hours before kickoff. Many players are the same, especially on the day of particularly significant matches like the South Africa game – even Martin Johnson. I remember sitting with Johnno in the dining room before a big Six Nations match, the nerves were churning and we were pushing our food around our plates without much interest in eating any of it. We weren't saying all that much as we thought about the challenge ahead when Johnno looked up and said: 'Why the hell we put ourselves through this, I just don't know.' The match against the Boks was an evening kickoff, which is the worst of all possible scenarios because it means you have to spend a whole day hanging around trying not to let the nerves get to you. In an ideal world I'd like to play all internationals and big club matches straight after breakfast so you could just get up, shower, throw back a fruit shake and, with your eyes barely open, run out down the tunnel and get on with it.

We had not lost to South Africa since the contro-versial 'video replay' defeat in Pretoria almost three and a half years earlier and we knew that if we played as we had over the previous twelve months or so we were likely to win. But there was always the X factor and four years earlier the once-in-a-lifetime display of Jannie de Beer had taken what had started as a largely well-balanced match and swung it very decisively in South Africa's favour. You never knew what might happen. Jonny Wilkinson could be injured in the first five minutes, Martin Johnson could be sent off . . . you just never knew what might happen.

The stadium, packed to the rafters with English support, was a fabulous sight and sound. At this stage we simply had no idea of the level of interest back home throughout the tournament, but if the atmosphere in Perth that evening was any indication, we knew that there would be a good few pubs and bars jumping and buzzing with excitement 12,000 miles away in England.

It was, just as everyone had expected, another immensely physical game. How could it have been otherwise? But on this occasion the Boks played it fair and square, and if there was any sly stuff going on it was no more or less than any other match in which two teams throw themselves at each other in a controlled frenzy. I picked up a neck-cum-shoulder injury in that game which I wouldn't properly shake off until March. I had my head over the ball trying to protect it when their lock Victor Matfield, who had a storming game, absolutely cleaned me out in the first half. It was a totally legal challenge but it was very, very robust and that just about summed up the essence of the contest.

I remember that the South Africans had made a decision to speak Afrikaans during the match – I had only ever heard them speak English in our previous encounters – and it was strange lying at the bottom of a ruck listening to them all jabbering away in this alien tongue. Throughout the game, standing at inside centre, I could hear their veteran scrum-half Joost van der Westhuizen screaming encouragement to his forwards like a banshee. What a warrior. You had to admire the man. This was his third World Cup, after heaven knows how many knee reconstruction operations, and there he was still throwing himself into the fray like a demon.

Shortly before the interval I made a dreadful mistake. It was 6-6 at this stage and I was standing behind the posts as their fly-half Louis Koen, who was having a shocker, lined up a penalty, having already missed two. He missed this one as well and as I caught his wayward ball I turned to the linesman David McHugh and said: 'I can't believe this guy has missed another kick!' and with that I tossed the ball to Jonny Wilko for the dropout, thinking nothing of it. Then the whistle blew and I realised in one dreadful, heart-freezing moment that I'd forgotten to touch the ball down behind our try line. That's not a schoolboy error, it's pre-school toddler group. What a prat! They had a scrum 5 yards from and directly under our posts, the best position in the house from which to score a try because you can go either way and the defence has to spread itself thinly. It's not quite the equivalent of a penalty in football but it's better than a free kick on the edge of the box.

None of the England boys seemed aware of what had happened – at least, nobody said anything or shot an evil look at me. It was TCUP time: just get on and do the next job. For what happened next I will be in eternal debt and gratitude to our scrum-half Kyran Bracken.

How he was even on the pitch that day God only knows, because his back was in a terrible state and he had had to wear a corset for most of the week and still couldn't touch his toes at the start of the match. It was their put-in, the ball shot to the base of their scrum and it seemed fairly obvious that they were going to do a back row move and come open to where I was defending. At that moment I was thinking that not only was I the one who gave away the incredibly daft penalty but I was also going to be the last line of defence and I had better damn well make the tackle. Just as these thoughts were rushing through my mind, I saw Kyran dive in and tap-tackle Van der Westhuizen and nick the ball. Seconds later the ball was landing somewhere in row Z halfway up the pitch. I was tempted to run over and mob Kyran, but I think I had made quite a big enough arse of myself for one passage of play. Had they scored a try and a conversion and gone in 13-6 up at the interval, the momentum would have been with them and we would have faced a battle to turn it around in the last forty minutes.

At half-time I apologised for my blunder but it was brushed aside and we were urged to forget, move on and concentrate on what lay ahead. The second period was about fifteen minutes in and Jonny had edged us six points clear with a couple of penalties when I found myself involved in the decisive moment of the encounter with a chance to redeem myself. From a scrum in the middle of the park, Lewis 'Mongo' Moody, playing in place of the hamstrung Hill, set off like a demented cheetah in an effort to charge down a kick by the hapless Koen. Alert as always to nicking a try, being the 'goal-hanger' that I am and knowing also that Mongo was a man perfectly at ease with the world when applying his face to a flying boot, I set off at a canter behind him waiting to feed off any scraps.

Sure enough, Mongo lunged at Koen, smashed down the kick and the ball squirted backwards towards the South African line. By now I've got a nice 15-yard start on everyone else – believe me, with my pace I needed it – and I knew that if I stayed cool then I was going to score. The pitch was very dewy by this stage because it was quite late at night and, figuring that the ball would skid along the surface quite smoothly, I aimed to summon up every last iota of my modest football talent and side-foot it over the line. The pitch had an enormous deadball line and so I had a massive target to hit. I could hear the chasing pack like a stampede behind me as I took a couple of touches with my boot and the ball bobbled into the zone. Now all I had to do was touch it down. I say 'all' but that was a more difficult challenge than it may have looked because the ball could veer off at a weird angle leaving me groping thin air unless I got it right. I remembered Alex Sanderson in Marseilles six weeks earlier when he missed out on a try by snatching at the ball and so I waited for the moment when the ball was bouncing downwards and there was no chance of it catching me out, and then I fell on it with the breath of fifteen Springboks heaving at my back.

There was a good photograph shot of me as I stood up holding the ball in celebration, but then Mike Tindall turned up, leaned over my shoulder and stuck out his massive tongue. In that one instant my moment of glory turned into an Alice Cooper album cover. Jonny converted to make it 19-6 and you could feel that the game was over from that point. Two mighty forces had collided and there was little in it before we breached their defence and the great spirit they had shown slowly seeped away. Jonny nailed two more kicks and we returned to the dressing room 25-6 winners.

After about fifteen minutes Clive pulled me aside and suggested that now might be a good time for him to tell the boys about my predicament. He summoned the whole squad and said: 'I know you all want to abuse Will for not putting the ball down in the first half, but he's off home for a bit and we don't know when or even if he'll be back with us . . .' To a man every player in the squad wished Caro and I good luck. That was a good moment. Whether I would be back to join them for the rest of the tournament was now in the lap of the gods.

The plan was that we would tell the press just before I flew out the following morning so that I wouldn't get badgered at the hotel or in the airport. But someone had leaked the news and Peter Jackson from the *Daily Mail*, who seems to find out everything, came up to me and his first question was: 'Is Caro all right?' I knew he knew, but I blanked it and said, 'Everything's fine, thanks.' Stephen Jones of the *Sunday Times* had apparently got hold of the story, too – almost certainly from a Harlequins source, I discovered later – and being a fairly tight pack of friends, the rugby reporters often share their information.

That night I went out for a quiet drink with Ben Fennell and his wife Amy and we were sitting at the back of a fairly busy bar when my mobile rang. It was Nick Keller, my manager, and he said: 'Put down your drink, get in a taxi and get back to the hotel. The story's in all tomorrow's papers. I know you are just having a quiet pint but it ain't going to look very good if a tabloid snapper gets you slumped over a glass in a downtown Perth bar. It could be taken out of context.'

He was absolutely right and seconds later we were out on the pavement. We couldn't find a taxi anywhere, so Ben flagged down a passing car, gave the driver about £100 in Australian dollars for a ten-minute journey and asked him to drive me back to the hotel. The bloke looked at me as I climbed into his car as if he had just woken up and found himself starring in an episode of *The Dukes of Hazard*. Before setting off in the morning I talked to the press and told them the full story. They've always been pretty good to me and I have never been badly turned over by them. At the end I asked them to urge their editors to leave Caro and me alone for the next week or so and that we would return the favour by keeping them informed of what was going on. I could trust the rugby reporters, but it was the newshounds back home I was a little anxious about.

When I went to check in at the airport, Clive Woodward, bless that man, had booked me into first class which meant I had my own bed and duvet, and, together with the sleeping pill from the team doctor, I would arrive in England feeling reasonably refreshed. It was my birthday that Monday when I went home to Southfields, dropped my bags and had a shower before setting off to the hospital. I have never had a rock 'n' roll, paparazzi moment where I've ended up chinning a photographer and smashing his camera, but I came very close to it that morning as I hurried to get off to see Caro. When I sat down behind the wheel of my car I looked up to see a photographer snapping away at me with his car rammed right up to my bumper and it took me about five minutes to get clear.

I had no idea what to expect as I headed up to Caro's room in the hospital and it was with painful memories resurfacing that I made my way through the corridors of the Chelsea & Westminster to see her. If, however, I had done nothing more than walk in and straight back out again and then boarded the next flight back to Australia, my journey around the world would have been worth it. Caro was sitting up and looking incredibly well. She had spent most of the last week either unconscious, or semi-conscious, sweating profusely, pale as a ghost and with a heart racing at two hundred beats a minute at times. Although it remained touch and go as to whether the operation would prove to be a success and her cervix would hold tight for the duration of the pregnancy, she looked far happier and more relaxed than I could have possibly imagined. I would miss the game against Samoa at the weekend, and have to battle to get my place back in the starting XV, but I knew I had done the right thing by coming home for a week. I trained twice a day at the gym in between my time at the hospital, and also watched all the World Cup games each morning which felt a bit weird.

I flew back to Australia on Saturday, feeling infinitely better about the world than I had done a week earlier. It was still going to be nerve-racking right up to the birth itself, but by the time I boarded my flight the situation was no longer critical. When I got off the plane at Singapore, I turned on my mobile and there was a message from Caro telling me to get to the television as quickly as possible because England were in danger of losing to Samoa in Melbourne. She must have just left the message because I watched from the airline lounge area as Balshaw and Vickery piled over for tries to seal victory. What I hadn't really taken on board was a substitution cock-up involving Dan Luger which led to us having sixteen men on the field for a brief moment just before the final whistle; when I rejoined the squad a full-blown row about the incident had erupted and there was a danger we could be docked points and be forced to take a different route through the knockout stages.

The England coaches have always been very strict on the smallest details of a match and one of the rules is that at no point should we ever be playing with fourteen men. So when Mike Tindall went off with cramp on the far side of the pitch, Otis, who was running the bench, received orders from Clive up in the stands to send on Dan Luger. The touchline official, rightly, wouldn't let Dan on until there was a break in play and there followed an altercation which ended with Otis sending him on regardless. Whether the officials are right or not, you have to do what you are told and Otis admitted his error afterwards. When Dan ran on, Tindall returned to the pitch at almost exactly the same time and for a few seconds we had a player too many on the park until the coaches spotted the mistake. The fact that the score was 35–22 to us when the incident took place and there were just thirty-five seconds left on the clock was irrelevant. It was a balls-up and it was right that we should be punished. To the glee of the Australian press the incident also sparked another round of Pommie-bashing. What seemed like a trifling incident at the time soon became a major problem and the press were swarming all over us. It was open day on 'arrogant' England again.

There had been a few sniggers in the rugby world when it was announced that a QC, Richard Smith, would be joining the England squad for the tournament, but his invitation was justified in this episode as he set about applying his expertise to making sure England were not punished too severely. Many of our rivals were saying that we should have been docked points and some of the more comical Australian commentators even suggested that we should be thrown out of the tournament altogether, but in the end we received a £10,000 fine and Otis was given a two-match touchline ban.

After the Samoa game the squad flew up to the Gold Coast where we would remain for the quarter-final, which would probably be against a rapidly improving Wales, if we beat Uruguay as expected and results in the other group went to form. This was another of the rewards of winning our group because, had we lost to South Africa and finished runners-up, we would have ended up crisscrossing the country in aeroplanes and thus felt that much more stress and strain as a result.

On our arrival there on Monday (27 October) the management immediately ordered us out to have a night on the town. They didn't actually say 'Go and get drunk, boys', but they were very keen that we relaxed. That was great management I thought because, with no disrespect to the Uruguayans, our next opponents, there was not a cat in hell's chance that we were going to lose that match and the back-up staff felt it was important that we had at least a small amount of downtime in what was a long, punishing campaign. I had just arrived back from England, my body clock was all awry, and so for me it made good sense to have a decent drink and get back into a steady sleeping pattern. Well, that's what Dr Jason Leonard told me anyway.

The following day we had a game of football and I for one couldn't hit a cow's arse with a banjo. I love my football but I'm no Wayne Rooney and in this particular match I was so poor you might have thought I was a Stockport County or Macclesfield Town player on holiday. My own efforts to apply lace to ball were funny enough but there was one particularly comic moment during the kickabout and inevitably, the comedian was Mark 'Ronnie' Regan. On this occasion the butt of his humour was our full-back Josh Lewsey, who for some obscure reason goes by the nickname of 'Tinker'. It was an incredibly windy day and at one point a cardboard box went cartwheeling across the pitch and Ronnie shouted out: 'Oi, Tinker! Quick, your f***ing house is blowing away!'

Perhaps Josh was still smarting from Ronnie's banter when we took the field against Uruguay but something was certainly driving him on as he ran in five tries in our 111–13 victory. In a match when you have the better part of a hundred points on the board, and when you are running at some very angry and humiliated opponents, it is sound advice to offload the ball as quickly as possible in order to avoid getting splattered. Unable to take any points off you, heavily beaten opponents will often settle for a few lumps of you instead, thus avoiding injury becomes the main priority in these games. While the backs were playing pass the parcel with the ball against Uruguay, our monsters up front were getting stuck into the dirty work. They were loving it, and if that's the way they got their laughs on a rugby pitch, you weren't going to find me suggesting it was about time they let the rest of us have a go, too. At each restart following a try the Uruguayans kicked the ball long on and whoever caught it would find himself a few seconds later being pulverised by a fleet of South American bulldozers. Like the Georgians, the one thing that the Uruguayans were very good at was tackling. Most of the time it was Lawrence who shouldered this ball-carrying task, but midway through the second half, Iain Balshaw screamed for the ball – I can only presume with a view to setting off on a mesmerising sprint to score the try of the competition. It all was going very nicely to plan until, roughly two seconds after launching his glory run, he got completely wiped out under a pile of Uruguayan brawn and had to be stretchered off. I came on as a replacement for him, and as an old family friend I felt gutted for him because it seemed as if he would be ruled out for the rest of the tournament (in the event, he would see a slice of the action right at the end).

The other significant episode of the game came when our flanker Joe Worsley was sin-binned for a high tackle and as he left the field acknowledged the applause of the fans who were giving him a standing ovation. The following morning we woke up to headlines reminding us, as if we needed to be, that we were a bunch of arrogant bastards. Joe expressed his regret afterwards, but it was just sheer absent-mindedness on his part. The man hasn't got a nasty or arrogant bone in his body.

After the match we moved down from our Gold Coast base into an extremely good hotel in the centre of Brisbane to prepare for our quarter-final clash with the Welsh, who finished their group D games by giving the All Blacks a mighty scare before going down 53-37. They put the frighteners on us, too, as it turned out, and there is no doubt that we came extremely close to losing a match which eventually finished 28-17 in our favour. I thought the Welsh played brilliantly and had they been just a little more streetwise and savvy it could have been them lining up against the French in the semi-final because we were definitely there for the taking that evening.

We knew Wales could hurt us – they were superb against New Zealand – but we were surprised by how hard they came at us and they hit us with two tries in the first half from Stephen Jones and Colin Charvis. The first came from a rare mistake by Tinds when he kicked the ball straight down Shane Williams' throat on the wing. Standing in Williams' way was our lock Ben Kay who, for all his other qualities, is not necessarily the man to whom you would go first to stop a winger half his size, twice his speed and with twice the skills. Williams went around big Ben like a speedboat around an oil tanker and then shot upfield before Jones went over to complete a fabulous, sweeping move. (When he was brought up on his missed tackle in the post-match analysis, Ben said: 'How can I have missed a tackle when I didn't get within fifteen yards of him?')

Charvis then went over from a lineout and when the half-time whistle blew, we were 10-3 down and, strangely for that squad, we all looked and felt absolutely shattered. There was an amusing moment when we were heading down the tunnel to the dressing rooms and two of the Welsh fans crowding over the walls started screaming abuse at me: 'Rodney Trotter, you're f***ing shit, you are. Rodney Trotter, you are going to win fuck all . . .' Lawrence Dallaglio was behind me and started peeing himself with laughter at this and I could hear him chuckling, 'That is very, very funny.' The Welsh lads then clocked him laughing and turned on him, saying: 'As for you f***king Dallaglio, you are f***ing shite as well. The Welsh boys are going to f***ing kill you.'

We certainly weren't laughing by the time we reached

the changing room and Clive set about reorganising us to try and turn it around. He decided to take off Danny Luger, who hadn't been at his best, put Tindall on the wing and bring on Catt so that we would have kickers at ten and twelve. It proved to be a tactical masterstroke. Shortly after the break, Jason Robinson made a fabulous burst from the back, his cheeks puffing like bellows as he slalomed at an angle from our left to the far right through the Welsh midfield. At this point in the story I'm tempted to follow the flattering storyline widely reported in the newspapers. As Robbo was weaving his magic, I was about to earn myself heaps of praise for my 'uncanny positional sense' and my nose for how events are going to unfold. Jason was bombing in the general direction of the corner flag, so I started jogging up the touchline on the off-chance that he might somehow manage to work his way through half of Wales and end up somewhere in my vicinity. Suddenly he was in the clear, Welshmen languishing and gasping in his slipstream, and there I was lumbering up on his outside, to take his pass and fall over the line for the try that supposedly swung the match in our favour. 'Uncanny positional sense'? I'd love to claim that, but the truth is I was so totally and utterly exhausted that I was collapsing out on that side of the pitch, miles from where I should have been, and it was just a superb coincidence that I happened to be passing through the area when Robbo came flying from nowhere.

Jonny Wilko then slowly turned the screw with a string of kicks to goal and although the Welsh hit back with a third try through Martyn Williams, we had just enough left in the tank to hold out. I had to go off after about sixty minutes, to be replaced by Stuart Abbot, because I was so shattered I could barely put one foot in front of the other. I was so drained that the doctors considered putting me on a drip and after the match I slept almost solidly for three days before I had fully recovered. All the travelling and the events of the past couple of weeks had caught up with me and we had also put in a massive week's training in the build-up.

We had looked extremely jaded against the Welsh and it was to the credit of the management that they had the humility to concede they had probably got it wrong that week by overdoing the training at our facilities at Brisbane Grammar School. It was piping hot for much of that week and our exposure to the strong sun sapped all the energy from already tired bodies. After the Wales match they decided to change our training time from the morning to the evening when it would be cooler. This was a mini-masterstroke, not least because the semi-final – and the final, if we were to reach it – were both evening kickoffs and it made sense to attune our bodies to playing at that time of day anyway. From the Wales game onwards, we rested far more than we trained and in the end I think the executive decision to ease up on the practice sessions made all the difference between glory and failure because I am not so sure, judging by that Welsh game, that we would have had enough left in reserve for the final, let alone one that could go to extra-time.

Our defence, so solid for so long, was now a major area of concern and you had to go back a year to find the last match when we conceded more than one try. Defence is crucial. If you don't concede a try in a match, 95 per cent of the time you will win. I can't remember ever losing an international game in which we haven't conceded a try.

Defence is all about organisation, technique and communication. The massive hits you see are spectacular but the real defensive work you don't see or notice: getting into the right position, talking to each other, taking your man down in such a way as to give you the best chance of turning the ball over. By and large you have the ball for about 50 per cent of the time in a match and traditionally all training and tactics focus on that half of the game. The ball is only 'alive', as it were, for about twenty-five minutes of the match and as a back you probably only have the ball in hand for a total of a minute or so in the whole match if you're lucky (unless you are the hooker or scrum-half or a greedy bastard like Austin). The front five probably have it for about fifteen seconds. When Phil Larder explains rugby to you like that, it's so blindingly obvious it slaps you in the face. Why haven't I ever thought of rugby like that in the past?

Phil has played a major part in England's success by opening our eyes about all these hitherto unseen facets of the game and since working with him I have really grown to enjoy defence. I still prefer life with the ball in hand, but in recent years I have enjoyed the challenge not just of the tackle itself but the manoeuvring and reading of the game involved. When I first turned up in an England shirt, everyone said I couldn't defend and there was a large element of truth in that. Even around 2000 I know they were nervous about picking me because of question marks over my defence. But slowly, and thanks largely to Phil Larder, first at Leicester and then with England, I have got better and better at it. By the time of the World Cup semi-final, it was said in the programme I was 'probably the best defensive inside centre in the world'. I take enormous pride in that, because I have always been able to pass and catch.

The media were full of France being the form team of the tournament heading into our semi-final and many were predicting that they were going to do to us just what they had done to New Zealand four years earlier and give us a surprisingly good hiding. We knew they could beat us, too – it's almost tedious to point out that they can beat anyone on their day – but I hope it doesn't sound arrogant to say that not for a minute that week did we think we would lose to the French if we performed close to the high levels we had reached in recent times. We had beaten them in the Six Nations and stuffed their second team in September while our seconds were unfortunate to lose to their firsts by a point in Marseilles. The momentum was all ours; the hex was on them.

The papers were full of bizarre stories contrasting the alleged strictness of our routine with the laid-back approach of the French. There were lots of pictures of them lounging about on beaches and pleasure cruisers while we were apparently cooped up inside our hotel with our caps pulled down over our heads wetting ourselves with nerves. While it is true to say that we didn't spend the whole week necking cocktails and doing karaoke, you'd be stretching it to describe the atmosphere in our Sydney hotel as 'tense' unless by that you mean lying by the pool, going to the cinema or occasionally popping down to the beach or out to a restaurant. By now, however, there were so many thousands of England fans camped outside our hotel that getting a few hundred yards down the road could take you all morning and we were perhaps not as visible as we had been earlier in the tournament.

If there was one great story, or photo opportunity, that the press missed out on that week (thank heavens), it was the sight of the entire England squad training in glorious sunshine wearing full waterproofs. Otis was convinced that it was going to be roasting hot and humid on the day of the match and being the imaginative and unconventional character that he is he wanted us sweating away in hothouse conditions. On the day, of course, it lumped it down with rain and was actually quite cold. Michael Fish, your job is safe.

At this stage of the World Cup, you could have excused us for feeling a little paranoid. Everybody seemed to hate us – and you had to take that as a perverse compliment because why slag off someone you don't fear? For as long as I had been playing with England we had gone out of our way not to sound in the least bit arrogant, we always said nice things about the opposition, we never crowed in victory, nor made excuses in defeat, our fans were brilliant ambassadors and we played some good rugby. But we still got abused wherever we went and, to be honest, we have loved every last insult. We have thrived on it so much that it has become tempting to wander around and really wind people up, just so we could get a face full of abuse back to get us going.

And is there a rugby nation on the planet that hates us more than the French? Or one that we hate more? In the world of international sport, there are two parallel worlds: one is called reality, the other is what you say to the media. Before a match against France we are invariably asked for our views about them and we dutifully reply: 'Lovely country, great food, Napoleon Bonaparte top man, super wines, such flair, Joan of Arc, Thierry Henry etc. . . .' But we're actually thinking:

'subsidies, blockades, Agincourt, dodgy politicians, overboiled vegetables and Sacha Distel'. Likewise, they make similar noises about us in their press conferences down the road, trotting out: '*le grand respect pour l'équipe de la Rose*' and admiration for 'the Houses of Parliament, Winston Churchill, double-decker buses, The Beatles, David Beckham and lovely parks . . .' But they're actually thinking: 'crap weather, Marmite, Benny Hill, overcooked meat, warm beer, appalling trains, hooligans and "Swing bloody Low" . . .'

I'm slightly playing devil's advocate with our French cousins here but the point I'm trying to make is that, in international rugby especially, you have to make yourself hate all your big opponents in order to fire yourself up and feel the importance of a match more keenly. When you look across at your opposite number you want to be seeing a man with horns and a tail, not wings and a halo. You don't want to be buddies with someone when it all kicks off and the boots are flying in. Friendship and rivalry don't really mix in spite of what they might tell you – not, at any rate, in the cut-throat world of international rugby.

In the build-up to the semi-final the French had apparently decided to ditch the customary pre-match diplomacy (and bare-faced lies) about the opposition, and let us know what they were really thinking. You know when you've got the upper hand on a team when not just their press boys but also their coaches and players start lining up to pour abuse on you. It's the last resort of the soon-to-be vanquished. If you can't beat them, insult them. Bernard Laporte, the French coach, boldly announced that the whole world hated the English and Jo Maso, the manager, called our backs 'diesels' and described theirs as 'well-oiled Ferraris'. What planet had he been on? Imanol Harinordoquy, their number eight, who seems to hate us even more than the rest of them put together, came out to inform the world that – go on, have a guess – the England team were a bunch of arrogant so-and-sos. None of us could actually recall having a conversation with Imanol, except to exchange traditional pleasantries at the bottom of the ruck, but there you go, that's modern international rugby for you. Harinordoquy was part of a great back row with Serge Betsen and Olivier Magne but of the three it was Betsen we feared most, the quiet one doing all the hard work on the floor, not the show pony.

After losing their way a little as a team France have improved considerably in recent years and that has been partly down to Laporte ordering them to improve their discipline and partly down to the increase in the amount of cameras around the ground. Which is all a great shame from our point of view because winding up the French had become almost a national sport by the time Brian Moore had finished with them in the mid-nineties. It was simple: you pressed the right buttons, they lamped you and either got sent off or conceded a penalty and England won the match. But they seem to have cut out all that these days, brought some greater pragmatism and structure to their play and are shaping up to be a pretty awesome outfit over the coming years.

The story of our semi-final against them was that they scored an early try when Betsen went over from a lineout and then, to put it into technical language, our forwards beat up their forwards. It was Richard Hill's first game back since pulling his hamstring, and he later said the try was his fault because he should have wrapped up Betsen. It was typical of Richard Hill to try and shoulder the blame, but the truth was that we should have won our own lineout. There was, however, no panic in our ranks when they went in front and we slowly, relentlessly, came back at them and drained their strength and will. It was attritional warfare rather than all-out assault on their lines and as we turned up the pressure, the cracks in their defences inevitably began to appear. Their winger Christophe Dominici was sin-binned for tripping Jason Robinson, but injured himself in the process and never returned to the action. The other wing, Aurelien Rougerie, a fabulous player who could have wreaked havoc if he ever got the ball, was hit by a huge tackle and had to go off. Jonny Wilkinson was the embodiment of composure and accuracy itself as he slotted kick after kick. His opposite man, Frédéric Michalak, the darling of the tournament up until then, simply went to pieces and I imagine that was as poor a game as he's had since he was a schoolboy. Before the match, there had been many comparisons made between Michalak and Wilkinson, but on the day there was no contest. It was a case of the master and the apprentice. Michalak is a fabulously talented player and I'm sure he will have plenty of days in the sun, but he was well and truly wrapped up that evening. Richard Hill, 'the Silent Assassin', showed why he would be many people's first name on the list for a World XV as he harried and hassled Michalak to distraction. Michalak was substituted with about twenty minutes to go, but by then the damage had been done and England were in total control.

As it had been raining steadily all evening, we weren't running the ball as much as we would do in good conditions and I had spent much of the first half chasing kicks or standing in the midfield watching the forwards pummel each other. I wasn't really having a great impact on the game, in short, and as we headed down the tunnel it struck me that this was a type of game perfectly suited to the particular skills of Mike Tindall, who had started on the bench that day. Tinds is known as 'the Salmon' in the England camp because there is no one better at jumping for the high ball and when Clive Woodward asked me, as the so-called 'captain of attack', whether I had any thoughts on the game, I said I had no problem if he took me off and put Mike on in my place.

I didn't want to volunteer myself out of a World Cup semi-final but I felt I should tell it as I saw it. It was as a team, as a unit, not as a collection of individuals, that we had forged our success over the previous years. There had always been a very selfless, all-for-one, one-for-all spirit in the England squad under Clive and I felt I had to put my hand up and be honest. It was just a question of getting to the final, whatever it took, even if that meant playing Jason Leonard at fly-half and me at hooker. Clive, however, ignored me, as people tend to, and as it turned out Tinds was soon on the pitch anyway because Mike Catt hobbled off with a calf injury.

This match was all about the forwards and the two fly-halves, and ours were superior in both instances. Victory was never really in doubt once you saw that our front eight, magnificent to a man once again, were almost smiling as they set about their friends from across the Channel and you knew it was well and truly over for France when Betsen kicked Matt Dawson in the head in the second half. Daws needed stitches in the wound, but it was Betsen, not normally a dirty player, who needed his head examined because, in one stupid act, he effectively killed off any lingering hopes of a French recovery.

In all the post-match analysis the general French reaction seemed to be: 'We are not making excuses, but the rain really made a difference . . .', the implication being that had it been dry their Ferraris would have sped and swerved around our lumbering diesels — those lumbering diesels being, if I may remind you, Dawson, Wilkinson, Greenwood, Catt, Tindall, Lewsey, Cohen and Robinson. Do us a favour. First of all a team has to get the ball in order to be able to run with it and there was no chance our white orcs on steroids were in any mood to be sharing it that night. Secondly, I think Clive Woodward got it just about right when, a couple of months later, it was put to him for the umpteenth time that the rain had made all the difference that night in Sydney. He replied that, yes, indeed, the rain had a big impact and that if it had been dry the French would have been stuffed even more comprehensively.

So the diesels returned to their hotel for a week to prepare for the final while the well-oiled Ferraris were driven to the airport and flown back home for some emergency servicing. Normally it's the gaskets that have blown with the French but on this occasion I gather there was a problem with the choke.

Chapter Ten

W E NOW STOOD just one match away from fulfilling the dream we had not dared dream over the previous four years and if there was one man, among the dozens, who had done more than any other to get us into this position, it was Clive Woodward. He had taken a lot of flak after the 1999 World Cup, and there was no question he was vulnerable for some time afterwards, but far from taking a cautious, steady-as-she-goes approach and return England to the narrower type of rugby we used to play, he became even more expansive and ambitious in his vision, and even more demanding and bullish with anyone he thought stood in his way, and that included his employers at the RFU, many of whom were keen to show him the door and kick him up the pants on the way out.

His personal story is a fascinating sub-plot in England's quest to win the World Cup. When he first took the job in 1997, he also owned and ran a very successful business. After the 1999 failure, he received a letter from an Irishman claiming he knew why England were not as successful as they should be and that, if we wanted to know the reason why, he was to get on a plane and meet his correspondent in a pub in Dublin. Most people would have chucked the letter in the bin, but being a man prepared to try anything, Woodie went to Ireland and met the man, who told him he could never be totally focused on his job as head coach while he also had his own business and was financially independent. Clive saw the sense and sold his business shortly afterwards.

How many people would have done that?

In his first two years in charge Clive had hired some of the best specialist coaches in the world but he wanted to bring in even more so that there was not a single area of our preparation that went neglected. When we landed in Perth for the start of the 2003 finals, there were nineteen back-up staff on the plane including our own personal chef, a QC, a vision coach, a media liaison officer and a throwing coach. They were all top-class people, but they were all being paid for by the RFU and if we had failed to return home without the trophy in November, there would have been cries of 'What a waste of money!' echoing down the corridors of Twickenham for years to come. Once again, Clive had put his head on the block and, although it would have been very unfair, his head would have been the first to roll in the trials, judgements and executions that would inevitably follow.

For me, the man can do little wrong, and if in years to come he ever needs a favour from me for himself or his family, he need only pick up the telephone any time of the day or night and ask. He's been nothing but good news for me since he gave me my first cap. I have earned more than fifty caps under him, won a World Cup under him, he stuck by me when Freddie died, he stuck by my wife and me when she looked like losing our second child, his wife went to see my wife in hospital when I was 12,000 miles away, he stuck by me when I wasn't playing in Leicester's first team, and he has been extremely generous in his support of the charity work Caro and I have done since Freddie's death. The list goes on. Once in a while we've had our disagreements about tactics and strategy, but Clive encourages open conversation and feedback from all around him and what is said always stays behind closed doors. He lives by the strict principles he sets down for the rest and he nurtures and protects his players. Have you ever heard him slag off a player or coach in public? You won't hear me slag off Clive Woodward in public or in private.

By the time we had beaten France to reach the final, most of Clive's doubters and critics had long been won over, but there were conditions attached to the admiration. Yes, England had played some fabulous rugby in the last three years. Yes, England had beaten all-comers to become the world's unofficial number one team. Yes, he had proved himself to be a great tactician, man manager and organiser. But what would it all mean if we went back to England with nothing but losers' medals to show for it all? The hard work could be blown in eighty minutes.

The press and fans were all over us in the week leading up to those eighty minutes and we couldn't walk outside our Manly Pacific hotel in Sydney without being swamped like The Beatles at the peak of their fame. It was crazy. If you went out of the front door it would be an hour before you went anywhere. We ate our meals on the first floor of the hotel and regardless of whether it was breakfast, lunch or supper, there was always a sea of red and white ebbing and flowing beneath us. Jonny Wilkinson was mobbed so badly when he walked out of reception that he took to creeping out of the back door wearing dark glasses and with his collar turned up and his cap down – he couldn't have drawn more attention to himself if he had worn a Mr Chuckletrousers clown uniform and gone around on stilts singing 'Ain't nobody here but us chickens'.

At this stage, though, we still had no notion of the scale of the excitement and the support back home. We knew we were making a bit of a splash, but it was not until we were engulfed by a tidal wave of fans at Heathrow on our return that we fully understood the level of interest there had been throughout the tournament. Caro certainly was in no position to gauge the mood of the country because she could see or hear no further than the four walls of her hospital room. I spent most of that last week asleep or on the phone home and two days before the match Caro gave me the best possible news when she told me that her operation had proved so successful that they were allowing her to go home the following day. A month earlier we had been informed, at the worst point, that the baby had about a one in five chance of surviving, but now Caro would be settling down on our sofa at home to watch the World Cup final, happy in the knowledge that the odds had shortened significantly. It had been an incredible turnaround, thanks in great part to the magnificent team at the hospital, and I would now be able to take the field on Saturday with as light a mental load as I had been carrying since arriving in Australia.

I was, meanwhile, slightly worried that I might have sown a seed of doubt in Clive's mind when I had volunteered to go off against France and at the start of the week he said to myself, Catty and Tinds that three into two didn't go and that he'd let us know which of us would start the final when he'd had a good think and made his mind up. When he finally pulled me aside and told me I was in, my emotion was two parts relief and one part joy. Clive also went for Tinds instead of Catty, figuring that his greater power would be more effective against the equally bullocking Stirling Mortlock who had played a blinder in Australia's superb, unexpected victory over New Zealand in the other semi.

The Australian press were slightly disorientated by now. After the Wallabies scraped a 17-16 win over Ireland in the quarter-finals, the media had turned their guns away from England and on to their own boys. They had called for the head of everybody they could possibly think of in connection with the team, but they were now unanimous in their opinion that the Wallabies were, in fact, one of the great teams of all time and heroes to a man after their truly titanic win over the All Blacks. 'We're So Proud' ran one headline. The New Zealanders, by contrast, came in for a barrage of abuse from all sides, not least from their own people. They had given the impression for months and years that, when it really mattered, they were going to blow everyone else away and that they had nothing to learn from anyone, least of all any of the Northern Hemisphere countries. Now, just as they had been in 1999, 1995 and 1991, they were on a plane home without the trophy.

I'd like to be able to tell you that the England squad did something incredibly special and interesting on the day of the most important rugby match of our lives, such as sacrifice a stray dog to the gods of rugby out by the hotel swimming pool or attend a chanting and meditation ceremony led by our high priests, Phil Vickery and Trevor Woodman. But in fact it was all very mundane and my day was not untypical. I rose fairly late, had some breakfast, watched a video of

Scarface, had a late lunch, returned to bed, went to the final team meeting and then got on the coach to take us back to the Olympic Stadium. There was an incredible buzz about the place – how could it be otherwise with a screaming mob of England fans on our doorstep? – but, if anything, we were trying to blank it all out in an effort to stay calm and focused and avoid being over-whelmed by nerves. Nor was there anything especially dramatic about that last team get-together and Woodie's final words were simple, basic messages, sound common sense rather than anything Churchillian. The general upshot of his talk was that we were to leave nothing on the training ground and then nothing in the changing room once the game was underway. But above all we were to enjoy it, he added. It was a World Cup final, for heaven's sake.

I have never seen a video recording of the 2003 World Cup final and so my memories of the immediate build-up, the match itself and its aftermath remain raw and pure, undistorted by subsequent analysis and revision. I'm going to recount it to you as I remember it, image by image, moment by moment, and I will recall it in 'real time', so to speak, to try and get across the immediacy and excitement of the occasion. If you are reading this book, it is a reasonable supposition that you would have seen the 2003 World Cup final as and when it happened, you would have read all about it in the newspapers and discussed it with like-minded enthusiasts. The only fresh input I can bring to the party is to relate it to you as I saw, felt and lived it there and then on the day.

After the final team meeting we leave the hotel and there are still thousands of fans causing a happy commotion outside, screaming, singing and backslapping. It is fairly quiet on the bus. There's not much chat, but Tinds' compilation CD is playing and most of us are alone with our thoughts. I'm sitting next to Matt Dawson as normal. A light drizzle is falling. The eight players not involved, together with most of the back-up staff, have already left for the stadium. All eight – Joe Worsley, Mark Regan, Julian White, Andy Gomarsall, Paul Grayson, Stuart Abbott, Dan Luger and Simon Shaw – have been superb throughout the tournament and you feel a twinge of sympathy for them that they cannot be directly involved in the action.

In the plush changing room we all have our own named lockers with individual seats. Reg the kitman has laid it all out, fifteen to one, around the room, and we start to get changed. Dallaglio is wandering around the room getting a bit 'street' and gangster on us, telling us to bring 'Every tool we've got . . . it's gonna be a scrap . . . they've been slaggin' us off . . . digging us out . . . we're gonna f***in' show 'em . . .' He's giving it the full Lenny McLean-style chat. He is pumped. The other forwards don't need much encouragement. They are all doing their Incredible Hulk thing where they turn from perfectly ordinary human beings into rampaging, frothy-mouthed monsters. Soon they will be in the showers smacking each other about. I'm sitting in my cubicle reading the match programme.

The atmosphere during the warm-up is incredible and the fans are being urged to set the world record for the biggest crowd noise ever. Half the crowd is English, and most of them are concentrated at one end. Jonny Wilkinson is a lone figure practising his kicks. Back in the dressing room a few of the coaches are taking it in turns to have a word. Andy Robinson is going around talking to the forwards. Phil Larder has a word with everyone individually about defence, as he always does. 'Keep talking to Tinds, hit low, drive your legs . . .' he tells me.

It's almost time to head out and Johnno calls us together into the centre of the dressing room for his team talk. There is nothing tactical and technical in what he says – the coaches have done all that. 'We've taken some shit, we've been through some shit, but there is no other band of lads I'd rather walk out into a World Cup final than you lot . . .' I know he isn't just talking about throwing away Grand Slam matches or tough tours or criticism in the press – he is talking about all the shit which we have been through as human beings. For me it means Freddie, for Lawrence it may have meant the death of his sister, for Ben Cohen it may have been his dad who was murdered in 2000, for Mike Catt it may have been his daughter who was very ill at birth, for all of us it was Nicky Duncombe . . . There is a great electric charge in Johnno's words – it isn't going to win any poetry awards but it speaks plainly and directly to all of us. We are bonding very tightly at this moment. Johnno doesn't actually need to say anything at all at times like this. You just need to be in his presence. An incredible man. This man spills blood for the cause, he never takes a backward step, he never moans. These next couple of hours are probably the end of the journey for him, I am thinking as I stand in the huddle listening.

There is a knock on the door. It's time to go. We file out into the tunnel. In normal circumstances, the away team walks out followed by the home side, but today we are side by side, just as the footie lads do. I am last out as always and Tinds is in front of me. Mortlock and Flatley are next to us and Tindall turns to them with a big smile and says in his broad Yorkshire accent: 'Now then, fellas, this is why we f***ing play rugby, isn't it? Listen to this noise. Let's get it on. FANTASTIC!' I look across and the two Australians are completely stony-faced. There is no banter coming back from them at all. Are they nervous or do they just think Mike Tindall is a twat? Tindall's sheer joy gives me a big lift at any rate. He is right. This is bloody magnificent. The Olympic Stadium in Sydney, England versus Australia, the world champions against the number one ranked team in the world, a roaring crowd, the pubs and clubs of England stuffed to the rafters, people with their tellies tuned in all over the globe from tiny little Polynesian islands, to Antarctic ice stations to British Army tents in the Afghan mountains. If I can't enjoy this . . .

They get two anthems for some reason, 'Advance Australia Fair' and 'Waltzing Matilda'. (Is that really an anthem?) We have 'God Save The Queen' and they are booming it out around the stadium. I feel the goosebumps and the shivers, but I want 'Land Of Hope And Glory' too. It starts and they score very early on, doing an England on us, when Stephen Larkham – what a player – puts up a perfectly executed cross-kick for Lote Tuqiri, who outjumps little Jason Robinson out on the wing. I have to admit to myself that that is brilliant. Flatley misses the conversion. Maybe he's thinking of Tindall. We get into the game, and start to find some rhythm. It feels good. Jonny slots two penalties and we are 6–5 up. The rain is still falling steadily, but we are throwing it around a bit. It is a massively physical encounter with huge hits all over the pitch. The pace is frenetic and the ball is slippery. There are lots of mistakes. Anything can happen here, I'm thinking. Larkham has a burst mouth and is in and out of the blood bin.

There are ten minutes to go before half-time when Ben Kay only has to fall over the line in the far corner to score, but the big idiot drops the ball for about the first time in a year. I can't believe it. Big Ben just doesn't drop the ball, he's got hands like buckets with adhesive linings. If he had scored, it would have been game, set and match to us. I turn round to see Jonny lying motionless on the ground after putting in another massive tackle. Wilko is the last person to stay down if there is nothing seriously wrong. It looks very, very bad and I'm standing there thinking: 'Get up, Wilko, come on, mate, just get the f**k up. We need you.'

He finally gets up and very soon he is slotting another penalty. Tinds puts in a huge tackle on their captain George Gregan, lifting him off the ground and running him into touch. Then we get the try we deserve and I have a small part to play in it. From a lineout I take the ball into the midfield and get walloped by about four of them, but I manage to keep the ball in the ruck and squeeze it to Daws, who goes blind. Dallaglio takes over and makes a storming run before offloading to Jonny, and I see Robinson flying up on his shoulder. We are in here! No one is stopping Billy Whizz from here. Jonny plants his pass right in the bread basket and Robbo bombs over at the corner and punches the ball into the air. The crowd are going potty. Jonny converts and we are cruising at 14–5 at half-time.

Early in the second half I make my only defensive mistake of the game. Mortlock is charging straight at me and then cuts inside with a small but sharp change of direction. Mortlock had scored a brilliant breakaway try in the semi, and, as I lie on the ground, I'm cursing because I'm thinking I've let him in for another. If a forward misses a tackle more often than not there will be another at hand to clean up but when a back misses one everybody notices. I turn round fearing the worst but there is Jonny – I love that man – cleaning out Mortlock. Danger averted. I am annoyed with myself because I have been tackling well and throwing my head into places I don't normally like to go, like Tuqiri's feet going at 30 mph.

I am not having a spectacular game, but I am doing all the basics right and making a handful of important contributions to the cause like everyone else. Somehow they are back in it at 14-11 after Flatley bags a couple more penalties. These bloody Aussies don't know how to die. We are playing better than them but the points have dried up. There are a few minutes to go and we are almost home when my moment of glory opens up before me. The ball is bobbling towards the Australian line and it's a straight race between me and Matt Rogers. It's about football skills now and if I can just get a boot to it, I'm in for a score no question, but Rogers, credit to him, slides in and beats me to it by inches. There are less than two minutes to go. I turn round to talk to Mike Tindall but he's not there. It's Mike Catt. What's he doing there? I see Tinds getting treatment on the touchline. The big fairy has got cramp.

There are seconds to go when the scrum collapses and the referee Andre Watson awards a penalty to Australia. Oh my giddy aunt. No way. I can really, really do without extra-time. The lungs are burning, the legs are wading through wet cement. Flatley slots it under massive pressure. That is very cool work I'm thinking. It's 14-14. 'How did that happen?' I'm wondering. We are the better team and yet we didn't score a point in the second half. It shouldn't have got anywhere close to extra-time. We should have had it in the bank by half-time and then turned the screw in the last forty, Wilko nailing them with his kicks. You have to respect the Aussies, they're hard-nosed bastards and just keep coming back at you.

Clive comes on to talk to us. Wilko cuts him off halfway through and says: 'Woodie, sorry but I've got to go' and then runs off down the pitch to practise his kicking. The rest of us go into a huddle. Again nothing sophisticated or technical is said: 'Just get the ball, keep it, run hard, give it everything, leave nothing on this field, you've got ten minutes each way and then it will be over. Let's make sure we f***ing win it. We are still controlling this game . . .' It's not so much the message as the communication and the bonding that's important now. There is nothing to learn. We know what to do. It's another band of brothers moment as Johnno urges us to make one final push. I am looking around and I see my team-mates with hands on knees gasping for breath or having a wound bandaged and I'm thinking, 'He was there for me at Freddie's . . . I've been playing with him for ten years . . . Yeah, I'll put my head in where it hurts for him . . .' When you read about happy or unhappy squads in the media, you might think that's just paper talk or psycho-babble, but it's true. It makes all the difference. We may or may not have been the most talented rugby team at the World Cup, but nobody could touch us for camaraderie and looking around at us I just know that was going to carry us over the finishing line. I watch us all being patched up by the back-up staff and I am reminded of the scene in Monty Python's *The Holy Grail* when the knight has all four limbs chopped off one by one, but he's still squirming about on the ground looking for a scrap.

Early in extra-time I am standing next to Flatley at a breakdown and I find myself congratulating him on his penalty to level the scores. 'Fair f***ing play, mate. You've got balls as big as a house. Great kick.' It has to be said now, not later. If I say it afterwards, win or lose, it is meaningless, perhaps patronising. Moments later we have a penalty after Johnno is taken out in the lineout. The boos are deafening as Jonny lines it up, but cool as ever he slots it and we are 17-14 up. The crowd, who have gone quiet in periods because it's so tense, start cranking out 'Swing Low'.

We are scrummaging superbly, but referee Watson doesn't like it and keeps blowing his bloody whistle.

Phil Vickery has been brilliant but Clive takes him off and sends on the maestro Leonard. Very clever move that. I can see Jason immediately having a quiet chat with Watson just trying to take the sting out of the scrum issue so that we don't concede any more pens. I have seen it and heard it all before and there is no one better at schmoozing a ref than Jason Leonard. Everyone likes Jason the Fun Bus with his Essex-boy patter. His conversation with Watson will have been going something like this: ''Ello, Andre. All right, mate? I'm coming on now and if you have any problems with the scrum, you come and have a word with me and I'll sort it for you, guv'nor. You're right, it's been a bit funny, but you've made some good decisions, but don't worry I think we'll be all right now . . . There'll be no penalties in the scrum. If you want, I'll even go uncontested . . .' You don't do that when you've won just a few caps. You do that when you are winning your 113th.

Everyone is going down with cramp and players seem to be coming and going. I notice that Iain Balshaw and Lewis 'Mongo' Moody are on the pitch. Who's gone off? Time is passing very quickly. These twenty minutes of extra-time are the most critical of my career but they are passing in a flash. There are about five minutes to go and I put in a massive tackle on Rogers and we get a penalty because he fails to release the ball. A minute later Watson is blowing up again and giving them a penalty in our half. What the fricking hell was that for? Was it against Johnno or Backie? I have no idea and nor does anyone else it seems. Flatley is under immense pressure again as he sets the ball up and prepares to kick. He does it again and I'm certainly not congratulating the bastard this time around.

A minute or so before the critical moment of the entire tournament, and of our rugby careers, we have Australia almost back in their own twenty-two when the ball is spun back to Rogers to clear. Just as he did against Louis Koen in the South Africa match, Mongo takes off and launches himself at Rogers and he gets so close to charging him down that the Aussie full-back half slices his kick into touch. Mongo has won us some yardage that could prove critical in the dying moments of extra-time. Rogers has got a kick like a cannon and had there been no pressure on him, his kick would probably have been fired deep into our territory and it would have taken a titanic effort for us to get back into a half-decent attacking position. We didn't know it right then, but in my view Mongo had just won us the World Cup.

There is about a minute or so to go, and we are looking at the nightmare of sudden death. Then it all happens very, very quickly, as if someone has pressed the fast-forward button. Steve Thompson launches a long throw to Moody at the back of the lineout and it is absolutely bang on the money. Thommo has copped some abuse over his throwing from time to time but right then, under enormous pressure, he delivers it on a plate. Mongo snaffles it and pops it to Daws. He feeds Catt who gets smashed, but looks after the ball. The ruck is formed and Wilko for some reason is screaming 'Pissflaps! Pissflaps!' (I found out reading the *News of the World* a few months later that 'Pissflaps' is a private call between Daws and Wilko when they are going to go for a drop goal. Thanks for telling us, lads.) Daws, thank God, ignores Jonny and as he steps away from the ruck to pass, Cockbain, their flanker, moves wide and creates a small gap and Daws is through it like a rat down a hole. I'm following him but there is no way in a million years the greedy little bastard is ever passing that ball. He is, in fact, right to hold on to it because the ball is greasy and by doing so he has reduced the chance of a knock-on or a turnover. He goes down in the tackle and I follow straight in to clean out the ball and hold off the gold shirts until the cavalry arrives. We are almost in drop-goal territory now and you can feel the sudden charge of excitement in our ranks. Neil Back is in the scrum-half position, and although he's a great handler of the ball, you really want your scrum-half, your best passer, to be in the slot for this one. Bang on cue arrives Johnno, Captain Marvel himself, who crashes forward and gains Jonny some extra yards and allows Daws to get up and feed the critical pass. At this point I am leaning on an Australian to keep his grubby hands out of the mix.

I'm in the ruck in front and the ball has to sail over my head to get to the posts. Daws has a quick look to get his bearings. This is the critical moment and he doesn't want to screw it. He can't dummy because he will concede a penalty. You are not allowed to con the opposition into offside, but what he does is sheer bloody genius. Instead of dummying, he merely looks up and immediately three of them step offside. Technically, it is a penalty to us but referee Watson doesn't hold out his arm to signal advantage being played. Why not? I wonder. But there is a second advantage anyway because it means the three transgressors have to take a step back, thereby giving Jonny a tiny bit more space to work in. Daws spins the ball back hard and flat to Jonny who drops it on to his right foot (his 'other' foot) and he lets fly with what can only be described as a duck that's just been shot. He's struck plenty of absolute beauties in his time, but this one is ugly and it's tumbling about all over the place in the air. But who bloody cares? The bugger's going through the sticks. Half the crowd is a happy red and white riot. The other is a sea of still gold. There's no real reaction from us at this point. There are about thirty seconds left on the clock. They've come back at us twice already and they could do it again unless we keep our heads. All we have to do is get hold of the ball at the restart and kick it out. Sounds simple but in the 100th minute of this nerve-fraying, leg-cementing, psychedelic, pinball drama of a rugby match, we are taking nothing for granted.

Realistically, there is only time for one more play before the ball goes dead after the hooter sound. But it is still time enough for them. They rush the restart and fail to make the right call, I think. All game they have been stacking their forwards right and kicking to Tuqiri on the left and he's been getting the ball back for them. On this occasion, though, they take it in the direction of their forwards when half of them aren't ready. That is a big balls-up I am thinking. Our prop Trevor Woodman catches it. Under most circumstances, with all due respect to our cousins in the front row, you don't want your props under the ball at a moment like this but Dougie, as he is known for some reason, bags it. At this point I find myself in the fly-half position next to Cattie with Wilko away somewhere on the other side of the pitch. I am not meant to be there because we want Catt, not me, to kick for touch to end the game. If I kick and fail to make touch, the game is still alive. It is essential Catt, who has a great kick, gets this next ball. So for the greatest moment in my rugby career and one of the very greatest moments in my life I go down on all fours like a dog and watch as Catt pummels the ball into row Z, triggering as he does so the biggest party in English sport for almost forty years.

At this point all I want to do is just jump up and down and hug somebody. It's sheer delirium. I'm blind. I could take my clothes off and run around here I'm so bloody hysterical with joy. I turn round and fall into a

PR opportunity that people would pay millions for. There is England's hero, Jonny Wilkinson, and we're hugging away with all the world's cameras trained on us and we're shouting 'World Cup! World Cup!' over and over again. Everyone is hugging everyone and the crowd are going absolutely potty. It's total pandemonium in my head and all around me. I don't know how long Jonny and I are jumping up and down for, but we suddenly have one of those moments when we both seem to realise our hug has been going on quite long enough and it is time to move on.

The emotion is huge. Everything is intense and extreme. One moment I am delirious with joy, the next I'm shedding up and thinking of Freddie. He is meant to be here in the stadium with Caro. But where is he? Is he watching? Is he as proud of his dad as I am of him? It is several minutes before I stop crying. Champagne appears from somewhere. We set off on a lap of honour. I soon get caught up in a very bizarre, potentially ugly scenario, involving my brother Tom, my sister Emma, some New South Wales policemen and a very drunk, fat and angry Australian man. I've got Tom and Emma on to the pitch so that they can pose with me for a picture, but I turn my back for a moment and when I look round again all I can see is Tom's shoes sticking out of the crowd about four rows back. The police think he is a hooligan and have hurled him back into the seats. My brother is a lot of things but one thing he's not is a hooligan. (He's actually a lawyer.) He is absolutely furious, and is shouting blue murder at the police. 'He's my brother, you bastards! I'll have you for common assault and actual bodily harm! I'll have you in court, you animals!' I'm trying to sort it out and calm everyone down, telling Tom to leave it and I'll see him with Mum and Dad and Emma later. I'm also trying to tell the police to cut my brother some slack. Here's my moment of glory and I'm trying to get my brother out of being nicked. While this is all going on, this big Aussie guy is pouring out a torrent of abuse at me, going: 'You f***ing wanker' over and over. Tom turns on him and says: 'What did you call my brother?'

'What's it to you, you Pommie w***er?'

It is getting very ugly indeed, especially for poor old Tom who one minute is out on the Sydney pitch having his picture taken smiling from ear to ear and the next he's upside down in row D and then finds himself face to face with a very big, very drunk man who wants to beat seven shades of shite out of every Englishman he comes across.

Tom, who had had nothing to drink, is going nose to nose with this big Australian when I have to butt in because they are getting ready for the presentation ceremony. I tell Tom to leave it and I will see them all later. 'What was all that about?' I ask myself as I trot back down the pitch.

There is an amusing episode when we are being

called up on to a hastily erected podium for the presentation ceremony and about forty of us step up on to it at once. As we are standing up there we see Lawrence Dallaglio screaming his head off still down on the turf a few yards away, but there is so much noise we can't understand what he is saying. We think he's so happy that he's lost it a bit and is shouting for joy. He is, after all, an emotional man, our Lol. We are waving at him and he is waving at us. Then we realise he is in fact a long way from being happy because his feet are stuck under the podium with about 1,000 stone of rugby player bearing down on them. Prime Minister John Howard then hands out all the medals very, very quickly and he barely stops to say anything to us as he whizzes along the line. It is not that he is being unsporting, but he has been told to hurry in order to meet the tight television scheduling.

We all get a roar from the crowd as the medals are dished out. Jonny and Clive both get huge roars but the biggest, quite rightly in my opinion, is reserved for Martin Johnson. Then it is time for Johnno to receive the Webb Ellis trophy and I notice that even then he's thinking clearly under pressure (TCUP). When he is handed the cup he takes the base off and then puts his hands on the lid to stop them falling off when he goes to lift it.

We run around the pitch to parade the trophy, each taking it in turns to hold it aloft, and it is now, with the adrenalin from the match subsiding, that I notice that my shoulder is absolutely bloody agony. The tight shirts we are wearing aren't doing it any favours but the only tracksuit top I can find to keep it warm belongs to Louise Ramsay our manager who is about 5 foot 6 inches tall. I feel camp and ridiculous running around in it singing 'We Are The Champions'. I am a cross between Freddie Mercury and Rodney Trotter.

It feels like we have been out on the pitch for days when finally we retire to the dressing room. By now we just want to get out there among the fans and have a few drinks, but first we have to shower, get dressed and deal with the press. It's already getting on for around midnight. No ice baths tonight, just an awful lot of beer and champagne. Prince Harry comes into the changing room and starts mucking about with us. Top lad. Howard, the Australian PM, comes in and he can't be more charming and gracious if he tries. The only Aussie player I notice is Stirling Mortlock. He seems like a good man and we chat for ten minutes before swapping shirts.

Tessa Jowell, the Minister of Culture, Media and Sport (the so-called Minister of Fun), is in the room for some reason. God knows who invited her. Most of the lads are wandering around half-naked by now and they don't recognise her as she stands about amidst the celebrations not quite knowing what to do in a room full of bare-bottomed men. There is a highly amusing moment when a group of us are trying to have our photographs taken and she is trying to slide in on the shot from one side. As we are taking our positions Mongo Moody turns to the Minister of the Crown and says: 'Look, sweetheart, I don't know who you are, but can you f**k off? Can't you see we're having our picture taken?'

All of us have got our cameras out and it is a surreal sight as we all walk about taking pictures of each other taking pictures of each other. As my dad always says: you can't bottle it, but try and remember as much possible. I take about forty pictures and someone takes one of me and Tinds with Prince Harry giving me a nipple tweak. It is all slightly mad. I have my shoulder looked at by the medical staff and they suggest that thirty or forty pints of lager is the ideal treatment for this kind of injury. Tindall and Dorian West are fighting about what music to put on. Tinds wants his gangsta rap, Dorian wants The Clash. Before heading out to meet the press Johnno says: 'Don't get too pissed for a few days. You want to savour every moment of this, suck it all in and remember every last detail.' And absolutely no one in the squad pays a blind bit of attention to him. It is the only time any of us has ever ignored our great leader. The eight lads who weren't playing had been on the sauce for a few hours and they were desperate to get into town. (Joe Worsley had emptied out some of the squad's energy drink bottles and filled them up with vodka and juice.)

The press conference is the most enjoyable one I have ever experienced and there aren't too many tough questions to field. Finally we are on the coach heading into town and we notice that getting away from the stadium looks like a nightmare for the fans because there doesn't seem to be any transport running and they are all walking. (My cousin Diana, Jonny Wilko's girlfriend, told me it took her four hours to get back and she ended up missing most of the post-match party.) On our way there we have a mildly embarrassing moment when the coach pulls up alongside a bus stop at some lights and there are about two or three hundred Australian fans standing there looking pretty crestfallen. We imagine that we are going to get some amusing banter off this mob, maybe even some proper abuse, and so we cram up against the window, jump about in celebration and sing 'I shagged Matilda'. We aren't taunting them, it's more a bit of childish horseplay, but we are surprised by the reaction. Far from getting pelted or abused by these fans, to our shame the whole lot start applauding us, to a man and woman. Whoops. A little red-faced and sheepish, we applaud them back. That wasn't meant to happen. I like that about the Aussies. If you beat them fair and square they'll take their hats off to you.

We had hired out the Opium Bar in Darling Harbour for a post-final party, win or lose, for all the players, their families and friends. At first it is all pretty quiet. The adrenalin has long worn off and the immediate, ecstatic excitement of victory has faded a little, while the physical fatigue is slowly enveloping our battered bodies. As the night wears on the tempo and atmosphere begin to heat up and we end up in a place called the Cargo Bar. Our entry en masse is arranged by my Australian friend Thynney who knows absolutely everyone worth knowing in New South Wales. As far as I'm concerned the man who owns the Cargo Bar should have received a knighthood with Clive Woodward in the New Year's Honours list. Even though there are dozens of us there, he hands us an account card, the 'card of power' as it becomes known for the rest of the evening, and he tells us we can stay as long as we want and have as many drinks as we like, all on the house. It is a great party. I look up at one point and I am met with the sight of Mike Tindall, Lawrence Dallaglio and Prince Harry playing the bongos together. How often in a lifetime will I see that? I have a good chat with the Aussie Test cricketer Damien Martyn. God knows what he is doing there. Then there is Foxy, a great friend of Thynney, and the former Test player Daniel Herbert, and to the great amusement of the England boys he is wearing full Wallabies kit, down to the socks, boots, head tape, vaseline and gumshield. This is the man who after the semi-final win against New Zealand slipped over the advertising hoards and did a lap of honour in full Wallabies kit, to the delight of the whole squad who knew him well. The rest is a blur and at nine o'clock in the morning I collapse on to my hotel bed. I am one very tired, very happy, very drunk world champion.

The IRB awards dinner was staged the following night and, quite honestly, a formal dinner was the last thing any of us wanted to attend, especially those who had yet to go to bed (see Mr J. Leonard). I did a Radio Five Live interview from there that night and though I wasn't exactly three sheets to the wind I had been no stranger to the tankard for the previous twenty-four hours and proceeded to make a complete tit of myself. Knowing my football allegiances, the producers had arranged for Manchester City striker Shaun Goater to be on the show, too, and I have a dim and mildly embarrassing recollection of breaking into a rendition of 'Feed The Goat And He Will Score', a City favourite sung to the tune of 'Bread of Heaven'.

Exhausted, hung-over but deliriously happy we boarded our plane, named *Sweet Chariot*, for the flight home on the Monday. As we went through security, we all had to empty our pockets for metal, but each time Matt Dawson went through the archway metal detector the alarm buzzer kept going off. Back and forth he went to the bemusement of the Australian security people who could find nothing metal on him. 'Oh, hang on,' said Daws in mock surprise and unbuttoned his shirt. 'It couldn't be this thing, could it? It's just a silly old World

Cup winners' medal.' Pathetic but highly amusing at the time.

We made a pact that we would drink as far as Italy, and we had a great time as Jase and Cattie, two of the veterans, held court with some great stories. By Singapore we could hold out no more and by the time we took off again, most of us were sound asleep. There was a feeling on that flight that a special period in our lives was coming to an end. Yes, we would all get together to go and see the Queen, and many of us would meet up again for Six Nations training in the New Year, but it did feel as if we were coming to the end of a much longer journey than the one we embarked upon that evening. After all the festivities died down, we knew that that side, which had been together for years, would never play together again. This particular adventure was over. As soon as the final whistle sounded on Saturday, one era came to an end and another began there and then.

We landed at Heathrow at four o'clock in the morning and staggered off the plane a little bleary-eyed. Originally Caro had planned to come and meet me off the plane but when I called her she said it might not be a good idea because she had heard there were a couple of hundred people there and that, being pregnant, she didn't want to get caught up in any jostling. A couple of hundred? No chance, I thought. It's four in the morning. We collected our bags from the luggage carousel and were about to head off through Customs when the police came in and said it was probably best if they took us out in ones and twos. Ones and twos? What's that all about? The officer looked at us and smiled. 'Just wait and see, it's going absolutely mental out there.' Jonny, Johnno and Clive, the big three, were the first taken out and as the automatic doors opened there was a deafening wall of noise. I was among the last to leave with Lawrence and it was a simply amazing experience. We were absolutely mobbed and as we tried to push our way through the place was reverberating to 'England, England . . . Swing Low, Sweet Chaaaaaariot . . . Ruuuule Britannia . . .' There must have been about ten thousand there and when we got on to the bus it could barely move because it was surrounded by so many fans.

An hour earlier we had all been in a coma, but now the adrenalin was in full flow again. Finally, we got to our hotel at Pennyhill Park, truly exhausted by now, and after a quick bacon sandwich we set off for our homes to see our families again. It was a wonderful feeling staggering back through the front door of my London house at the end of this magical adventure. There was my wife, looking beautiful, healthy and happy, getting nice and tubby about the waist. There was Rufus, the Norfolk terrier, snapping at my heels and there was Caro's mum who had held the fort and looked after her so brilliantly while I was away. And there, upstairs, looking ridiculously comfortable, was my own bed. I belly-flopped on to it and as my head hit the pillow I was away into another world.

Maybe it was all a dream.

Afterword

TWENTY-FOUR HOURS AFTER stepping off the plane at Heathrow I was back in training with Quins ahead of our match against Leeds at the weekend, but I pulled up when it became obvious that the shoulder I had damaged again in the World Cup wasn't going to hold out. In the end, I was sidelined for over four weeks. Several of the England squad, however, either played or were on the bench for their clubs that weekend – which was total madness if you ask me as we were all battered and exhausted after seven back-to-back, high-intensity internationals. The physical legacy of the World Cup lived on for months as half the squad were either forced to carry their knocks, or were so badly injured they couldn't even play and, in some cases, had to undergo operations. The Southern Hemisphere sides have two or three months off after the World Cup because it was always the end of their domestic seasons, but we were straight back on club duty. In an ideal world, the clubs should have given us until the New Year to let our bodies recover.

It was true that all the functions and celebrations in the wake of our victory took their toll on the squad, but there was no avoiding them. A lot of the public wanted a piece of us, to join in the celebrations and share the moment and we were only too happy to oblige because the fans had been magnificent to us. There were also your friends and families who, naturally, wanted to take you out and hear about the World Cup from the inside. Function followed function, one engagement after the next, right up until Christmas. It was pretty crazy throughout that time and our feet barely touched the ground as we jumped from one venue to the next, one television camera to another, but a line was finally drawn under it all when we went to one last function on 20 December. It had been a fabulous month, lapping up the congratulations and taking the backslaps, knowing we were living through a very special period in our careers. Enjoy it while it lasts, we thought, because the backslaps can quickly turn to brickbats, as we were soon to discover in the New Year with our Six Nations defeats against Ireland and France.

The highlight of that mad, media-frenzied month on our return was unquestionably the double-decker bus parade around central London a couple of weeks before Christmas. We all met up at the InterContinental Hotel where we boarded the two buses and set off up Park

Lane. We had seen media reports saying up to a million people were expected to throng the route and we thought that sounded a bit far-fetched. Our suspicions appeared to be confirmed during that early leg of the journey where a handful of fans, some dog walkers and a newspaper seller were the only ones there to give us a wave. This is going to be a bit embarrassing, we all thought. We're going to be waving to bemused Japanese tourists on Oxford Street before turning up in Trafalgar Square to be greeted by a handful of diehard England fans.

However, as we came under Marble Arch and turned right into Oxford Street we were greeted by the most spectacular sight. Stretching out before us for about a mile were tens of thousands of people awaiting our arrival, all of them presumably on sick leave from work. The players were in the front bus with Clive while the coaches and the back-up staff were in the one behind us and as they edged their way down I was amazed by how many people I recognised in the throng. The champagne was flowing, endless strains of 'Swing Low' floated on the air. You may have seen for yourself the waving flags, the people hanging out of office windows and climbing the lampposts and you probably saw us grinning from ear to ear with our cameras and mobile phones, once again doing our best to bottle and preserve the moment forever.

We turned into Regent Street, which was heaving,

too, and by the time we got to Trafalgar Square you had to wonder if there was anyone left in England to fill it, but it was absolutely crammed to every corner. What a truly awesome sight. What would it be like if England ever won the football World Cup? The question-and-answer session with the BBC followed before the Mayor, Ken Livingstone, seizing the publicity moment like any good politician, took the microphone to say a few words. You will see plenty of pictures of the England squad in recent years with one or two of the players making an 'L' (for 'loser') gesture with their thumb and forefinger above someone's head. It's just one of those silly rituals or in-jokes you tend to get when you have a group of men together on tour for weeks on end. The joke is normally left behind in the training camp, but while Ken Livingstone was saying his piece you can see Steve Thompson making an 'L' sign above his head. Well, I thought it was funny anyway. We weren't, it seems, doing that well with the politicians, what with Mongo telling Tessa Jowell where to get off in the dressing room at Sydney and then Thommo making childish signs above the Mayor's head. You just had to hope that everyone would behave themselves at Downing Street later.

Next stop, Buckingham Palace. After picking up our wives and girlfriends back at the InterContinental we drove through the Palace gates and were led into a stunning room packed with incredible paintings by

Rembrandt, Renoir and Canaletto. This was a world a million miles removed from the madness of Trafalgar Square, all padded carpets and multi-million pound art on the walls. The girls were waiting in a room laid out for tea next door (Caro says the Queen's scones are the best she's ever tasted) while we the players were waiting like excited schoolboys for Her Majesty to arrive through a pair of double doors at the end of the room. We had had some special moments over the previous few weeks but I have to confess my heart was beating double time in anticipation. It was partly the hushed elegance of the place that made you feel a little edgy, but mainly the prospect of meeting HRH, the woman whose name we blast out at the start of every international match, the figurehead of the country we represent each time we take to the field. The doors were swung open and first through the door was a pack of corgis and dorgis, snuffling and sniffing and wagging their tails, a few paces ahead of their famous mistress. At this great moment in our lives, I could hear Mark 'Ronnie' Regan whistling to the dogs and whispering, 'Here doggies!'

That morning one of the tabloids had splashed a very silly story about Mike Tindall becoming close friends with the Queen's granddaughter Zara Phillips and as Her Majesty approached to greet us, there was even more sniggering as a few of the lads were going: 'Here she comes, Tinds, your future grandmother-in-law . . . Christmas'll be nice here, mate . . .'

During the tea that followed Danny Luger and I wandered off to have a sniff around with our cameras and found ourselves in the throne room and I was within about a yard of sitting down on it when the door was flung open and a very stern-looking official snapped: 'May I ask what you think you are doing in here, gentlemen?'

'Er . . . nothing, nothing, we're trying to find the toilets. Sorry, sorry,' we said in squeaky schoolboy voices before beating a hasty retreat.

The evening was to end with a Far Eastern-themed testimonial dinner for Lawrence Dallaglio in Battersea Park but first it was off to Downing Street for an hour or so of hobnobbing with politicians of various hues. It had been an incredible day in the middle of one unforgettable month, but by Christmas I wanted to disappear into the shadows and go on a strict fast. There was a bit of sniping here and there that the cocktail party circuit would be the ruin of the team and there was an element of truth in that, but only a small element. We didn't have any England training days over that period and we were not as strict about our diets, but as professional athletes we all still looked after our bodies as far as our injuries would allow between the functions. For my part, it was important that I didn't get carried away at the parties because at any moment I could get a call from Caro or her doctor telling me to get to the hospital at the double. I couldn't think of anything worse than Caro going into labour or having to have an emergency operation and me rolling up three sheets to the wind whistling 'Land Of Hope And Glory'. Even more important was that I didn't drink between the functions in case I had to drive Caro to hospital myself.

The bigger concern for many of the players was that they were being asked to play in hugely important league and European games when their bodies had had no chance to recover from the massive exertions of the World Cup campaign. As a full contact sport, unlike football, rugby pounds the body like no other. Rest is essential and you could mount a reasonable medical argument that eating canapés and drinking the odd glass of champagne is time infinitely better spent than battering a body that has already been taken to the limit of its endurance. You only have to look at the string of injuries still afflicting the England squad months after the event to understand the damage and the wear and tear sustained in an intense campaign which to all intents and purposes began back in July with gruelling fitness programmes at Pennyhill Park.

Every week that passed on my return from the World Cup was a cause for mild optimism because it meant that the baby was that much closer to having an uncomplicated birth. We were ticking off the weeks as they went: 28, 29, 30 . . . they say that, born under 24 weeks, a child has virtually no chance of survival, but the chances increase proportionally with every week that passes. I wasn't quite leaning over Caro's stomach and shouting 'Go on, my son!' – partly because we didn't know if the baby was a boy or girl – but we were both quietly willing him/her to the delivery finishing line and when we got to week thirty-six, the blind fear we had felt when Caro was rushed to hospital back in October had turned to a mixture of mild apprehension and tremendous anticipation. For the first time Caro could walk down the street with a look of happy expectation on her face. Her irrational fears of inadequacy had almost, but not quite, disappeared. The suture which had held everything in place was due to come out on 29 January and you didn't have to be a prize-winning gynaecologist to guess that dramatic events would not be far behind. We were due to play Brive away in southern France that weekend and without me even having to ask him Mark Evans, Quins director of rugby, insisted that I had the day off, not least because Brive is two and a half hours from the nearest airport.

The suture came out as scheduled and almost immediately the rumblings began and grew stronger and stronger. At 6.30 on Saturday morning Caro woke me up and told me she felt the time had come although she couldn't be sure. She disappeared downstairs as I tried to rouse myself and a few minutes later I heard a collective 'Oh, my Lord!' from Caro and her mother and I was out of bed like there was a bomb under it. Caro's waters had broken, and five minutes later we were in the car and back on that familiar route up the Fulham Road, street for street the same one I had taken on the night of Freddie's birth.

In the event the labour lasted almost twelve hours. The cervix, so wretchedly 'incompetent' in the past, was now refusing to budge an inch. In these moments, and I can speak only as a male of the species, all you want is the baby out safely . . . and fast. I imagine it is the same for all fathers but after our experience with Freddie I was perhaps doubly urgent. I tried to appear as cool as possible, nonchalantly filling in the crossword, running errands here and there as the midwife, Pamela, a lovely Irish girl, looked after and encouraged Caro. Between two and four that afternoon she was in a lot of pain and I began to pace the delivery room floor like a polar bear in captivity. Then the moment finally arrived – it was bang on 7.30 – and it all happened with astonishing speed. Out he came (for it was clearly another lad!), but there was no noise and my instant reaction was 'Come on! Say something!' They gave him a bit of oxygen, gently slapped him about a bit, put him under one of those special heat lamps and within seconds there was a little reedy bleating noise. It was the best noise I've ever heard, worth a thousand Twicken-ham roars rolled into one. You can have my World Cup winners' medal – this was the true moment of glory I had been dreaming of for the past eighteen months.

There was a curious twist to the day. Once Archie had been given the all-clear we had to leave the delivery room and go to the one that had just been allocated to us. Caro and I both clocked it as soon as we entered, but neither mentioned it for fear of upsetting the other: this was the room in which Freddie was born and had died. At first I felt a little uncomfortable as all three of us settled down for the night, but very quickly it dawned on me that this was perfect. There was a wonderful symmetry to it all and it was as if the whole thing had been arranged by a higher authority. It felt like Freddie and Archie were there together.